GREAT
STORIES OF
MEN
AND THE
ANIMAL
WORLD

GREAT
STORIES OF
MEN
AND THE
ANIMAL
WORLD

SELECTED AND CONDENSED BY
THE EDITORS OF READER'S DIGEST
WITH AN INTRODUCTION BY
JAMES HERRIOT

Volume One

The Reader's Digest Association, London, Sydney, Cape Town, Montreal

FIRST EDITION

Published by
The Reader's Digest Association Limited
25 Berkeley Square, London, W1X 6AB

For information as to ownership of copyright
in the material in this book see last page

Filmset by MS Filmsetting Ltd.,
Frome, Somerset

Printed in Hong Kong
by Toppan Printing Co., (HK) Ltd.

CONTENTS

INTRODUCTION

by James Herriot

As I look through this treasure house of animal stories I marvel anew at the vast spectrum of interest in this field. There are so many ways of being involved with animals.

I have spent a lifetime in treating the ailments of domestic creatures and this in itself is a wide and fascinating scene. Unglamorous, perhaps, by comparison with the exotic experiences of the authors in these volumes, but just right for me.

As a boy, I decided to be a veterinary surgeon because of my fondness for dogs and cats. I grew up in a city, knowing nothing of farm life, and I envisaged my future career quite clearly: I would be dressed in a white coat standing under the brilliant lights of a spotless operating theatre, ministering to the needs of the small animals which had always captivated me. But fate had something different in store for me. I qualified during the depression of the thirties when jobs were scarce, and before I knew what was happening I found myself among the lonely farmhouses of the Yorkshire Dales, trudging through the mud and snow in winter, burned by the sun in summer. I had become a doctor of farm animals, and that is what I am today. This gave

me another kind of joy: an appreciation of working in the open air and a delight in the rural scene which bred a compulsion to write about it.

Yet I still cannot regard myself primarily as an author. The deepest satisfactions of my working life have come not from literary success but from the little triumphs of my veterinary life. Saving the life or easing the suffering of an animal in some remote environment with nobody to see it happen—this has been a strange fulfilment.

I wonder if the great writers who appear in these volumes feel as I do. Perhaps their greatest pleasure has been derived more from their work with animals than from their writing about it. Be that as it may, the books they have produced reflect their dedication, and are a thrilling bonus for animal lovers and readers everywhere.

These books are classics, many of them old friends of mine like *Man-Eaters of Kumaon* which held me spellbound in my youth, and the unforgettable *Ring of Bright Water* and *Born Free*. Lorenz's *The Year of the Greylag Goose* is here with its fascinating mix of science and a breath of the wild, as is Hans Hass's exciting and beautiful *Diving to Adventure*; while in *Bandoola*, J. H. Williams brings the majestic world of the elephant to us as nobody else could.

Farley Mowat's touching and witty *Never Cry Wolf* takes its place naturally among the winners, and it is good to see my fellow veterinarian, J. Y. Henderson, in such company. He treats a greatly different kind of patient from mine but his adventures in the circus are a joy.

Michael Morcombe paints a vivid picture of wildlife in *Australia: The Wild Continent. Lords of the Arctic* is a spectacular and absorbing study of the polar bear in its environment by Davids and Guravich, while in *Caught in Motion*, Stephen Dalton displays the astonishing virtuosity of his animal photography. And how do you classify Gerald Durrell, one of my long-time favourites? He is inimitable, and *The Whispering Land* shows him at his best.

As I have said, I wonder whether I am a vet or a writer, but I do know that I am a reader and I think I can recognize excellence. This collection of animal books has that quality.

James Herriot

BANDOOLA

A CONDENSATION OF THE BOOK BY

J. H. Williams

ILLUSTRATED BY NEVILLE DEAR

Bandoola, a magnificent bull elephant born in the Burmese jungle, grew up to work and fight alongside the man who trained him: his devoted native oozie, Po Toke. Their story is told by J. H. Williams, who came to Burma from England as an inexperienced young man and later learned to manage huge elephant herds for the Bombay Burma Corporation, making a home in the jungle with the girl he married. He writes evocatively of the exotic, dangerous world which he came to know so well; of his colleagues, brave, reckless and hard-drinking men; and above all of the noble elephants who worked the vast teak forests so tirelessly.

J. H. Williams, who also wrote another classic animal book, *Elephant Bill*, encountered hundreds of elephants in his long career. In his own words, "Bandoola was the most interesting and challenging animal with whom I have ever had to deal."

1

I N AN EARLIER BOOK I wrote a little about Bandoola, that magnificent elephant, and his oozie, Po Toke. I have chosen his name for the title of this book, not because it is exclusively about him—it is not intended as the life story of an elephant—but because Bandoola was the most challenging animal with whom I have ever had to deal.

He and Po Toke were pioneers; before I had ever thought of going to Burma, they had already proved many of the theories which I was mistakenly given credit for working out. They were both most interesting characters, with great virtues and also weaknesses.

Bandoola killed a man, but he was not a killer. Po Toke ended his life as a dacoit, or brigand, but this was the result of the peculiar conflict between his nature and his time, already apparent when he christened the baby elephant Bandoola after the great Burman patriot, General Maha Bandoola.

In November 1897 Po Toke was an elephant boy of fifteen. Fifteen may not seem a great age, but the Burmese mature young. He had already picked the girl he wanted to marry, and he had chosen well. Ma Pyoo was beautiful and she was also the daughter of the contractor who owned the herd of elephants with whom he worked. Po Toke was ambitious and for the last year his thoughts had centred on his charge, Ma Shwe, who was carrying a calf. Po Toke never knew who the sire was, but he suspected a wild tusker.

Wild elephants consider it the duty of the whole herd to protect an elephant carrying young, but in captivity the "auntie" system prevails. Instinctively, elephants realize that to protect a young calf against the tiger two elephants are needed, and for a whole year before the birth the expectant mother and her "auntie", Mee Tway, had grazed together in preparation for the great and dangerous occasion.

Every oozie is excited when his elephant calves; but Po Toke was especially excited. He was penniless, and he felt that his fortune was bound up with that of Ma Shwe's calf.

Ma Shwe and Mee Tway selected a site for the birth where the creek made a crook-shaped bend. That meant they were protected on three sides by water. There were plentiful supplies of elephant grass, which meant good fodder. And in the centre was a gigantic nyaung tree, to provide shade.

The mother and the auntie spent a considerable time circling the tree and stamping down the grass, until they had flattened an area the size of a circus ring. By nightfall the maternity ward was complete.

There was little fuss about the birth, though for half an hour there was great tension as Mee Tway went round and round the tree on guard. Then the sun rose and revealed the tubbiest little male elephant calf ever born.

By the time Po Toke arrived, the calf was tottering about. His trunk was just a deformity of a snout which he could scarcely move; and his small piggy eyes were surrounded with wrinkles as deep as those of an elephant over three score years and ten. His complexion was the kind of purple you get by mixing blue and pink in a paintbox. His little tail touched his hocks and insects were already teaching him its use.

When Po Toke called to the mother in a loud voice, Ma Shwe rumbled a sort of purr of pride, a pride which Po Toke shared; for this was his calf as well as hers. He came over and patted the calf, congratulated the mother and guided the little gaping mouth to the mother's teats between her forelegs. Mee Tway was grazing about twenty-five yards away. "Don't stray too far!" shouted Po Toke in a friendly way, and then left the maternity ward, whistling to himself.

At noon he set off down-creek to visit his charges again. As he approached the maternity ward, he called aloud to warn them of his coming. In answer came great elephantine rumblings to say that all was well with them.

He stayed with them during the afternoon, and before he left he gave to Ma Shwe and Mee Tway a ball of molasses each. He made another ball, spat in his hand and rubbed the ball in the saliva. That he gave to the calf to sniff so that it could learn his smell.

As the sun went down, the clearing seemed to be illuminated with a green eerie light. This was the time when some of the jungle dwellers were stretching and licking paws and rubbing sleepy eyes awake. Po Toke knew that the coming night would be the most dangerous of all nights for his calf. As he went down to the creek on his way to camp, he saw that Ma Shwe had walked the fifty yards to the river to drink during his absence and Mee Tway had done likewise at another time. A good mother, a good auntie: they would not leave the calf unguarded.

A YOUNG FULL-GROWN tiger waited in a cane break four hundred yards away across the stream. The tiger had chosen his lair with the same jungle instinct as the elephants had chosen their maternity ward. Soon after sundown the breeze would shift to downstream as the hot air rose from the valley. So he had made his lair below the clearing, ready to work upstream against the breeze after crossing the river.

He knew a calf had been born by the rumbling sounds of pleasure made by the mother. He sat up and washed his face as Po Toke went by along the creek. The only sign of his excitement was the twitching of his tail.

In the teak-harvesting camp there were fourteen men. Married or single, they lived in bamboo huts with thatched roofs, on posts raised four feet above the ground. They were a hundred miles from the nearest jungle village. Yet they were happy and contented. The rice store was full and the jungle itself provided all the other things they needed for flavouring their curry.

That evening Po Toke was happier than any of them. He tied his long hair in a knot and encircled it with a crimson piece of silk. He changed his daytime lungyi of indigo blue to one of vivid scarlet, and over his shoulders, which normally were bare, he put a coat of native cloth. For this was the Burmese courting hour, and he had been invited by Ma Pyoo's mother to come to the veranda after the evening meal.

Po Toke ate with the bachelor oozies, squatting round a large bowl of rice. Ma Pyoo ate with her parents and her aunt in the privacy of their hut. A veranda ran along one side of the hut, and it was there the young oozie found her waiting for him, alone.

They talked about the future, as the young do who are in love but still too poor to marry. They talked of the elephant born that day, which Po Toke insisted would be an elephant of all elephants, and of how one day

Po Toke, with Ma Pyoo as his wife, would own a camp of elephants like this one, and by then maybe this calf would be the prize of all his charges. When the time came to say goodnight, he did not kiss her; he just pinched her little toe and went down the bamboo steps. When he got back to his hut most of the oozies had already gone to bed, and the camp was in darkness except for the glowing embers of the fires beneath the scattered huts.

BEFORE IT WAS DARK the tiger left his lair and crossed the creek a long way below the elephants' pitch. He worked stealthily upstream until his sensitive nostrils picked up the scent of the newborn calf on the evening breeze.

Then for a time he squatted motionless on his haunches, working himself up for the attack. He knew that he could not seize the calf until he had stampeded both the adults. He must spring on the back of one and so lacerate her that she fled for safety; then he must unseat himself and stampede the other long enough to give him time to seize the calf and carry it off.

But before he could attack, he knew that he must circle the clearing, because the best line of attack was from upstream. His patience was superb. Twice he moved up within fifty yards of the clearing, but each time the breeze was coming downstream too fast for him to risk his scent being carried to them when he moved above.

The moon rose higher and higher, but it was not till well after midnight that the breeze dropped. Utter silence fell on the jungle, a silence so deathly that few human beings can endure it without making some sound or movement to reassure themselves. But the elephants made no sound. The two adults stood side by side, as unmoving as statues; and between the forelegs of his mother stood the baby calf, as motionless as they.

The tiger was fifty yards out, and he had decided to make his attack from the creek side. Four times he circled without crackling a leaf or a twig—the perfect hunter. His poise was low on the ground. He moved forward with his powerful hind legs tensed under his body, ready instantly to spring.

At last he saw an elephant's flank clearly silhouetted, and only ten bounds and a leap away. His enormous power was released as he bounded forward and with a seven-foot spring landed on Mee Tway's back. His forepaws dug deep into the barrel of the elephant's back, their vicious grip holding his weight, while with his hind claws he lacerated the wretched elephant's shoulders.

For a second Mee Tway was taken by surprise. Then, bellowing with panic fear she was off, making for the nearest jungle, where she could shake this savage terror from her back.

As she reached the edge of the elephant grass the tiger retracted his claws and slid off, as a child might slide from a bareback pony. Immediately he turned and bounded back to attack Ma Shwe, standing under the nyaung tree, the calf huddled between her forelegs.

Ma Shwe took one chance. As the tiger checked before her, she took a pace forward and lashed at him with her trunk. With a lightning swing his right paw struck. The sharp claws struck home and Ma Shwe bellowed with pain; for the trunk is the most sensitive organ of the elephant. But she did not stampede. She replaced her off forward foot to protect the calf, who hadn't moved an inch.

But in that moment the tiger sprang up on her withers. His fore claws dug their hold and his hind claws tore at her flesh. She shook herself to fling him off, but still she didn't stampede and still he clung and tore.

Then suddenly something struck her with the force of an avalanche. She sank to her knees with the impact, without damaging the calf. And when she rose again, the murderous weight was gone. Mee Tway had returned, goaded to fury by her wounds, and charged at the tiger clinging to the mother's flank.

The king of the Burmese jungle fell to the ground. He was badly hurt in pride and body, but he managed to slide away to his jungle lair.

Now the two defiant elephants stood side by side once more, blood streaming from their wounds, but the calf untouched. They raised their heads and trumpeted a challenge to all the tigers of the Ningyan forest.

Po Toke had been still awake when Mee Tway broke the stillness with that first bellow, as the tiger dug in his claws. He leaped up and in a moment the camp was in a tumult, moonlit figures running to get bamboo firetorches and scare off the tiger.

Now, with their spears in one hand and the torches in the other, they came hopping down the creek from boulder to boulder, Po Toke in the lead. They had no fear of tigers, these men who were as much at home in the jungle as any animal. It was the tiger who was afraid of the bounding torches and the yelling voices. For a moment he watched the fires dancing down the creek, and then he slunk into the shadows of the jungle.

They expected to find the worst when they entered the arena. But when, holding their firetorches high, they came to the nyaung tree, there stood Ma Shwe and Mee Tway side by side, rumbling alternate sounds of terror and delight. A sudden dread made Po Toke bend down and thrust his torch as near as he could to the mother's bleeding trunk. He saw two tiny, frightened eyes. The calf was safe. He stood between his mother's forelegs, with his ears shaped like two maps of India cocked forward.

"Oh, Mother! He lives!" Po Toke yelled, and then, with joy in his heart, he called to the little elephant. "Come out," he shouted. "Come out, you brave warrior! Show yourself, Maha Bandoola!"

And so the little elephant was christened Bandoola, after the great Burmese general who had fought and died for the independence of his country in 1824. For Po Toke, as well as being a great oozie, was a great nationalist.

2

The wounded elephants and the calf were taken to the camp immediately, so that the adults could have their wounds treated. But the calf Bandoola did not matter to anyone except Po Toke and Ma Pyoo. The contractor and the older men were agreed that trying to rear elephant calves was a waste of money. It would be twenty years before they were any use in hauling timber. It was much cheaper to capture young elephants from wild herds and train them by breaking their hearts and spirits.

Po Toke was too wise to argue. He believed that baby elephant calves born in domesticity would learn and work far better than any captured elephant. But he could only prove it by example—the example of Bandoola. So he relied not on logic but on love.

It was fairly easy for Po Toke to persuade Ma Pyoo that he was right about Bandoola, because she was young and she loved him. It was not so easy for Ma Pyoo to persuade her father that he should keep and train Bandoola. He loved her, but he had known all that there was to know about elephants since before she was born. If the calf survived the strain of the forest life when his mother was back at work, well and good, he answered.

Ma Pyoo bided her time. She waited until her father went down with a worse attack of malaria than usual. Then, as she soothed his burning forehead she whispered, "Will you give me Bandoola as a pet?"

"Yes," he groaned.

From that day onwards Bandoola became almost as important as Ma Pyoo herself. Nobody, not even the contractor himself, knew that this favourite daughter had promised the baby elephant to Po Toke as soon as they were married.

News passes fast in jungle camps and riverine villages. It was soon known that some wonder calf had been born and christened Bandoola after the great patriot. At four months he was so independent that he strayed well out of sight of his mother. He was so imitative that he aped his mother's every movement. When she squatted at the order "Hmit" ("Sit down"), he tried to squat too; and at the order "Tah" ("Get up"), he rolled over in play. He lay still in the water to be tickled when Ma Shwe was scrubbed, and they said that by the time he was five years old he would need no breaking. He would be one of the few calves born in captivity to equal any animal of the wild. Could anyone doubt that Ma Shwe had been mated by the Bwetgyi Monster, the great wild tusker of the Ningyan forest, to bring forth such a prodigious calf?

So ran the rumours. And they weren't without their foundation in fact. Some calves are nuisances, crowding at their mothers' heels on the dragging paths. But Bandoola kept clear and made the most of the best days of his life, like a child, before being claimed for discipline and responsibility.

To Ma Pyoo and the children in the camp he was a pet. He would pretend to have been left behind by his mother and then suddenly scuffle after her. Everybody looked and laughed at him; and that was why he did it. But he also had the sort of accidents which all children have. He was stung by a bee. He split a toenail. He poked the tip of his trunk into a pot of hot oil. He walked on burning cinders which he thought were cold. These are the sorts of accidents which are part of education.

But there are experiences which leave a mark to last a lifetime. And Bandoola had one of these.

He was showing off how he could run, and suddenly the ground gave under him. He had plunged into a swamp. His forelegs sank deep and the more he struggled, the deeper he went. He rolled and struggled even more violently as panic possessed him; yet all he seemed to be doing was digging his own grave.

He sank until the cold mud lay beneath his tail at one end and his chin at the other. He was helpless. He couldn't even struggle any longer. His little piggy eyes turned skywards.

The largest tusker elephant in the camp was summoned, and ropes were made fast, not without protest, to Bandoola's tail and around his neck. Then the pulling started. The Burmans took no notice of his squealing. They urged the tusker to pull harder. And suddenly, with a pop like a champagne cork, out he came.

It was an experience which Bandoola never forgot.

FOR FIVE YEARS Po Toke planned for the calf's training and by the time Bandoola was five years old Po Toke could make him stand still merely by gripping the point or lobe of his ear.

His ambition was to train Bandoola by kindness instead of by breaking his spirit. He went to Ma Pyoo's father and asked for permission to arrange the training in his own fashion. The contractor, like many an old man faced with the challenge of youth, granted permission in such a way that if the experiment succeeded he could claim some of the credit for it, and if it failed he could say, "I told you so."

Po Toke found two trees which grew so close together that they would make a fine head for a pen. With the help of his campmates he drove in two uprights and fixed stout timber rails horizontally from them to the trees.

Then he asked for permission to visit the old Ponna, the astrologer, at the Shinbyuyan Monastery eighty miles away, who could cast Bandoola's horoscope. With clear instructions as to the day and hour the training was to start and what offerings and rituals would be necessary to placate the jungle spirits, Po Toke returned to the camp. The other oozies listened to what he had to say in silence and respect. His certainty that he was right about Bandoola made him naturally a leader of the oozies.

Bandoola was already ripe for training. For a calf of his age he was unusually independent of his mother. Ma Shwe's new oozie said that often when he went into the jungle to track and recapture the mother elephant for work, there was no sign of Bandoola. But he always returned to camp a few hours later, rolling in like a guilty schoolboy who has been off on some exploit of his own.

When the day fixed for training came, Po Toke, the camp-followers, and even the contractor himself attended ceremonial prayers to the jungle spirits at the base of the two trees.

At the head of the pen they had built a little shrine shaped like a Burmese doll's house, thatched with a grass roof. About it burned sixteen candles, one for each year of Bandoola's life to come before he could be considered a full-grown animal. His childhood days were over and the discipline of school years was about to start.

The system of training captive elephants which Po Toke had devised was entirely his invention. He greased the inside of the pen with fat from a roasted bear, then onto a heavy branch protruding over the pen he fastened two jungle-made pulley blocks. Through each he threaded a rope. At the end of one rope there were two nooses, through which San Oo, Ma Pyoo's thirteen-year-old brother, could slip his legs. At the end of the other was a block of heavy ironwood. The pulling ends of both the ropes were tied to the sides of the pen independently.

Near the camp clearing Ma Shwe stood motionless, chained to a tree. Young Bandoola was loose, and very curious to know what all this commotion was about. Po Toke and the eight men under him ran to the training pen. Ma Shwe's rider unfettered her, mounted, and began to follow them. Bandoola came behind.

When they reached the pen, San Oo was in position, silently dangling over the pen with his legs in the nooses. The contractor went into the pen, holding out a whole bunch of bananas to Bandoola. Bandoola was interested, but suspicious. Life, he had found, was good, but never quite as good as that. He now stood in front of his mother, but he made certain that his hindquarters were in touch with her trunk.

The contractor came towards him and offered him a banana. Bandoola tried to snatch the whole bunch but the contractor dodged back, and clambered over the side. Bandoola felt his mother's head pushing his rump forward and followed the contractor into the pen.

Ma Shwe's oozie had urged her forward. He held her tight while two oozies slipped two stout bars behind Bandoola's legs. And there he was— trapped. Ma Shwe, who had long lost interest in her son, went away without a sign.

Bandoola lunged out at the timber bars with his hind legs. The bars resounded but they didn't give an inch. He tried this way and that, furious at the indignity of being trapped. But it was no use and soon he gave it up.

The moment he did so, a banana came through the bars of his prison. He took it. There was another, and another.

Every now and again for the first half hour he would burst out in a fit of temper, but every time he was calmed by bribes of titbits passed to him through the bars.

Gradually the excitement died down. Bandoola stood still. He could not even steady himself against the bars to get a purchase because the bear-grease was now well smeared and his hide just slithered against it. The chattering ceased. Very slowly San Oo was lowered onto Bandoola's neck, immediately behind the wide head.

The moment San Oo took his seat the storm began again. Bandoola shook himself. That was no good. Then he nearly stood on his head with his hind feet resting on the top of the bars behind him. San Oo was immediately raised, but the moment Bandoola regained his normal position, down came San Oo on his neck. This time Bandoola stood on his

hind legs and screamed with temper. But San Oo did not care, because he was dangling on his rope up near the pulley block, well out of reach.

Bandoola stood on his four legs again and immediately San Oo was sitting on his neck. This time the young elephant tried to reach him with his trunk and tear him off his rope. But a sharp rap from San Oo's cane on the tip of the trunk taught him better.

Then he swayed to one side, and very nearly did succeed in crushing San Oo's left leg between his body and the side of the pen. But not quite. Bandoola was beginning to learn that these men possessed a determination which was more powerful than his brute strength. Without a let-up San Oo was raised and lowered onto Bandoola's neck for about four hours. Finally he let San Oo sit his full weight on him for three whole minutes, then, the next time he was let down, for half an hour. Bandoola was becoming reconciled.

Now the heavy block of wood over the elephant's back was raised and lowered just as San Oo had been, but whenever the block was raised San Oo jumped on Bandoola's head. The object was first to show him that he could stand his rider's weight without discomfort, whereas the weight of the wood was intolerable; and then gradually to force the elephant to collapse his forelegs out in front of him and his back legs out behind. The moment it was clear that this was going to happen, the elephant men started to chant, "Hmit! Hmit! Hmit!"

At last Bandoola collapsed, with San Oo on his head, and the log now resting lightly on the middle of his back. His spirit had not been broken, but it was being firmly mastered.

After fifteen minutes the weight was lifted, but Bandoola made no effort to get up. The chanting began again, but with a new word of command. "Tah! Tah! Tah!"

He got up wearily, but immediately the voices changed to "Hmit! Hmit! Hmit!" down came the weight once more; and down went Bandoola under it.

This went on until he even lost interest in the bribes of sugarcane proffered through the bars. He was performing his first movements under control almost without knowing it, he was so exhausted. And at last he could do no more. He sat down and he couldn't rise again. San Oo remained on his neck, now talking to him in sweet tones. The day was won.

It was evening before Bandoola rose again. He drank some water from a bucket. He was cramped and he was tired—so tired that he did not notice when his forefeet were shackled. The prison bars behind him were quietly withdrawn. Around his body, passing behind the withers and behind the elbows, they fixed a circle of rope, which San Oo gripped with one hand. There was no certainty that Bandoola, once out of the pen, would not become a bucking bronco. He tried at first to struggle, but the shackles held him, and he developed a sort of long stride-hop in his journey to the tree to which his foot was to be chained for the night. Near the tree was stacked a mountain of bamboo fodder. Then he was left alone, to munch and meditate. And from that night began his life as a draught elephant.

At dawn the whole camp visited him and Ma Pyoo brought him some cooked rice rolled into balls by her dainty hands. He didn't seem frightened that the ordeal of yesterday would be repeated. Po Toke and San Oo spent the whole day with him. San Oo was on and off the elephant's head continually, and by sundown Bandoola was completely under control. Po Toke had proved his method of training. An elephant could be mastered by patience and kindness.

Even the contractor praised Po Toke's achievement. "Of course," he added, "Bandoola is a very clever elephant. But it will be sixteen years before he begins to do any real work."

3

Despite the difference in the lengths of their gestation, men and elephants have roughly the same rate of development, the same span of life. Bandoola and I were born in the same year; while I was at school, he was receiving his education from Po Toke and San Oo. Together we embarked on adult life.

Bandoola was born at a time when dacoity or brigandage was rife throughout Burma. But by the time he was five years old it was rapidly dying out. Forest areas which had been the hideouts of dacoits for years became safe again; and those of the British teak-trading firms which had managed to survive the troubles began to expand their activities. New leases were granted by the British government easily enough, in difficult and more inaccessible forest areas. The problem was that there weren't enough elephants. For years no wild elephants had been captured to replenish the captive herds; hundreds of captive elephants had gone astray during the troubles and rejoined the wild herds.

In the meantime the contractors who owned elephant herds had doubled, and in some cases trebled, their prices; and when the question arose of working difficult forests, they flatly refused. If the teak trade was to be expanded, the companies had to build up elephant herds of their own. The old jungle salts who had survived the bad times were sent out through the forests to see what they could do.

One of these was a man called Bruce Walker. He was buying elephants for a British firm which had held forest leases under the Burmese kings for many years, and had decided to open up the forests of the Upper Chindwin.

So it happened that one day in the year 1903, Bruce Walker came in search of elephants to the camp where Po Toke worked. Bruce had acquired in his youth a remarkable knowledge of the Burmese language, by attending the monastery schools. He understood and liked the Burmese way of living and of doing business. So when, in answer to his statement that he was out to acquire a herd of a hundred elephants, the contractor told him flatly that he had no elephants for sale but that he had an excellent five-year-old calf called Bandoola, Bruce Walker laughed and said that he was interested in no animal, male or female, under twenty or over forty. But he consented to look at the five-year-old all the same. The shortest distance between two points in Burma is never a straight line.

Po Toke demonstrated the animal's points: how obedient he was, how magnificently developed, and not a training scar upon him. "Yes, yes," Bruce agreed, "but, you see, we want to work these forests now, not in sixteen years' time." He was not impressed by the prodigious Bandoola, but he was impressed by Po Toke, who in his own way was equally prodigious. He was only twenty, but the manner in which he handled Bandoola showed that he had a way with elephants that was quite exceptional. The thought occurred to Bruce that, despite his youth, Po Toke might be the very man he needed as head elephant man, or Sinoke, to move his new herd of purchases up to northern Burma.

"Come and see me this evening in my tent," he said.

Before he arrived, Bruce had already discovered that Po Toke had been to the Mingin Monastery School; that he was going one day to marry the contractor's daughter; that he had *auza*, or deep respect from the other elephant men in the camp. It was an excellent report, and it decided Bruce to offer Po Toke the job of headman, despite his youth, at a wage which it would seem impossible for him to refuse.

But he did refuse; and being pressed, he said that nothing would separate him from Bandoola and that he wanted to marry Ma Pyoo; and anyway perhaps the contractor would not give him permission to leave. He gave the impression that he considered himself as much the contractor's property as were Bandoola and Ma Pyoo.

It was an attitude that pleased Bruce. He sent for the contractor. When the contractor arrived, Bruce told him nothing of what Po Toke had said to him or he had said to Po Toke. He merely asked how much the contractor wanted for Bandoola.

"I cannot sell Bandoola," answered the contractor. "He belongs to my daughter, Ma Pyoo."

They sent for Ma Pyoo. While they waited for her, Po Toke explained to the contractor what Bruce had suggested. He was excited. But the old contractor merely smiled. He squatted on his haunches and began drawing in the sand, as if calculating the price for Bandoola. Then he turned to Bruce and said, "I am an old man. Perhaps it is time for me to sell all my elephants and retire to the village where I was born. In that case Po Toke can do as he wishes, and the price for Bandoola can be the dowry for my daughter's marriage."

"And how much do you want for your elephants?" asked Bruce.

The old man went through his elephants one by one, naming a figure for each, except Bandoola; and Bruce, knowing that in Burma these things are matters for careful bargaining, agreed that he would buy the elephants, but the exact price would be settled later.

Then Ma Pyoo arrived at the tent and made her obeisance to the Thakin, and her father told her that he had sold all his elephants, with the exception of Bandoola. Was she prepared to sell Bandoola, and if so how much would she want for him?

Ma Pyoo laughed. Looking at Po Toke, she explained that though her father had given her Bandoola, she had promised him to Po Toke when they married, so that she really could not sell him.

Then they all laughed, including Bruce, who now knew that he could save his face for buying a calf elephant by spreading his price proportionately over the prices of the other animals. He knew also that the old contractor would not be difficult in his bargaining, because this offer gave Po Toke the chance of becoming a well-paid Sinoke and marrying his daughter, who was now of age.

The price which Bruce agreed to pay the contractor for Bandoola was five hundred rupees, which made a satisfactory dowry for Ma Pyoo; of this amount he spread four hundred and fifty rupees among the nine grown elephants and wrote down Bandoola's price at fifty rupees, which made a satisfactory entry in Bruce's accounts. With Po Toke thrown in, he had got a bargain.

IT TOOK PO TOKE six months to collect into one watershed all the elephants which Bruce had bought.

In the meantime he was very happy. He had married Ma Pyoo and together they were going to his home in the Upper Chindwin forests. Only one thing slightly marred his happiness. While the contractor owned Bandoola, Po Toke could always fancy the elephant was really his. But once the letter "C" was branded on Bandoola's rump, he, like Po Toke,

would be working for the company. If they were to keep together, Po Toke would need to use all his guile and ingenuity.

The march to the Upper Chindwin began in late September. There were a hundred and sixteen elephants in all and they departed in batches of seven to nine at intervals of three days. Po Toke and Ma Pyoo led the first party, a group of nine elephants with Bandoola, harnessed with a miniature pannier and laden with some of Ma Pyoo's smaller chattels, wobbling along behind.

The last of the elephants did not arrive in the Upper Chindwin until April of the following year. On the journey two elephants died from natural causes, but there were no other casualties. The hazardous crossing of the Irrawaddy River was made on bamboo rafts without a hitch. Bruce congratulated himself on his choice of Po Toke as headman, and was so pleased with the condition in which Bandoola arrived at the end of the long journey that he gave instructions that the calf should join his six travelling pack elephants, under San Oo.

This delighted Po Toke. San Oo was a splendid young oozie. Every day Bandoola was with the pack elephants he was learning something new. In the course of the eleven years he spent as a pack animal he covered thousands of miles and visited every forest area in northern Burma in every season of the year. But any attempt to use him for rice transport was always foiled by Po Toke, who knew that there was a danger of galling his back through overloading.

At the age of fifteen his tusks began to take the shape which is called Swai Gah, after the posture of the Burmese dancing girl, with arms bent upwards and outwards. This gave him a rather wicked appearance when he raised his head and cocked his ears. Those who did not know him were careful not to pass too close when they met him in the jungle.

By that age he was already as well developed as most young tuskers of twenty or over. And he had something which none of them possessed. His spirit had not, like theirs, been broken. His lifting power with his trunk or tusks was as great as theirs; but the obedience which he gave to his oozie sprang from trust and not from fear.

When Bruce saw how well Bandoola was shaping, he wanted to put him straight onto timber work. It took all Po Toke's obstinacy to fob him off; and by the time Bandoola was seventeen, even Po Toke had to agree that he should do harder work than transport, or there would be a danger of his going on *musth*, the periodical state of frenzy that adult elephants are prone to; and if he went on musth he would have to be chained up and would lose condition. But even so Po Toke won the concession that before

Bandoola was put in dragging harness he should be given a couple of years pushing and lifting logs with his head, tusks and trunk.

So for two years Bandoola was sent to Moo River among the old crock elephants, where logs stranded on sandbanks had continually to be rolled back into the main channel; a form of work reserved for pensioned tuskers, suffering from old age or deformities that made them unfit for harness.

It was almost the last order which Bruce Walker ever gave. For war had broken out in Europe and, like many British forest assistants and managers, Bruce Walker volunteered for service and was killed in action. So for the duration of the war Po Toke took over practically the whole of Bruce's work of organizing the timber extraction, and during this time he had to leave Bandoola almost entirely to the care of San Oo.

The Spanish influenza epidemic, which swept the world in 1918 and killed more people than the worst war in history up to that time, penetrated into the heart of the Burmese jungle in a virulent form, and word came to Po Toke that San Oo was dead. He liked his brother-in-law and was sorry he had died so young. But his first thought was for Bandoola. After thirteen years with San Oo how would Bandoola react to another oozie?

Picking the best man he had, he set out with him at once for the Moo River. The time had come, he decided, to move Bandoola to the Gangaw Forest and break him to his main task of hauling timber in the camp of Maung Aung Gyaw.

Bandoola had come of age.

4

Bandoola was a rare elephant in his generation, born in captivity and educated to man's service not through cruelty and the breaking of his spirit, but by the indomitable patience of Po Toke. He represented a new generation of elephants.

In the same way, the men who joined the firm of Bombine after the First World War represented a new generation of forest assistants. We approached life in the Burmese jungle and the management of elephants differently from our predecessors. We were ripe for the ideas of Po Toke, which appeared to the senior men in Bombine as sentimental, unpractical, uneconomic.

But I am anticipating, for I did not meet Po Toke or Bandoola immediately I joined Bombine. My initiation into jungle life came with the help of Willie, my first forest manager. It was Willie who pronounced the dictum: "In this country there is the choice of two evils—women or the bottle. Choose which you like, but don't mix 'em."

Willie had chosen the bottle. Though I would never have dared to mention it to Willie, it was my dream that one day in the future, when I myself was a forest manager, I should find a white woman who would share life in the jungle with me. Meanwhile I kept up an extensive correspondence with almost every girl I knew in England. "Damn lot of snippets!" Willie remarked, looking at my mail. "The only people worth writing to are your mother and father. Besides," he added, "think of the incoming mail. All these letters take up room. What about my cheroots? What about my whisky? What about my cheeses? The damn runner can't carry *everything*."

So letters were out and cheeses were in. And they were, I admit, delicious cheeses. Willie would regularly have them sent out specially from England, Wensleydales and Blue Cheshires, the date of their dispatch carefully calculated so that they should not reach their prime before arrival. He knew how to treat a cheese to perfection, and he had it served dressed in a starched white napkin with all the pomp to be found in a London club.

After letter-writing was banned I looked round for some other hobby, anything which would serve as an excuse to get out of range of Willie's sharp tongue. He made everything a challenge, and though at first I thought it was just pure damn cussedness, I came to realize that it was his way of putting one on one's mettle. He inspired an almost vindictive loyalty, the desire to prove that one wasn't the fool he took one for.

"If you want something to do," he said one morning, "we'll play cricket. You make the pitch, I'll provide the bat and ball. You ought to get a nice pitch ready by teatime with the help of the oozies."

He sat back in his chair and slept, while I mustered a gang of elephant men and set them to clearing the jungle.

The more roots of shrubs and grass I pulled up, the more I despaired of ever getting a smooth pitch. My oozies worked sullenly on in the blazing sunshine, plainly indicating that this was not their favourite form of insanity. Every now and again I would look across at Willie, placidly asleep in his chair. At last, in desperation, I went to my tent and removed the dhuri—a mat about six feet by four—from beside the camp bed, and pegged it to the ground with bamboo stakes. As I drove home the last stake, Willie woke up and went into his tent.

He came back with two cricket stumps. One of these he planted at one end of the mat, the other he handed to me. "These Burmans can't bat or bowl for toffee," he said, "but they're jolly good fielders." He placed them in a circle round the camp clearing, which wasn't fifty yards across and contained our two tents. He set the field as if for rounders, and to Po Pyan, his head servant, he assigned the position of wicket keeper, a position which from Po Pyan's expression of resigned disgust he had clearly occupied before. "You bat first," he said to me. "No scoring. No runs. Just bat." He took a grubby tennis ball from his pocket, paced out fifteen paces and made a mark. I squared up, gripping the stump with both hands.

Willie bowled a straight underhand ball and I played it. The second, an off-break, passed me and Po Pyan caught it with a sigh. The next was a full toss, and I let fly for a brilliant six. It was a satisfying sock. How many trees and bamboos it hit before it came to rest I do not know. But when at last it sank into the dense jungle, I turned to smile at Willie; only to find him standing a couple of yards away from me, his face purple with rage. "Do you think tennis balls grow on trees, you idiot?" he asked. I could not have felt more shame if, on being declared "Out" at the Oval, I had clubbed the umpire over the head with my bat.

It was ten minutes before the ball was found, and long before then I had reached the miserable conviction that the least I could do to make amends was to get myself out. I need not have worried because Willie's next ball took my stump clean out of the ground.

"My innings!" Willie declared with an ominous note of complacency in his voice. He took the stump and surveyed the fielders.

I gave him a well-pitched spinner. He cut it, with a twist of the wrist which amazed me, all along the carpet of the jungle clearing to an oozie, who fielded it and threw it in to me. The next he went forward to. It came back to me like a rocket. He played every ball. He let nothing past him. With a straight stump and an eye like a hawk, he placed his shots all round the wicket.

Cricket has never been my favourite game; but my fanatic loathing of it dates from that afternoon. When it had been going on so long that I felt I could scream, I suddenly had an inspiration. "Hadn't these oozies better track and catch their elephants?" I said. "You remember you told me to check each evening or some would be missing in the morning."

"We draw stumps when I say, and we move camp when I say," Willie answered, and nodded his head to a waiting servant to bring the tray with whisky and soda. He downed a stiff glassful in a gulp and as he saw me licking my lips, took up his stance and called out, "Play!"

So once again I reverted to off-spin, leg-spin, googlies, bumpers. It made no difference. My strength failed long before the light. At last he called, "Last ball!" If only he would take a final swipe and lose the wretched thing for ever! But no! A beautiful stroke, telling but restrained. As the fielder returned it to him, he placed it in his pocket and said to me, "Remember to put this dhuri back in your tent. The night dew would spoil it, and it isn't yours."

Apart from having to bowl to Willie whenever I met him during the next few months, I never played cricket again in my life. But I never told Willie with what abhorrence I regarded the game, for it was the beginning of the thawing process. As I got better at the game, so Willie in his unbending way unbent. And I didn't realize that these games were not in fact a torment designed especially for me, but that Willie, who was a well-known bat in county cricket, was keeping his eye in for a tour with the Free Foresters when he returned to England on leave.

During one of our inspection trips I had an unpleasant task when we visited Po Toke's camp. I had already conceived an admiration for Po Toke, but one of the questions on which we could never see eye to eye was the medical treatment of the animals. Po Toke, who believed in faith, had allowed an enormous abscess on the chest of one of his tuskers to go untreated. This he had at first hidden from me because he was ashamed. We both of us awaited Willie's inspection with trepidation.

The best method of defence is attack, and when we came to this tusker,

I went in front of Willie to the elephant's head. I tapped the tusker under his lower jaw and the animal raised his head with his tusks resting almost on my topee. I felt the abscess. It was twice the size of my fist. I looked back at Willie, expecting some comment, perhaps even a word of advice. But he said nothing; he just looked sick.

"It's ripe," I said. "I think I'll open it up now."

He made no comment, moving away as if in disgust.

"This is my hour," I thought, and turning to Po Toke I asked him in Burmese for a knife. Po Toke drew from a sheath on his hip an ivory-handled dagger. Seeing it, the rider bent down and said something to the tusker which I did not understand but which I took to mean, "Now behave yourself."

I stabbed the abscess with the dagger, and the pus poured down the animal's chest and foreleg. I cleaned the abscess out with my fingers, then syringed it with a dilute disinfectant, which I also used for washing the animal's leg and my own hands.

The whole thing took about five minutes. "Well," I said, much relieved, "I think that's that, sir." It was a nice job, and I considered that if I had not earned any praise, at least I had avoided a rocket.

Willie approached and, remarking rather grimly, "We'll talk about it later," he continued his inspection.

After Willie had taken his first whisky of the evening, he turned to me. "Didn't Po Toke tell you that animal was dangerous?"

"No," I said; "but in that case why isn't it down in the inspection book?"

"It is, as you'd know if you'd taken some trouble to read Burmese. It's a wonder the animal didn't knock your block off."

"Well, why didn't one of you stop me operating?"

"For precisely the same reason that the animal *didn't* knock your block off," Willie said in a tone which, despite the ambiguity of the words, made me feel that this was the kindest thing he had said to me in six months.

Willie took another drink and then said, "You've got to watch out for Po Toke. He knows a lot about elephants. But he's not a Bombine boy. We bought him with that elephant Bandoola. He's very good, but there's something I can't quite trust. Watch him as you go on."

It was the first hint I had received that I would have the chance to "go on". In a few months my probation year would be over and my future depended on Willie's report.

During the rainy season I had three attacks of malaria. Though I had been used to that during the war, I never got a more welcome letter than

Willie's note to say it was time that I came out of the jungle for a change. He met me on the main river, and we had one night together before we boarded the steamer for the three-day trip to headquarters.

I had not seen him for three months. I think he was rather shocked at my appearance, because the fever had been severe. He was so pleasant that I almost felt he would have given me six innings to his one.

"By the way," he said, "you've got an overdraft and I've been told to say the company is worried about it."

"I'm even more worried about it," I answered, not adding that it had piled up through keeping pace with his thirst.

"I'm glad to hear that," he said. "I'm not against a man drinking, provided he can afford to."

Then he told me that I was not only confirmed in my appointment, but I was to take over a large district to relieve a senior assistant. "Your new forest manager will be Millie," he said. "You may think that I've been an absolute devil this last year. You're quite right. I have, deliberately. You'll find Millie a much nicer man than I am, but I trust you to serve him just as loyally all the same."

That night I found myself at last accepted, and the acceptance was all the dearer because it had been so hard to win.

Aboard the river steamer there were other passengers. The skipper and the engineer we knew already, but in addition there were an American oil-driller called Jake who was as tough as hell, his Cockney assistant, a miserable little man, and lastly a missionary who was a meek and gentle creature.

Our cabins surrounded a small furnace which was dignified by the name of The Saloon. As if it wasn't already stifling enough, the American oil-driller raised the temperature even higher by emitting a stream of blasphemous obscenities whenever he opened his mouth.

After dinner he wanted to play poker. Our eyes all turned to the missionary. "I don't know how to play," he said, "but I'm game to learn on condition you'll moderate your language for the rest of the evening, Jake."

This offer won the oil-driller's heart. "OK, Mister Sky Pilot, it's a deal. Goddamn it if I'll swear again tonight."

The skipper and the engineer excused themselves on the grounds that they would have to be under way at dawn. The saloon table was cleared and Willie suggested that instead of poker, we should play Northern Farmer, which is much the same but rather simpler.

We played for a couple of hours. The missionary, with beginner's luck, held wonderful cards and played them shrewdly. The American, deprived of his freedom of speech, was slightly down and so was I. I remembered what Willie had said about my overdraft, and knowing that I could ill afford to lose any money I began to play hesitantly, which is a fatal thing.

When it came to the last round, however, we were all a little reckless. The pool built up until it contained about seven hundred and fifty rupees (fifty pounds, which in those days was a lot of money). By that time there were only two of us left in, the Cockney oil man and myself. It was my turn, and I had a five of spades. If I chucked my hand in, the Cockney would clear the pool. If I called him and won, I would share the pool; but if I lost, I would have to pay another seven hundred and fifty rupees, which I hadn't got.

My card lay face down on the table. I looked at the Cockney. He had on his face an asinine smirk. He was sitting pretty. I felt incapable of making a correct decision. I turned to Willie.

To any of the others Willie's face would have appeared expressionless. But I, who had studied it over the past year for the slightest variation of mood, could read plainly the gathering disgust at my hesitation. He might as well have said outright: "If you don't call him, I'll never speak to you again."

"All right," I said, as much to Willie as the Cockney, "I'll see you," and I turned up my five of spades.

"You sure?" said the Cockney.

"I'm sure."

The Cockney turned over his card. It was a four.

At six the next morning I was awakened by a cool hand on my forehead. I opened my eyes. Willie had a glass in his hand. "Drink that!" he said. "Champagne and stout. Do you a world of good."

It was the last order he gave me as my No. 1, and I obeyed it willingly and then went back to sleep.

I saw him a few times before he departed on leave. From somewhere in England I received a laconic postcard. "How goes the cricket? I got a century yesterday. Keep fit." I was in camp with my new forest manager, Millie, when it arrived. I passed it to him.

"You may not realize it," Millie said. "You've only known Willie for a year, and I've known him for twenty. You've been very highly honoured."

Millie was a complete contrast to Willie, a man of the most gentle disposition, a strange man to find in the jungle. I can never think of Millie

without seeing him in front of me on the march, with two inches of his white underpants showing below his blue shorts. He had little feeling for animals, seldom came very near to his elephants, and seemed to take it for granted that I knew as much as he did. It was his method of teaching, because it forced me to pick up his knowledge by attention.

This may sound as if he was inefficient. He was not. But he was by nature a reader, a student. He was not apparently interested in the inspection of elephants. But their droppings he would read most studiously. He could recognize these more easily than he could the elephants' heads. Every elephant dropping he came across in our working area he would examine, prodding it with his shooting stick. Usually he had no comment to make, but occasionally he would say, "Look at that, Mee Too's been eating earth again. I don't like that." Prod, prod. "Um. Elephant worms again." Or, "Poor old Kah Gyis. Beginning to show his age. Bamboos passing through him like string."

It was not until Millie's digestion gave out too, and he went sick for a long period, that I appreciated he knew four hundred elephants in that forest by their digestions. Henceforward one of my precepts of elephant management became, "By their droppings ye shall know them."

5

Bandoola and I did not meet till we were twenty-three; and Po Toke, who introduced us, made the most of the fact that we were the same age and both embarking on our adult life in the jungle, and facing similar problems. He did his best to instil in me a sense of responsibility towards the first product of his training methods. He was a pioneer of the theory that calves born and trained in captivity were far more suitable for perpetuating the elephant herds than wild elephants captured and broken in spirit. I was completely converted to his views, and so were a number of forest managers and assistants. The times were changing.

But individual training did not prove a success. There were only one or two oozies with any outstanding gift for training; none with the genius of Po Toke: and no trained calf ever developed in the same prodigious way as Bandoola. The decision was taken to start a number of training camps with a school of young elephants in each, and Po Toke was appointed general trainer.

In a sense it was a triumph for him. His theories and methods had been officially accepted. But it meant that he could no longer keep an eye upon Bandoola, and that was why Po Toke appealed to me.

I was so convinced of the rightness of Po Toke's methods that I made every effort to see that during Bandoola's early years of dragging timber he was not overworked. But the senior timber assistant immediately above me had very different ideas. He was a man called Rasher, nearing the end of his time and violently opposed to the newfangled methods of elephant training.

When we met periodically, we thrashed out our arguments in camp over whisky: for Rasher, like Willie, was married to the bottle. "You're crazy," he said. "Just because an elephant lives roughly as long as a man, you pretend he has the character of a man. I've never heard such unmitigated nonsense."

I felt at a loss in answering, for the truth was that Rasher was nearly crazy. He was tough and hard on animals, but he drove them no harder than he drove himself. He had the frantic willpower of the alcoholic.

It was a Goanese doctor in a small upcountry station who took me on one side and warned me that if Rasher was to get home on his retirement leave in three months, I should have to remain his constant companion in the jungle until it was time for him to go.

The prospect terrified me, as only those who have lived in the jungle can appreciate. Even living there with one's greatest friend makes one want to scream at times. But Rasher and I had nothing in common. My interest in elephants was young and intense. His had disappeared years before, and nothing had taken its place except the bottle.

He frightened me, I don't mind admitting. Looking at him, red-faced and jittery, I had a nasty premonition that I might be looking at myself a quarter of a century older. "Women or whisky," Willie had said. The idea of taking a Burmese mistress did not attract me; and though I liked drinking, I was horrified by the later stages of these marriages to the bottle. I loved the life, but I wanted a woman of my own race who would share it with me. And what woman in her senses would?

Meanwhile, I racked my brains for something which might give Rasher some new interest, and I found it in my camera. He had never done any photography and he grew interested in a set of photographs I was trying to build up, of game tracks. He wanted to try his hand, and it was wonderful the change that came over him.

He wanted to photograph elephants; his enthusiasm suddenly revived as he realized that instead of seeing them every wretched day of his life, he would soon see them only in zoos. He cut down his drinking because it hindered his hobby.

One evening we agreed to do some flashlight printing. We rigged up my tent as a temporary darkroom. We set up the table and laid out the equipment: the red developing lamp which smoked malodorously, the trays of liquids, developers, fixers and washes, and spare glasses of all necessities.

Before we started, Rasher was by his standards stone cold sober. But he fixed himself an extra large whisky and water and placed it on the table before him. I was to fire the magnesium pistol, while he held the printing frame.

"Right ho! Lights out." Except for the glow of the developing lamp we were in darkness. Everything went well for a time. He worked with enthusiasm. And then the urge to drink came back to him. "Wait a minute," he said. He picked up his drink and drained it in one.

Then he sprang up, spilling liquid from the plates and knocking over glasses as he staggered to the tent flaps. Everything was ruined.

"What the hell's the matter?" I asked, furious.

"I've drunk the bloody hypo," he groaned, and collapsed.

For a week he did not smoke or drink whisky. The glass of hypo combined the effects of Epsom salts and mustard water. After that, Rasher's passion for photography vanished. "Pure waste of time," he said.

The Goanese doctor congratulated me, when I saw him next. "You did a wonderful job," he said.

"It wasn't me," I answered. "It was the hypo."

Rasher went home. He had fifteen thousand pounds in capital, the savings of a lifetime; and three years, he reckoned, in which to spend it. They say he spent six months of every year in a nursing home for repairs and maintenance, and the other six months over-lubricating the works.

When he died at the end of the three years, his whole estate, amounting to one hundred and fifty-eight pounds, was bequeathed to the RSPCA.

AFTER RASHER LEFT, I saw Bandoola every month or six weeks. As far as the disposition of my elephants was concerned, I was now my own master; but I learned very soon that in the jungle a man is never completely his own master, far less the master of his elephants. It seemed to me that the real master was the monsoon, and his innumerable servants were the leeches and the malarial mosquitoes.

Not long after Rasher went home, a man came to my camp and asked to see me. He told me that he had come from the camp of Maung Aung Gyaw. I asked him how things were going there. They were not going well, he answered, not at all well. Bandoola's oozie was useless. "Bandoola is on his first musth," he said. "The oozie cannot recapture him. The whole camp is terrorized. Bandoola is dangerous. There is no telling what he may not do." He went on to tell me that I should offer a reward for Bandoola's recapture; a reward which I fancied my informant hoped he would collect himself.

But I merely said I would visit the camp myself. I wanted to learn something about musth at first hand.

I had sat near campfires and listened to old Burmans giving their ideas about it, as though it was a form of madness or possession. But, even though I myself had never seen an animal on musth, I was convinced that there was nothing abnormal about it unless the sexual urge was to be considered abnormal.

When I reached Maung Aung Gyaw's camp, Bandoola had been lost for five days, and all the elephants in the camp were chained to trees as a precaution against the demon Bandoola, ranging at large on musth.

I had brought with me Kya Sine, my hunter. Together we set out to track Bandoola. Kya Sine led and I carried a shotgun only, as I was not hunting him. We followed his tracks to about five miles from the camp. There we saw the bleeding bark of the trees which he had been stabbing with his sharp tusks. We cut away from his tracks and went down to the riverbed, which was bordered by a mass of huge granite boulders. It was a sweltering hot afternoon in April. I was sure Bandoola was nearby. I could feel him, could visualize him standing perfectly still, waiting to charge us.

I told Kya Sine to sit in the shade of one of the huge boulders and wait until I came back. Then I began to work upstream. I was wearing rope-soled shoes, which were almost as silent as Bandoola's own feet. I had been gone about an hour when, looking over a huge boulder, I suddenly saw him.

He was not the Bandoola who had been described to me, stark staring mad on musth. He was the same Bandoola I had always known. He was down in the creek, standing under the shade of an overhanging tree. For a moment I thought that he was facing another elephant, but then I saw it was a boulder about his own size.

He seemed to be making some sort of obeisance to this boulder. His trunk swung from side to side in the movement which the Burmans call "rocking the cradle". And when this stopped he rocked his body from side to side, standing on alternate feet in the movement described as "winnowing the rice".

I watched him for a long time, during which he remained looking at the boulder as if in a dream. He was, I am convinced, imagining that the boulder was a beautiful female elephant and how he would pay court to her. The sexual manifestations of it were plain to see.

I left him at last and went back to Kya Sine and told him in a whisper what I had seen, imitating the motions of Bandoola's body with mine. "Musth has passed," said Kya Sine, excited. He now told me to sit and wait while he went to see for himself.

The time passed slowly. Then suddenly I heard Kya Sine give the order "Hmah," meaning, "Lift it up," and immediately after a crash like a rifle shot, as a branch of a tree which barred the elephant's path along the bank was snapped. I jumped to my feet, ready at any moment to climb the boulder for protection. But as soon as I saw Bandoola's head, with Kya Sine riding him, I knew that the time of danger had passed. I did not say a word, but followed them back to the camp.

We chained Bandoola to a tree and to my surprise Po Toke arrived soon after. He had heard the same exaggerated rumours that I had about Bandoola at large on musth.

We discussed Bandoola at length. We could not leave him with his present oozie, who was an utter failure. So we decided to attach Bandoola to my pack elephants and, with Po Toke riding him, to march to the training camp. There we would take the precaution of sawing off the tips of Bandoola's tusks.

We left the following day, and on the march early one evening Po Toke came to me and said, "Go upstream along the bank alone. Don't take even Kya Sine." I didn't question him. I knew from his voice that he was letting me into some secret of the jungle. I went upstream until I came upon Bandoola. This time he was not contemplating a boulder. He had with him a wild kheddar-captured elephant purchased in the Shan States which we were taking to Po Toke's camp for branding. I watched them mating that evening until it was almost dark, and for the ten successive evenings. Bandoola, I thought almost with envy, had lost his loneliness and found a mate; and I wondered whether Chit Ma would bear a calf the equal of the sire, though she was not the dam I would have chosen.

Po Toke did not take the possibility seriously. "They are both too young," he said. "But when Bandoola musths, it would be as well to keep him in the company of good dams of middle age."

6

The site of Po Toke's camp was a deserted village, centuries old. The only signs that the place had ever been inhabited were a huge cultivated tamarind tree, and nearby it a small pagoda, now little more than a mound of mud bricks overgrown with creeper.

To watch the operation of sawing off the tips of Bandoola's tusks, I took up my position on the pagoda mound. Bandoola was securely chained to the tamarind tree. All signs of musth had passed and once again he was as docile as any domesticated animal.

The tamarind tree was excellent for the purpose. Its bole was of great girth, and its massive branches, radiating out in the form of an umbrella, afforded complete shade. It looked as if it had taken about a century to grow and was good for at least another century.

Po Toke dipped his finger in red betel nut and lime and marked off where he was going to cut each tusk. As the first three inches of the tusk, which were to be sawn off, contained no nerve, the operation should

cause Bandoola no pain. Then Po Toke took up the handsaw. Bandoola watched him, squinting down his tusks. It was rather like a child at the dentist's for the first time, I thought. Po Toke caught hold of the tusk with his left hand and began to saw with his right.

For a moment Bandoola was quiet, then suddenly he jerked up his head and let out bellow after bellow of rage. Po Toke shouted to him to be still, but the elephant took no notice. The other attendants stood back, well out of the way. I could feel the air charged with danger.

Bandoola was securely chained to the tree. Po Toke had the advantage, he waited for Bandoola to quieten down. He spoke to him reassuringly. Bandoola was as silent as a coiled spring.

After a time Po Toke reached up and held the tusk in his left hand again. Suddenly the spring of Bandoola's anger was uncoiled. He put every ounce of his tremendous body-weight against his chains. But they held. Po Toke stepped back. Into his orders he put his full authority. But Bandoola took no notice. He turned around to face the tamarind tree, seized the tying chains in his trunk and jerked to snap them, but still they held. Then he raised a forefoot and stamped on the chains, already strained to breaking point. The fetters snapped. His forelegs were free.

The oozies fled. Po Toke ran up and joined me on the pagoda. We were helpless. There was nothing to do but watch the furious animal break loose. His rage apparently was concentrated on the tree.

Having got his forefeet free, he ignored the chains which still held him and, raising his tusks high up the treetrunk to give him leverage, he pushed with his whole weight and every muscle in his powerful body. A shower of leaves fluttered to the ground; the tree rocked; its trunk came back against Bandoola's trunk and for a moment he rested. Then he heaved against it again. Something snapped, a large root passing underneath him. He rocked the tree rhythmically; there was another snap, a third, then suddenly there was a rending, and the heaviest branch of the tree snapped and fell towards Bandoola. He saw it coming and screamed and tugged to avoid it, but the links of his chains did not part. With a volley of explosions as the roots snapped, the whole tree keeled over, fell on him and buried him from sight.

There is a silence of the forests which follows the crashing of a giant tree, a grave and tragic silence, as if something has suddenly died. Judging from the quiet and the absence of movement, I thought Bandoola was dead too, crushed beneath a tree far more massive even than himself. But when we examined him, we found that he was alive, lying flat on his side, still chained to the tree by his hind legs.

With incredible speed the elephant men got to work with saws and axes. We had no idea how badly Bandoola was injured. He lay quite motionless during the rescue. Then he slowly rose as if he were recovering from a severe winding. He was docile. He gave no trouble at all. But no one ever suggested again that his tusks should be tipped.

It was just as well, as it proved; for within two years he had a battle with a wild tusker which might have ended very differently if Po Toke's operation under the tamarind tree had been successful.

Bandoola was not on musth at the time. A wild elephant found him grazing peacefully alone, and challenged. There followed a duel, which no one witnessed, but the violence of which I could read easily enough from Bandoola's wounds and the tracks of the wild tusker.

I went after the wild tusker myself. I trekked him for two days as far as the mouth of the Sihaung River. There he disappeared into a sea of elephant grass into which it would have been suicidal to follow him. From his tracks I could see that the wild tusker had received the coup de grace from Bandoola's sharp tusks, as his droppings were heavy with blood. He must have died.

Bandoola's wounds were terrible, long deep incisions on the head and withers. I treated him for a year in Po Toke's training camp, which had now become a hospital for the sick as well as a school for the young. I had learned a great deal from Po Toke about training elephants; but I found it very difficult to teach him and other Burmese elephant men about curing them. Po Toke as a Buddhist believed that sick and injured elephants could be cured by faith; and I could not help feeling at times that he resented what I tried to do.

Bandoola's wounds healed remarkably well with treatment. He was the most wonderful patient I have ever handled, man, woman or animal. The day came at last when I could give orders for him to return to forest work.

That evening I was sitting at my camp table in front of my tent, feeling pleased with myself and the world in general. "Well," I told myself, "you've throughly deserved the fishing holiday at Patala which you're going to take tomorrow."

Then I saw Po Toke coming towards the tent, in company with Ma Pyoo. That was not merely unusual: it was ominous.

They both squatted near the table and I asked Ma Pyoo how she and her relations were. She answered politely that all was well, when suddenly Po Toke broke in. "Thakin, I wish to resign and give up my work."

I couldn't believe my ears. Po Toke was my most trusted assistant. "*What* did you say?"

He repeated his resignation, a resignation which meant abandoning Bandoola. I couldn't imagine why he was going, but I suddenly realized that he felt he could leave Bandoola because I was there to look after the elephant for him. "If you go, Po Toke," I said, "I shall go too." I almost meant it.

Both of them tried to smile off my threat of resignation, but I repeated it seriously.

Then Po Toke thought of a way out. Instead of resigning, would I allow him to go on long leave?

"That is a different matter," I answered. "And while you're away," I added, to put the conversation on a lighter plane, "while you're away, wouldn't it be a good idea to leave Ma Pyoo with me, just to make sure you come back?"

They laughed, and then Ma Pyoo said that she had heard I was going to Patala for the fishing. "Don't worry," she said, "you will catch a fish there and then you won't be lonely."

"What makes you say that?"

She smiled and answered, "That fish has no scales." There lay beneath her joke, and I suppose mine as well, a recognition of my loneliness and longing for a mate.

PATALA WAS A VERY isolated village of intermarried Chinese and Burmans. I camped about a quarter of a mile away, and on the first evening the headman invited me to come to their rice festival.

It was the biggest drunk I have ever attended. I joined in the party, danced round their pots of country rice liquor and took my drink through the same straws as they used. To me, accustomed to whisky, the drink was as soft as lime juice, though not as pleasant. But the Patalans grew drunker and drunker, the women even worse than the men.

I learned their songs. There is one I can sing to this day. "Choyin! Choyin! Chalin Mayin!" I don't understand a word of what it means and yet the air conveys to me a lovely sense of the forests and the hills.

When I went to bid the headman goodnight, he begged me through an interpreter to stay, as a compliment to them. So I remained until the communal pot was dry and the last dancers staggered off. Then the headman invited me to his house.

We went up some bamboo steps onto a veranda. Suddenly a most beautiful girl was produced from behind an inner bamboo-matting partition.

In height she was almost six feet and as fair of skin as a fair Spaniard. She wore her jet-black hair in two long pigtails which hung down her back far below her waist. She was of no nationality known to me, but she spoke the language of these people of Patala.

Standing on that veranda, with pigs grunting below us, and their stench rising steadily, she was an astonishing spectacle. She looked as if she had been taken from some prison den and dressed for the occasion in beautiful clothes. There was no smile on her face. Indeed, I could see from the way she looked at the headman, the interpreter and the others, that she hated them. Yet in the way she held herself, with her head up, exposing her long, slender neck, there was magnificent pride.

Everyone left us except the interpreter. "Who is this girl?" I asked. She had sat down. There were four smoky open-wick lamps burning on the veranda and their light seemed to caress her. I didn't like what was happening. It smacked too much of the slave market.

"What she is called we do not know," said the interpreter. "Her mother was a Chinese woman from this village, but she is dead. Her father was a

European officer—a Sit Bo—who passed this way to the Kuki rebellion many, many years ago. He is dead also. He was killed after sleeping in this village."

I could see the whole picture: a young British officer a quarter of a century before, as lonely as I was and frightened into the bargain, because he was going to quell a rebellion. I could understand that; and now I could understand this beautiful girl, *her* loneliness and her pride.

"She is unhappy," said the interpreter. "You will take her away and make her happy."

I shook my head. His arithmetic was wrong. If you add one loneliness to another, you don't necessarily get love or even companionship.

"Take her for ten days, then," said the interpreter. "You can leave her here again when you go."

The girl was lovely and I told the man to tell her so. She wore across her shoulder a brilliant red Chinese blanket like a chieftain. The interpreter spoke to her and took the blanket from her bare shoulders to pass it to me;

but she snatched it and flung it back across her shoulder. She got up and stood, looking like an angry matador. Then she turned and ran into the darkness of the veranda. She understood something the interpreter didn't.

I moved camp next day to fish and forget about red blankets. In my new camp I caught a baby otter. She was a darling. I kept her for six months and lost her without grief. She used to fish with me in the Upper Taungdwin. One afternoon while I was swimming I let her loose in a pool which was as clear as gin. She came back to the rocks three or four times and chatter-barked to me. Then I caught sight of three other otters schooling in the pool. The three soon became four, because Taupai joined their game and their company. It was the last I saw of her, sporting with them in the clear water. I said goodbye with a contented heart. She had found her happiness, even if I had not.

EVEN THOUGH I had learned Burmese, and took some trouble to understand the men who worked for me, I knew that I only understood a small fraction of what was going on in their minds; I was British, they were Burman. I, though the employee of a private company, was the government, they were the governed. It was a thing that had not worried me much until that evening when Po Toke came with Ma Pyoo and tendered his resignation. It gave me a shock. It made me realize that just as the camp was a clearing in the jungle, so my own tent was a little clearing in the camp.

I had noticed strangers in camps which I had visited; but there are always strangers—travellers, opium peddlers and so on. I suspected sometimes that these visitors had another purpose, that they were out to make trouble. But there was nothing on which I could put my finger.

About a month after Po Toke departed on his long leave to stay with his wife's relations, I was transferred to the same area—back to Ningyan. Immediately I got there I realized that rumours of discontent were well founded. I could feel the tension the moment I went into a camp, and my assistants found the same thing wherever they went. I discussed it with government officials, but the answer was that the resentment was directed not against the government but against the large teak-trading companies.

Perhaps the government was right, I thought. Perhaps the hostile feeling which greeted me in camps was not because I was British but because I was working for the T'Tai Bombine. All I knew for certain was that the feeling was hostile, and I didn't like it.

The first news which I received from my old forest depressed me even further. Bandoola was lost. Po Toke had heard rumours of his escape and though he was on leave he came to me to find out how true they were. I could tell him only what I had heard, but I added as a joke that maybe Bandoola had made up his mind to join us in Ningyan.

Po Toke did not smile. "He was born in Ningyan," he said. "Born and trained at the mouth of the Palway Creek, thirty-seven years ago. And if he's found, it will be at the Palway Creek."

One day, I thought to myself, when I am free, I'll go to the Palway Creek and look. But that day did not come for nearly a year, and if it had not been for a dog, Ba Sein, it would never have come at all.

Ba Sein was a Bassein Fishery Hound, a breed once listed by the Indian Kennel Association. It is supposed to have originated from a cross between bloodhounds, imported into the Burmese port of Bassein by Portuguese traders, and the common Indian pariah.

They bred very true to type. From the bloodhound strain they got their deep chocolate colour, the heavy jowl and lop-hanging ears; from the pariah, small, neat, sure-footed paws. The tail was peculiar, because it had the twist or twirl of a chow, though entirely unfeathered.

Bassein fishery men used them to guard their boats. They were savage with strangers and could be left for days and nights alone on the sandbank of the delta without deserting their charges.

I came by Ba Sein because he was in disgrace, in fact under sentence of death. He had dangerously savaged an Indian postman. I was taken in to see him at night, securely chained in a stable. He was marvellous. He bayed at me with the voice of a hound. He twisted his tail almost out of joint, begging for another home and yet another chance.

I walked straight in to him, patted him, unchained him and led him home to my bungalow. Next day I left on a forest tour. I had a number of reasons for needing a dog who could act as a sort of police guard. I was going to the Nanpo, which hadn't been worked for timber for thirty years. It was notorious as a hideout for dacoits. I was taking a lot of money with me, for I had an appointment with an elephant contractor. The Nanpo was ten days' march away and I would have an isolated camp each night. Even in the most peaceful of times that would have been hazardous, considering the amount of money I should have with me. But in addition to that, I had received a few days before an anonymous letter in Burmese threatening me with violence if I tried to open up the Nanpo. As I see now, the Nanpo was intended as one of the mustering centres for the coming rebellion. That first night there was no danger. I camped in a bungalow on the fringe of a village and slept in a securely-closed room.

Ba Sein was deliriously happy to be off his chain and given good food and constant attention. He was an extraordinary dog. He never slept or fully rested. Every time I looked up from my reading or writing, there he was, with his ears half cocked, perpetually alert.

Before I went to bed, I gave Ba Sein a mat in the centre of the room and told him to lie down. Several times during the night I woke up and flashed my torch on him; each time he was in exactly the same position, motionless but intent and wide awake.

For the following ten nights I camped in a tent. Ba Sein became more and more of a companion. His eyes fascinated me: as warm and brown as his short coat, they seemed fixed on something deeper and beyond anything I could see. The only thing that worried me was that he never slept. Whatever hour I put my torch on him he was awake and alert.

When I reached my destination, an eerie watershed with precipitous slopes to the headwater, there was no sign of the contractor or his elephants. But this did not worry me. They had a two months' march from the east and might well have been delayed a day or two. So I settled down to wait a few days.

The Nanpo Creek was a fast mountain stream and very rocky, with huge black boulders, fast runs of rapids and large pools where mahseer were plentiful. On the evening of my arrival I fished from near camp and caught two splendid eight-pounders.

The next day I decided to trek upriver. I would not take Ba Sein because the going was slippery and treacherous for a dog; but he insisted on following me. Three or four times I ordered him back to my tent sharply in Burmese, but I had not gone a quarter of a mile before he was with me again.

I knew it would be courting trouble to chain him up. So I asked the cook for one of the mahseer I had caught the previous evening and threw it on the floor at the entrance to my hut. "All right," I said. "Guard that, and if you're hungry, eat it." He sat on his haunches beside it and made no attempt to follow me.

I shot a barking deer for the pot that day and it was late evening before we got back, my gunboy struggling with it across his shoulders. There was commotion in the camp. "Your dog is rabid mad," my servants shouted. Ba Sein had threatened to savage anyone who came in sight of the tent. "Load your gun," they said, "you'll have to shoot him."

As I approached the tent, I called out, "Ba Sein, Ba Sein." But he did not answer. Then I caught sight of him. There he was sitting on guard beside the fish, just as I'd left him. He wagged his twisted tail at me. "Are you mad, Ba Sein?" I asked. "Mad?" he seemed to answer. "Yes, mad with delight!" and he rushed round my legs. We loved each other dearly.

That night for his supper he had baked mahseer, bones and all, in a bowl of rice.

The anonymous letter which had worried me before I set off passed out of my thoughts. It was good camping in the jungle with the sound of the babbling stream, and fish and game to fill the pot. Saw Maung, the contractor, arrived with eighteen elephants and six baby calves at heel. The contracts were signed; everything had gone according to plan; and we started back.

The trek was uneventful until we reached the bungalow, the last rest before the march to the main river. Ba Sein shared tea with me on the veranda and then we went for a stroll round the compound. The village seemed strangely quiet. It was practically deserted. I called to a man walking along the dusty road, but he hurried on.

I went back to the veranda, and suddenly I noticed that Ba Sein was not at heel. At the same moment there came a cry: "Thakin! Thakin!" It was one of the servants. I ran out, and there, kicking and frothing on the ground, was Ba Sein, apparently in a fit. I bent over him, and as I did so he went stiff. He was dead.

As I picked him up and carried him to the veranda, the recollection of the anonymous letter came back to me. They had poisoned Ba Sein because they knew that while he was alive they could not get at me. I yelled for my head elephant man. "Catch all elephants," I shouted. "We are moving onto the main river tonight."

My camp was never broken quicker. The elephants were loaded, the last one carrying the cold body of Ba Sein wrapped in a blanket. As we moved off, there were no villagers lined up to watch our departure, no headman came to pay respects. The village was deserted. And so it was all the way to the main river. We saw no one.

It was almost midnight when we arrived at the township headquarters on the main river. But the district bungalow was ablaze with light. The place was occupied by a posse of civil police. As I went in, I met a police officer I knew. He wrung me by the hand. "Thank God you're here!" he said. "The whole damned countryside's in the hands of rebels." He mentioned the name of a forest man I knew. "They got him this morning," he said, "murdered him for the firearms."

And that, I realized, is what would have happened to me if it hadn't been for Ba Sein.

7

For months after that, contact with elephant camps was practically severed. It became too dangerous for individual Europeans to travel through the jungle.

When at last we succeeded in re-establishing contact, by touring in armed parties, I found that in one case the rebels had borrowed a hundred baskets of rice and twenty elephants, leaving a message to say that they would be paid for as soon as the government was overthrown. My own elephant men had carried out the transport for them at the point of stolen firearms, rather than desert their animals.

On another of these tours a strange thing happened. We had twenty pack elephants, and I took the precaution of tying them up to form an outer defence perimeter to warn the pickets in event of attack.

At dawn the next day my head elephant man reported that a wild elephant had been heard visiting our tethered animals during the night. The same thing happened the next night, though we had marched at least ten miles during the day. A strong band of dacoits had recently camped nearby, so my suspicion was that they were using the elephant as a scout.

That night the elephant came again, and as he moved round the perimeter we could hear the tethered elephants ringing warning sounds with their trunks upon the earth. But no attack developed. We moved on again and the elephant moved with us, visiting each animal in turn during the night and disappearing before dawn. If it had not been for the rebels, I would have gone after him to satisfy my curiosity; but it was too dangerous.

One day, when we were nearing our destination, the mouth of the Palway Creek, the column suddenly came to a halt. I was in the middle and I pushed ahead to see what was wrong. From the lead I heard shouts of "Taw Sin! Taw Sin!" (Wild elephant!)

I went forward cautiously with the headman, and there, a hundred yards away, I saw a magnificent tusker indeed. But he was one I recognized immediately, though I had last seen him five hundred miles away. "Bandoola!" I said in a loud voice; and seeing me, he trumpeted furiously and fled, exposing as he did so the bold "C" branded on his nearside rump. Po Toke had been right. Bandoola had returned to his birthplace.

Several times during the day we saw him. There was no chance of going after him. We had to tether even our own elephants and hand-feed them, because of the danger of men getting separated and captured as hostages.

Po Toke was the man to capture Bandoola. But Po Toke had overstayed his leave and my suspicion was that he was in some way concerned with the rebels. Bandoola had become shy of men, we decided by that evening, but he seemed docile enough apart from that. So a young Karen oozie suggested that we try the method of capture which was known as *mela shikar,* and volunteered if that succeeded to ride Bandoola.

For mela shikar, the Karens select two full-grown female elephants of a steady temperament; on each are mounted two riders, one on the head in the normal position, the second on the centre of the back, holding a rope tied fast round the elephant's body. Even young wild elephants are often captured in this way, because an elephant usually does not notice a man mounted on another elephant, since he is above the scent line.

I agreed to try mela shikar, despite the dangers of leaving camp; and as we got down to it, all thought of rebels passed out of my mind and for a few hours I was really happy again, back in an old routine.

It was early evening when the two female elephants entered the sea of kaing grass, eight to twelve feet high, in which Bandoola was grazing. I climbed up a tree from which I could see the whole manoeuvre. Bandoola was out of sight but the tops of the kaing grass swayed when he moved. The two females I could follow because the oozies on their backs were visible above the grass. With amazing patience the females were steered to converge on Bandoola from either flank, so skilfully that, grazing freely all the time, they were unaware of what was happening.

Such an operation at any time is fraught with suspense; in this case there was the added hazard that at any moment there might be a rebel attack. It was all done in complete silence and in slow motion. It was rather like watching from a cliff the movement of yachts in the distance. They drew closer and closer. Then suddenly, when they were within a stone's throw of one another, the silence was broken by a chirp, a chirp I somehow associated with this lovable great animal Bandoola. It was made by placing the tongue between the teeth against the side of the cheek and then sucking air in, rather like the gee-up sound for a horse. The noise will carry a mile and is a signal of contentment and joy. It was as if Bandoola was calling to the females, "Come here. There's a luscious patch of green kaing where I am."

The heads of the four oozies were now very close together. So for a moment they remained. Then it was all over except to see them march out of the kaing grass in single file to the riverbed below me. First came Shan Ma with one rider only, then Bandoola, whose rider had merely stepped off Shan Ma's back onto his new mount, and finally Yinzin Ma with her two riders.

It had been beautifully done. When I congratulated the young Karen on his good work, he said, "My people say no captive elephant wishes to return to the wild, but if an elephant tries, it takes another elephant to convince him that he is wrong."

It was the same with the Burmese rebels. Police and soldiers only strengthened their determination. The rebellion was broken by the persuasion of sensible Burmans.

Bandoola was attached to my armed party for the remainder of our tour. He was in his prime. His size and strength set him apart among the pack elephants, like a shire horse in a cavalry troop, and his very name and presence gave us protection. For no Burman without a lifetime's experience of elephants would have dared, whatever his political opinions, to tackle so ferocious-looking a tusker, docile though he was in fact.

With the breaking of the monsoon and the capture of the rebel leader Saya San, organized rebellion collapsed. Resistance continued in isolated pockets, but the country returned to normal.

I tried to make contact with Po Toke. But he was living in a remote village where the rebels had been very active, and when at last he did come back I found it impossible to believe in his innocence. Why had he come to me just before the outbreak of the rebellion? Why hadn't he returned at the end of his long leave?

I was deeply disappointed in him—though perhaps it was my fault for taking him to be a simpler character than he was. But the trust which had once existed between us was shaken. I told him that as he had not returned from his long leave at the proper time, he had broken his service as far as I was concerned. I could not reinstate him, certainly not as a trainer. I confess I was shocked by his appearance. He was only about fifty, which is not old for a jungle Burman, but in the past twelve months he had aged tremendously. The sense of authority which he had commanded had declined. And yet I still couldn't deny that Bandoola could not be in better hands than Po Toke's.

So I decided to transfer him back to the Chindwin forests. He left me with a complete camp of ten elephants including Bandoola, and as a result of the information which I sent ahead of him, he was taken on, not as a Singaung in charge of a timber-extraction camp, but in a more subordinate position. But Bandoola was his leader animal and that made up for his loss of responsibility.

He could also pride himself on extracting some of the largest timber ever handled by elephants in Burma. The demand for long teak logs suitable for squaring had become so intense that a teak log of over fifty feet was like nugget-gold. Elephants like Bandoola, capable of handling these enormous logs, were even scarcer than the logs themselves. But thanks to Po Toke's good management Bandoola was never sick. In one season he was recorded as having extracted three hundred tons of teak an average distance of two miles from stump to floating stream.

8

I did not realize what a strain the rebellion had been until it was all over. It was not merely the threat of danger and the irritation of having to travel in armed companies. It was the fact that during that time we had been cut off from the outside world, from those casual contacts the value of which one does not appreciate until deprived of them.

The Indian touring circus were the first strangers to arrive at my forest headquarters after the troubles. The company of one's colleagues in a forest station begins to pall after a time. One longs for people who are different; and different these circus folk were. There was a Russian trapeze act, five men and one girl; a troupe of Filipino acrobats; a Canadian couple, a man and a girl with good horses; some French clowns who were funny on bicycles; some Japanese wrestlers who were fat but not funny at all, and a stunningly beautiful Italian wire-rope artiste, whose loneliness I felt it would be ungallant not to console.

Anyway, I arranged to give a midnight party for the whole troupe after the last night of the show, and promised that I would muster all the Europeans, of whom there were more than usual at the station because of the troubles. I had six young bachelor forest assistants, living in the large bachelor chummery, who were quick to make friends with the circus people, so that I soon found I had my rivals. Michael, Hamish and Peter all ganged up on me. "Of course, we know you're just giving it for her," they said, "but remember all's fair..."

Most of us had already been to the circus once, but we all turned up for the last night just the same. The tent was packed with Indians and Burmans, the colour of whose clothing was a show in itself. There were fifteen to twenty Europeans.

When it was over, it was arranged that those with cars should stay behind and bring the artists over to my bungalow in relays. The crowd had left after the last turn, the spectacular act of the Russian trapezists. The safety net was still in position, the ring was empty, the artists were in their dressing rooms changing.

We were growing tired of waiting. Hamish and Peter tripped out, imitating two of the Russian trapezists. One went to each of the enormous tent poles. They bowed to us and bowed to each other. "Hopp-la!" Together they started to climb the rope ladders, pretending to miss their footing, but always getting higher. It was a wonderful imitation of a professional tipsy act. Both of them arrived swaying on the trapeze platforms and as they bowed again to each other, there was a burst of applause from us below.

Without hesitation Hamish took the pole hook, leaned forward and pulled back the trapeze. "Hopp-la!" He pretended to fall, but hung on with one hand, precariously holding his balance.

Peter did the same thing. And then once again they solemnly bowed, amid our laughter and applause.

Then, to my horror, Hamish gripped the trapeze bar and swung from the platform into midair sixty feet above the safety net, followed immediately after by Peter. They were still clowning, pretending to lose grip and hanging on by one hand. Down below we stopped laughing. We all knew they would never be able to get back to those platforms.

It was impossible to tell exactly when they stopped playing the clown and tried seriously to swing themselves back, because their efforts were just as clownish. They were getting tired, their bodies becoming heavier every second. Hamish released one hand. "Hopp-la!" he shouted, and as he let go he waved to Peter. Whether he bent his knees or not, I don't know, but the net shot him back into the air like a popgun cork. When he stopped bouncing, he lay absolutely still in the rope net; whether dead or unconscious we could not tell, while Peter was still hanging on above.

Peter said nothing, but he began feebly to swing to and fro, and as he reached the end of a backward swing he too bellowed "Hopp-la!" and released his grip. Instead of falling feet forwards, he came down with arms and legs outspread like a flying squirrel, striking the net simultaneously with face, chest, stomach and legs, before he bounced up again and came to rest a dozen feet from Hamish.

Three excited Russians, shouting in their own language, swarmed up the ladders to the net and passed the limp bodies to the ground. That Hamish and Peter were now sober there was no doubt, but there was some question for a moment whether they were alive. Then they began to groan. No bones were broken. But I had not seen such welts since I was at school. For them the party was over.

"Well," said Michael to me, as we drove to my bungalow, "that's two out of the running for the fair Italian. That just leaves you and me."

But we were mistaken. She arrived at the party squired by a French clown. "You haven't met my husband, I think," she said. In her arms she was carrying a large parcel. "And by the way," she asked, "where can I put this?"

"What is it?" I asked.

She opened her beautiful eyes as if surprised. "It's baby!" she said.

WHILE I WAS ENTERTAINING the Indian circus, Po Toke was marching his elephants to the Chindwin forest. En route, Bandoola was intercepted and directed to a very specialized job, breaking up a terrific blockage of teak logs in the Wabobin Gorge.

The gorge was regarded by the Burmans as a shrine of the Nats, their jungle spirits. At its entrance, where the river flowed in between cliffs two hundred feet high, and again at its exit a mile below, stood two small snow-white pagodas. It was an eerie place which never saw the sun, except for a shaft of light about midday, the sort of place round which superstition gathers as inevitably as cobwebs in the dark corners of an unused room.

If we were to exploit the forest above, we had to float our timber through the gorge. And in the first floating season the monsoon was sharp and heavy. On the terrific floods the logs went through and only a very few jammed. But the next season the monsoon was lighter and more gradual in its coming. The floods carried the logs down and piled three thousand of them in a gigantic stack across the gorge.

It looked as if the only way of clearing them would be by blasting, which even if it did not call down the anger of the Nats, as the Burmans swore it would, would certainly antagonize the Burmans themselves.

The man with the misfortune to be faced by this problem was Gerry Dawson, a very gallant and generous fellow. He was well aware of the superstition against blasting, and before he blasted he wanted to see whether he couldn't unlock the jam by using elephants.

I was asked to advise on the practicability of using elephants. I went

along to see for myself. It was a fantastic sight. From above, the logs looked like matchsticks; as if a whole warehouse full of matches had been blown up and had landed in the gorge. But close to I saw that they were all locked and interlocked as if embedded in concrete. It was dangerous to walk over them.

It was difficult to decide what should be done. One could wait until the next monsoon. The thousands of tons of water might dislodge them, but then another three to five thousand logs would be arriving with it. It was too dangerous a gamble. The block might be worse than ever.

One could blast, but I didn't like the idea of blasting. After all, one man's superstition is another's religion. "Try elephants, Gerry," I said, "but the less said, the less even thought, the better." I found him nine tuskers, and I included Bandoola, whom I was sure the Nats loved.

The Burmans on the job were pessimistic. "The Nats will not let the logs go," they said, "if you anger them there will be tragedy."

But Gerry was young. He was strong. He got to work with his tuskers and reported that they had loosened the jam. "But I need more," he wrote, "if I'm to finish before the monsoon."

But I could not give him any more, and when the rainy season broke, I had to withdraw even the elephants he had. Gerry was not satisfied to leave it to the monsoons, or the Nats, to work things out between them. There were two enormous logs, over fifty feet in length, heavy logs and impossible for the elephants to move. In company with a dangerous atheist, Soo Lin, Gerry planned to free them with dynamite after all. They made a bamboo raft and crossed a pool to the base of what remained of the jam. There they placed their charges with long fuses and made their getaway.

The dynamite shifted the whole balance of the logs. They collapsed in a sort of avalanche. But the overhanging rocks in the gorge collapsed also. Long before the elephant men in the neighbourhood arrived they could hear Soo Lin calling for help.

What happened no one ever knew exactly, but the whole of Gerry's left forearm and wrist had been flattened to pulp. Gerry looked at it and pointed to Soo Lin's heavy jungle knife. "Cut it off," he said, "quickly."

Soo Lin struck as hard as he could. But he failed to amputate the hand. Gerry fainted. By the time the men had carried him out of the gorge to the top of the cliff, he had recovered sufficiently to ask for a small stone and a short stick. With his right hand and with the help of his men he applied a tourniquet inside his biceps and secured it. "Get me to main river headquarters," he said, "quick as you can." Then he fainted again.

For four days and four nights his men carried him on a bamboo stretcher. They averaged four miles an hour and they doped him with opium the whole way. The tourniquet was never released.

When they arrived at that small station, the one and only doctor was on tour. The only European was a civil policeman, the only nurse an English-speaking Karen girl of nineteen. It was obvious to both of them that an operation was immediately necessary. But who could operate? The policeman remembered that the Indian Sikh who was orderly to the police mules had some amateur veterinary knowledge. He summoned the man and ordered him to perform the operation. The nurse gave the anaesthetic and the policeman, holding a surgical book in his hand, supervised and accepted responsibility.

All things considered, the operation was a remarkable feat. The Sikh amputated above the pulped wrist, and when Gerry came round he seemed in good shape.

The next morning a qualified Indian doctor arrived from Sagaing. He examined Gerry, congratulated the unfortunate Sikh on what he had done but announced that an immediate operation was necessary higher up the arm. As the tourniquet had not been released, gangrene had set in.

Finally, Doc Harry arrived. He was one of those heaven-sent European doctors whose name was already a legend for miraculous cures. Doc Harry examined Gerry and then he shook his head. "I'm sorry, Gerry," he said. "There's nothing I can do now. It's too late."

Gerry asked if he might see the others, the policeman, the senior forest man and the other doctor. They came in with long faces, but Gerry grinned. "There are two bottles of warm champagne in the club," he said, "let's have a drink, and to hell with this arm and Wabobin."

The party lasted ten minutes or so. His eyelids began to droop and Doc Harry nodded to the others to go out. "Time you had a sleep now, old boy." Gerry leaned back on his pillows, his legs propped higher than his head. "I shall sleep all right, doc," he said, "and I shall dream of the happiest twenty-nine years of life a man ever had."

I expected that the death of Gerry would strengthen local belief in the Nats of Wabobin. But I was wrong. He had lost his life, but he had cleared the gorge of that enormous timber stack. When the monsoon came, the floods came thundering down, and with that monstrous load of timber they swept away the superstition attaching to the gorge. For years after that the logs passed through without a hitch and the Burmans worked without fear.

No one who works in the jungle calculates on a ripe old age as a near-certainty. But Gerry's sense of death at his elbow, his philosophy of "Eat, drink and be merry," seemed to me to have dated from the time of Paddy's death. Paddy was his greatest friend and a very trusting person, even after he woke up one morning to find that during the night someone had made off with his specie box containing fifteen thousand rupees. The police, to whom the matter was reported, arrested Paddy's head servant. He was charged and tried but the case was dismissed on the grounds that the evidence was insufficient.

Paddy was quite sure the servant was innocent; he replaced him while he was awaiting trial but afterwards he asked him to come back as head servant. The Burman was deeply touched at this sign of trust and for some years he served him with great devotion.

Then one day a confidential letter from the police arrived in Paddy's mail. It was seen by an English-speaking Burmese timber clerk, who immediately warned the head servant that the case had not been closed and suggested that the reason why Paddy had taken him back was to keep him under observation. The clerk, I imagine, thought that given this warning the head servant would be off.

Not a bit of it. The head servant said he was innocent and he saw no reason why he should give up a good job, just because the police were asking a few more questions. He appeared calm and unworried. He continued with Paddy in the usual way, but his mind was becoming unbalanced by worry as to what Paddy would reply. The next morning he took Paddy's tea into his tent at dawn as usual and finding him asleep he tried to kill him with a large jungle knife.

The wounds he gave were mortal, but Paddy had time to scream for help before he died. The uproar woke the camp but the head servant grabbed a loaded shotgun from under Paddy's bed and killed an old Burmese cook who came running to the rescue.

The servant got away through the jungle to the village monastery, where he sought asylum and confessed to the priest. Having done so, he committed suicide, a thing almost unknown in Burma.

It was a curious tragedy of good intentions. There is no doubt that it was the servant who had stolen the money from the specie box. Everything would have ended comparatively happily if Paddy hadn't been such a good man.

9

When I went into the jungle for the first time, I had highly coloured ideas of man-eating tigers and charging wild tusker elephants. But after a short time I came to realize that the wild beasts of the jungle were not my natural enemies. They had no desire to attack me and I had no desire to attack them.

I do not mean that I ever lost my fear when I was in the jungle. No one but a fool would boast such a thing. But I came to see that the things to be afraid of were not wild beasts, but the climate during the monsoon season, and the repulsive creatures that flourished in the rains; the black silent anopheline mosquito which carried malaria, the hookworm, the leeches on the dripping leaves and the tinea lurking in the mud.

The Burmans called this tinea Sin Wai, which being translated means Elephant Itch. It was, alas, not confined to elephants, though they were the principal carriers. In the rainy season the elephant tracks were churned into deep quagmires impregnated with Sin Wai, and I have known elephants kick themselves raw by continuous scratching of the hind ankles. They seemed, however, to find relief in standing in water.

Human beings become infected with Sin Wai through contact with the mud of the elephant tracks. Slow and wearisome though these were to us, there was no other way in many places because the jungle was so dense. It only affected the legs up to the knees, those parts of the body which came in contact with the foul mud.

During the rainy season one always had to take precautions against Sin Wai. The one hope lay in prevention. The Burman oozies used to urinate over their feet and ankles as their only preventative—I myself laced antiseptic with my hot washing water.

These precautions usually sufficed. But one year, while working out in one of Po Toke's camps, we got a bout of perfect Sin Wai weather. It rained very heavily for some days and then, when the tracks were deep in mud, the sun came out to hatch the thing.

It all began on the same day. As we came into camp, we all started to scratch, the elephants and I. At first small vesicles appeared on the skin, very irritating but not very angry in appearance. I smeared Vaseline over my feet and ankles, and if we could have got out of the jungle, perhaps I could have cleared it up. But the trouble was that every day I became reinfected. Sleep became impossible. I tried pricking the vesicles in the early stages with a needle dipped in pure carbolic, hoping that the burn would either kill the bug or stop the irritation. But it gave no relief.

Within a week, ulcers developed on my calves. In sympathetic reaction the glands in my groins swelled to the size of fists. It was impossible to stop scratching for a moment, impossible, even with the aid of whisky, to gain any sleep. I was in a high fever; my general weakness brought the malaria back. I lay down in my bed. My weeping sores ached, and made up my mind for me. It had been raining for forty-eight hours. The river was in torrential spate. But I had to get out.

That was easier decided than done. This camp of Po Toke's was five marches from the nearest river navigable by country boat or dugout; five marches through rain-sodden jungle along game tracks knee-deep in mud. And even when I got there, there were the Yoo Rapids between me and the main river where I must go to rest up. In these rains the Yoo Rapids would be impassable. I could only pray that by the time I reached the river the floods would have subsided.

I lay thinking on my bed. Planning to move took my mind at least for the moment off the agonies of the flesh. I should have to go by elephant. I thought of Bandoola, but it was Po Toke who suggested next morning that Bandoola should carry me.

I found that morning that I could no longer stand. I had to be lifted into Bandoola's cane "kah". Each stage of that agonizing trek was about ten miles. At every step Bandoola sank deep into the mud. Each foot he lifted made a loud sucking noise, and even his gigantic powers were sorely taxed.

Most of the time I was delirious. I remember in a moment of lucidity suddenly realizing that we were crossing a torrent of chocolate-coloured water, against which Bandoola was leaning his weight so far over that I was nearly falling out. But the great elephant knew what he was doing. His massive head and tusks ploughed a passage through the water like the nose of a submarine.

When we reached the hut on the Yoo River I knew that Bandoola could be of no more assistance. Propped on my camp bed I could see the river. It was in full flood. Branches were torn from the boles of trees and carried off. Ten miles below the rapids started, and it was suicide to try to shoot them. I was trapped. I would have to cure myself here.

I called for two empty kerosene tins and had these filled with water as hot as I could possibly bear on my ulcerous legs. The discharge from the sores oozed down like black treacle and the relief was such that I was able to endure the pain for as long as a quarter of an hour before collapsing on my bed again.

After two days the swelling in my groins had somewhat lessened. But the strain had brought on severe malaria. The floods continued and I was no nearer help. I was too weak, too giddy to care any longer....

Soon after that a dugout came down the river. And in it was one of the bravest and maddest forest men I ever knew, Colin Kayem. Like myself, Colin was fleeing from the rains, and had put in to wait till the floods subsided and he could shoot the rapids. "Thank God you're here," I said, and with that I resigned all responsibility. If it had not been for him, it is most unlikely that I should be alive to write this narrative.

He did not trouble to take my temperature. He knew that it was malaria. For a whole night he dressed and drained my sores, and by dawn he had me nearer normal than I had been for ten days. Then he shocked me by saying, "We're getting out of this bloody hole. I'm making up a crew of three volunteer boatmen to shoot the rapids." He made the impossible sound as easy as winking.

I was carried down to the dugout and placed in a deckchair, which just fitted the beam. There was no more talk of volunteers. It was "you and you" to the oarsmen. "And you," to a paddle-rudder helmsman. "I'll take the pole in the bows," Kayem said, "just in case we lose our way."

Hearing the "volunteers" muttering, Kayem turned on them. "What's all the talk about?" he said quietly in Burmese. "D'you think I'd risk it if I didn't know we could do it? There's only one man who'll drown if we capsize. And he's game to go, even if he *is* ill."

Under my canopy of a waterproof sheet, I had to smile for the first time in days. It was a perfect Kayem argument.

Two of my servants made up the boatload. We cast off from the bank. My elephant men who carried me down shouted and cheered. I wondered how many of them were really saying goodbye.

The muddy brown water, built up above the rapids, was flowing quite silently though at speed. The oars creaked in their rope runnels. The bow was taken by the current and as the helmsman shouted, we swung out and down and away.

For an hour we had fair going. Once, as we were passing, a high bank fell, and a dozen full-grown trees crashed into the river, sending a bore of water a foot high broadside at us and rocking the boat perilously. To me the excitement was a tonic. I asked to have the canopy removed.

"Keep well out on the bends," yelled the helmsman.

We were going all out now. As we neared the Ngapun Rapid the roar became terrific. But Kayem gave them no chance to pull in. He started singing the Burmese boat song "Hey Los! Hey Los!" as they strained at their oars. The helmsman, who was the owner of the boat, took it up and headed us straight for the broken water. Suddenly we were drawn into it. Desperately the oarsmen struggled to keep her head on. Then, with the waves dashing over the sides, we tore ahead through the channel and were down, baling out the water we had shipped in the comparative calm of the eddying pool below.

The Ngapun Rapid was the first but by no means the worst. Kayem drove us on to take the next, the main Yoo River Rapids, without a pause. I had shot these many times before in normal conditions, but they were devils even in the best of weathers. No one had ever tried to shoot them in floods like these. I lay back in my deckchair, too weak to worry but not too weak to picture what lay ahead, the five consecutive rapids and at the bottom of the last the sheer cliff, against which the river took a right-angled bend, forming a whirlpool at its base.

We could hear the rapids from a long way off. At first it sounded like a gentle murmur then, as we rounded each bend, the sound grew louder, at the same time deepening in tone. As we took the last bend it seemed like thunder echoing through the dense jungles and the surrounding hills.

Kayem, stripped to the waist, stood in the bows with his powerful shoulders braced, his spiked pole raised as if to meet some charging monster. No orders were given. The helmsman had it all in his hands.

The flood took our dugout and drove it forward with the speed of an outboard motor. Our bows hit the first wave of broken water. Kayem disappeared from sight in a cloud of spray. For a moment I thought we were going to dive under water. But the bows rose and Kayem appeared again. The water we shipped poured into the well and half drowned me. But the crew was intact and the two oarsmen, rowing like mad, still held our way.

The waves appeared to tear past us high above my head. It was one of the most alarming experiences of my life, momentarily expecting to be submerged, or turned turtle by a hidden rock, or dashed to splinters against a boulder.

We shot forward out of the flying spray. We had lost the race of water and now the current of the outer rim of the whirlpool caught us. "Swai! Swai!" yelled the helmsman. "Pull! Pull!"

But all the pulling in the world could not bring us back into the main current. We swung, drifting sideways, around the outer ring of the vortex, part of the flotsam, the floating branches making the slow corkscrew circuits to the sucking centre. I looked desperately for something which I might clutch to save myself. Then suddenly our craft swung out again into the outer circle.

We circled nineteen times, no longer now drawn towards the centre. We had strength enough to keep on the periphery, but not the strength to break away. For an hour this went on, then Kayem fastened a groundsheet to the end of his pole, and each time we came downriver he made a cast into the race, hoping that the extra pull would be enough to draw us out. One moment we were going with the whirlpool; the next we were plucked like a twig and carried broadside on down the race.

As the helmsman straightened up, Kayem turned to me. "Don't worry, old boy," he said, "you'll see Paris again."

I grinned in answer and then, the suspense over, I leaned back and went to sleep. I did not realize until later quite how ill I was.

10

It was almost Christmas before I was fit for the jungle again. I wanted to get back in time to supervise the crossing of the Upper Chindwin River by thirty-five of my elephants. Fortunately Willie, who from being my old taskmaster had become a very good friend, had sole use of the company's sternwheel paddle launch. He was doing his farewell trip on tour upcountry, and suggested that we should combine his Christmas shoot with an official trip to watch the river crossing. The paddle launch was a luxury ship, a miniature showboat with spotless white paint, a black stack, an upper deck with four comfortable cabins amidships, and saloons fore and aft.

There were two other guests: Millie, the connoisseur of elephant-droppings under whom I had served in my second year, and a young man called Tony, handsome and immaculate.

As soon as Tony and I boarded the launch, it was clear that though elsewhere folk might be waiting till Christmas Day came, in three days' time, Christmas had come aboard the launch several hours before. Willie and Millie had got a start on us, but as we went full steam ahead, Tony and I rapidly caught them up.

Willie made us all help with the decorations. He had a Wensleydale cheese the size of a wheel, doctored to perfection and swathed in damp muslin. All drinks for cooling were slung in baskets over the stern so that the paddle should keep them sprayed. The champagne at lunch was followed by Napoleon brandy. There were real crackers, and in place of Burmese cheroots, Coronas. Yes, Christmas started early that year.

It was Christmas Day for three days, and on the real Christmas Eve we came to the fords where the elephants were to cross. They were all congregated in a central camp. Early on Christmas morning Willie inspected them. Then they were released and we and the elephant men seconded to act as beaters for the day, shot until dusk over a lake where ducks and geese abounded.

We went back to the launch and had hot baths and then a Christmas dinner unequalled on any table in the land. We were all satisfied and tired. Suddenly Willie called for Po Pyan, his head servant, who appeared from the darkness of Willie's cabin where he had been squatting silently waiting to put Willie to bed, as he had done every night for the last fifteen years. "Clear the table," Willie said in Burmese, and then, turning to us, "Let's make it a *real* Christmas and play bridge."

"No," corrected Millie. "Bed is what you mean."

I got up and fetched the cards. I knew Willie. If Willie said bridge, then bridge it would be.

It was serious bridge, and the hours flowed past as smoothly as the river beneath us and the whisky down our throats. How many bottles were emptied I do not know; but the moment a glass was empty Po Pyan refilled it.

We had reached that stage of utter fatigue when even the thought of getting up to go to bed is an effort. The fifth rubber dragged interminably. But at last there was a hand which stood a fair chance of making game, rubber and bed. We were all left with three cards as Willie collected a trick from the table and laid it neatly in line with our tricks. We waited for him to lead. He sighed deeply. His left hand holding the cards flopped with them face downwards on the table, his chin sagged onto his chest. He was absolutely still. No sign of the heavy breathing of a man who has passed out.

We sat for some minutes. Then, looking very white, Millie rose from his chair and made his way in the direction of the fore saloon. Tony shrugged and followed on tiptoe.

I didn't know what to do. I had often seen Willie pass out, but never quite like this. I got up and joined them in the fore saloon. Millie was as white as a sheet. "It's terrible," he said. "Heart failure. I always knew it."

"Don't be ridiculous," I said. "I've seen him pass out dozens of times before."

"I've watched him passing out for thirty years," said Millie, "but never like this."

"I'm new to all this," Tony said, "but I must say I didn't like his colour."

"Well, you're the senior, Millie," I said. "You go back and shake him and see."

"I shall do nothing of the sort," Millie answered sharply. "After all, you know him best. And besides, it's your forest he's visiting."

"As a matter of fact," I said, turning to Tony, "I think you ought to go, old boy. He's almost a stranger to you. You'd find it less of a shock than we would."

Tony hesitated. Millie broke in: "That's unfair to Tony. It's your duty and you know it."

I went out. Willie was in exactly the same position as when I had left him. I could not touch him. If I tried to feel his pulse, I thought, he might wake up and accuse me of looking at his cards. Or he might not wake up.

Suddenly I realized that I deeply loved Willie, from whom I had learned so much. My heart grew cold with fear at the thought of him dead. I sat down opposite him with my three unplayed cards face down on the table before me. I picked up my glass and drank my whisky slowly.

As I put down my glass, it clinked against an ashtray; it was like a touch of magic. Willie's lips fluttered to a smile and, coming fully awake, he looked up at me blearily, then at the empty chairs. He turned his three cards face upwards on the table. "Game and rubber!" he said. "I knew you wouldn't leave me, partner." He heaved himself up and staggered the ten paces to his cabin. As he opened the door, I saw Po Pyan appear out of the darkness and catch him in his arms.

At dawn a few hours later, very few, I was awakened by Willie with a glass of black velvet in his hand, a fifty-fifty mixture of champagne and stout. "You had rather a thick night, partner," he said, "you'll probably need this."

At breakfast there was no mention of the night before. Willie, I noticed, looked far more alive than any of us.

The air was cold and there was a heavy morning dew. A river mist hung over the water. Occasionally the tops of the forest trees on the opposite bank appeared above the mist like a mirage, reminding me of the work ahead.

It was not going to be an easy crossing—the river at this point was about a mile wide—and I was anxious when at ten o'clock I left the launch. U San Din, a very old man, was in charge of the whole herd of thirty-five elephants, which was divided into five sections of seven, each under their respective Singaungs. Being all fully grown, they appeared an enormous herd stretched out along the shingly foreshore.

None of us had any idea which animal would lead. But we kept eight possibles lined up along the water's edge. Bandoola and all the other full-grown tuskers were kept far back from the river bank. The families of the elephant men crossed first in canoes, three or four at a time. Then the elephant gear was ferried over in larger dugouts.

In silence the eight possible leaders entered the water as casually as if they were going for their daily scrub. But though some of them went into deep water, not one would start to swim.

U San Din was being paddled up and down in a small dugout canoe. One could almost feel him praying that something would happen as a start. Then suddenly there was a commotion. A young female elephant came scuttling down the shingle, her rider working his feet behind her ears as if he was pedalling a low-gear bicycle. There was a tremendous splash as she entered the water. She waded into deeper water and lunged forward into the channel. For a moment she disappeared, rider and all; then she rose with the buoyancy of a cork. She was afloat, swimming steadily with a lovely action, a sort of slow lunging which totally immersed the rider every now and again as she dived. When he came up, he waved his hand to those behind.

Now one female followed after the other. They went out across the river in line ahead, launching into deep water like lifeboats.

Then the tuskers began to take off. Bandoola, by far the most massive, stood out even in the water. Soon every animal was away, strung out like gigantic corks on an invisible rope, stretched from where we stood to a point on the far bank at least a mile below us. The sight was marvellous.

Late that evening a message came that Bandoola had killed his rider.

It was apparently a wanton and unprovoked attack. Bandoola was tied to a tree while Aung Bala, the oozie, had been adjusting his forefetters. Suddenly the tusker gored Aung Bala, then knelt his enormous weight upon him and finally with peculiar viciousness tossed his body out of reach with his tusks.

When I reached the camp, I tried to discover the facts. Had Aung Bala been careless? Bandoola appeared completely normal, except that he was fettered and attended by two spearmen, one of whom was Po Toke. It was strange, and to me rather tragic, to see Po Toke, who had struggled so hard to train this elephant without cruelty, taking up a position with a spear.

I treated Bandoola with circumspection as I had no desire to follow Aung Bala. But from as near as I dared approach, I could see no spearmarks or signs of ill-treatment on him. Bandoola seemed happy and contented, normal in every way as he munched at his fodder. The only thing which was abnormal, as I suddenly noticed, was the amount of his fodder: whole plantain trees, sugarcane, bamboos, branches of nyaung.

Then I noticed another thing, which made me very suspicious. There were no droppings, and yet no signs that Aung Bala had done any cleaning up around his charge. I turned to Po Toke suddenly. "Who gave Bandoola all this fodder?"

"Aung Bala, just before he was killed," said Po Toke. But a shade too quickly. I was sure that he was lying, and I went straight to Helaw village, about half a mile away, where U San Din had taken Aung Bala's body to the headman's house.

At the steps of the headman's house, U San Din met me. "Dokha gyi (this is big trouble)," he said.

"You must expect big trouble from an elephant with an empty belly," I said. I looked at U San Din and I could see the shot had gone home.

He told me the story without reserve. Ma Pyoo had given Po Toke no children. For many years it had been their common sorrow. Now, either because he desperately wanted children or because Ma Pyoo's beauty had faded, or perhaps for both these reasons, Po Toke had sent Ma Pyoo back to her village and taken to himself a second wife, a girl of sixteen.

In this there was nothing contrary to the Buddhist religion. But Po Toke himself did not feel easy about it. For two days before the river crossing he had neglected all his duties as a Singaung. This would not have mattered much if Aung Bala had not been an opium eater. But U San Din admitted that for two days before the crossing Bandoola had been left chained with little or no fodder. The oozies, when I questioned them, stated that it was not two days but three.

When Aung Bala chained him again after crossing the river, Bandoola grew desperate. He tangled his chains and fetters, trying to draw attention to his hunger. But instead of giving him more to eat Aung Bala tried to untangle them, and the captive elephant saw red.

It was Po Toke who had betrayed their negligence by trying to cover it with that enormous amount of fodder.

As I returned to the launch late that night, there were strange thoughts in my head. It is very hard to fix responsibility. Was the responsibility Aung Bala's entirely? The break-up of Po Toke's marriage which I had envied for its apparent happiness, made Po Toke responsible for the tragedy. But then I remembered that during those two days of crisis, when Po Toke had dismissed the woman he loved most, and neglected the elephant who was his pride, I myself had been enjoying a protracted Christmas, shooting, eating and drinking.

Willie was waiting for me when I boarded the launch and I told him what had happened. "It's up to you to dismiss Po Toke or not as you like," he said. "But I agree that you cannot brand Bandoola as a killer in his history sheet."

So the killing did not go down in Bandoola's official record. But nothing that anybody could do would stop tongues from wagging. Every oozie would learn sometime or other that Bandoola had killed Aung Bala, but not necessarily the reason why.

The next morning Po Toke came to plead with me for forgiveness. He was heartbroken. It was easy enough for me to understand what had happened. It was not so easy to decide what to do. But there was, now that Po Toke had dismissed Ma Pyoo, only one constant thing in his life: his devotion to Bandoola.

"I ought to dismiss you," I said, "but I don't want to do that. After what has happened to Aung Bala, I can't employ you as a Singaung. But I'm willing to pay you the same wage, to be Bandoola's oozie."

"In the same camp?" He was thinking of saving his face.

"No, I will transfer you both."

Po Toke bowed his head in acceptance. The wage would enable him to keep his new wife. The charge of Bandoola was really all he cared about.

A very simple man, he had three ambitions, to beget a son, to manage the greatest elephant in the forest, and to see his country independent. All three of them in the end were frustrated.

11

One year I was sent in charge of a party to explore the uninhabited forests of the Northern Andaman Islands. There was only one thing which marred my excitement at the prospect, and that was the future of my Alsatian, Molly Mia. I could not take her with me and I was frightened that when separated from me she might pine, for she was as devoted to me as I was to her. Her devotion had become something of a byword.

On one stage of my march out of the jungle I decided to descend upon the camp of a man I knew, the chief conservator of forests, and spend the night with him. His camp was not far away and very soon I saw him fishing in a stream, and went over and chatted with him. He seemed delighted to see me and asked me to pitch down with him, so I pushed on to his campsite. It was on the high bank of the river, and as I crossed, I saw there were two tents instead of one. He had not mentioned that he had company, and I was in two minds about turning away when I saw a tall, slender girl in the clearing. She had seen me, and waved. I raised my Terai hat, feeling slightly ridiculous.

"My name is Susan," she said. "My uncle's fishing somewhere." She seemed, reassuringly, as shy as I was.

Molly Mia, who usually avoided strangers, ran across to her and allowed herself to be stroked.

"What a lovely dog," Susan said. "I know who you are, because I've heard all about Molly Mia. They say you're inseparable."

That we weren't inseparable I soon discovered. Molly Mia attached herself immediately to Susan, completely ignoring me. When Susan went into her tent, Molly Mia followed. While we sat round the large logfire listening to the chief conservator's angling yarns, Molly Mia crouched beside Susan's shapely legs.

At last, about midnight, the old boy took himself off. As soon as he left, I realized how useful his long stories had been. I wanted to be with this young woman but I couldn't think of anything to say. Merely to break the silence, I said, "If you'd like her, Susan, I'll give you Molly Mia."

She shook her head. "Let's share her," she suggested. "I'll look after her until you return from the Andamans."

That was a bargain as far as I was concerned. But I wondered how Molly Mia would feel about it. We stood up to say goodnight, and as we went to our respective tents Molly Mia went not with me but with Susan.

The next morning I said to her, "You'd better keep Molly Mia on a leash when I go." I said goodbye to the dog, rather hoping that there might be a bit of a scene, but Molly Mia merely wagged her tail.

"Well," I said to myself, as I started off, "if she's got Molly Mia when I get back, the only way I'll get her back will be to marry the girl."

And so it was. Susan and I were married on home leave and for our honeymoon we returned to the jungle.

I HAD ACHIEVED, after eleven years' hard work, what had been my ambition when I first came to Burma. I had found an Englishwoman whose pleasure in the jungle was equal to my own.

But married life brought its changes. For one thing, the manufacturers of camp equipment have never apparently turned their designers onto

the problems of matrimony under canvas. As far as I know, no one ever invented a double camp bed. One night Susan complained that there seemed to be a peculiar and rather offensive smell in her bed. When I stripped it the next morning, I saw that the leather thong which tautened the canvas had been smeared with a rank-smelling grease—fat from a roasted wild pig, as I found out later. I asked my servant what the hell he had been up to; and he grinned and said, "It stops it creaking." And that was as near as we got to special camp equipment for a honeymoon couple.

Soon after we came back to the jungle, I took a polo side from our upcountry station down to Monywa. This meant a three-day trip downriver in the firm's launch, a week's polo, and a voyage back. And the monsoon broke as we started back.

The river rose and on the third day floodwater prevented us from navigating the Kalewa defile in daylight. But the Indian Serang assured us that it would be quite safe for us to steam up to Kalewa and tie up there for the night, because we had a powerful searchlight.

The launch, with thirteen ponies on the lower deck and our polo party on the upper deck, made slow but steady progress up the defile against the swift current, the searchlight trained on the rock wall.

It is always exciting to steam through a gorge, even in daytime. We all stood leaning over the rails, watching the tear of the river swirling and breaking in little white waves which were caught by the searchlight, and towering above us the great cliffs on either side, and over all the stars. It gave me a wonderful sense of man's mastery, the way we chugged along, steering by the searchlight on the cliff.

Then suddenly all the lights went out. There was a feeling of silence, even though the engines were still running. It was merely the generator which had failed.

The current at this point bore hard against one cliff, and amid the yells of the Indian crew I expected at any moment to feel the crunching of the launch as in the darkness we smashed against the rock face by which we had been steering.

I ran to get a lifebelt to give to Susan, thinking as I fumbled with it that we must untie the ponies, to give them at least a chance. If we struck, it would be a matter of minutes before we foundered. I got the lifebelt free and ran back, calling to Susan. But she seemed to have disappeared.

Suddenly the beam of a torch leaped out, lighting up the cliff face towards which we were heading. The launch heeled over as the Serang swung her to starboard, away from the rocks; and Susan, whose torch it was, made quickly for the bows, keeping the torch beam steady on the cliff. She had saved us from certain catastrophe.

Fortunately at that moment the lights came on again. An Indian fitter-engineer had gone straight to the trouble and rectified it.

We were all shaken by this incident; but at the same time I was reassured. Susan would be the only European woman in the station, and during the rainy season she would not be able to come with me on my tours. There would be loneliness, and in times of sickness great responsibility. I knew now that I had married a woman of resource with a singular capacity for rising to a crisis.

Yet it was not very long before a crisis arose with which I feared she could not cope, since she was in ignorance of the danger.

Three days after our return to the station, we were all out touring our respective forest areas. To make the transition from bachelor to married life more peaceful, I had dismissed my old headquarters staff with one exception and engaged fresh staff, who would accept my wife's more ordered management of the household without question. The exception was Po Lone, a man who I thought might fit in with the new regime.

The monsoons were particularly heavy. Jungle-touring was grim. I had been on tour a month and had reached the camp where my old friends Bandoola and Po Toke were working, about three days' hard march from headquarters. I had hoped to receive mail there by jungle messenger, but there was none waiting for me.

It was late evening. The rain ran off the small thatched huts in sheets. The creek, already half in spate, was still rising. Everything in the dense forest was drenched and dripping, all elephant and game tracks were reduced to quagmires. I felt very depressed.

Aung Net left my hut and went to join my other servants. Aung Net was someone to be thankful for, a simple, loyal soul, who had been in my service since he was a village boy of fifteen. I knew him as I knew no other Burman. He grew up with me almost as my son.

Aung Net soon returned, followed now by the messenger San Pyoo. As he climbed the rickety bamboo ladder of my hut on stilts, he called, "Sak yauk byee." Mail had come.

San Pyoo looked dead-beat. The tracks were very bad. His manner struck me as slightly unusual, but then I knew he was an opium smoker. Aung Net emptied the mailbag and followed San Pyoo out. The mail was all a man could want: home mail from England, home mail from my wife and, besides official correspondence, a bundle of newspapers which I could read at my leisure.

Aung Net returned after a short time. His presence irritated me. "Don't bother me now, Aung Net," I said. "I am busy."

He went out but in two minutes he was back again.

"What *is* the matter, Aung Net?"

He knelt down. "I fear to tell you, Thakin. But San Pyoo says that Po Lone is poisoning Thakin Ma."

San Pyoo had been afraid to tell me himself, but when Aung Net brought him in, with a blanket round his shoulders and shivering with a malarial ague, he produced from a dirty piece of paper a grubby pill. "This was given me by Joseph the cook, who found it in Po Lone's pocket," he said. "Joseph says that Po Lone dissolves a pill like this in every drink he takes to Thakin Ma."

I took the pill and said, "And how is Thakin Ma? Is she ill?"

"She was riding a pony the morning I left," San Pyoo answered.

I sent them both away. The idea that Susan was being poisoned seemed impossible: and yet nothing was impossible in Burma. I nibbled the pill. It tasted like dirt but for all I knew it might be arsenic. God knew there was enough of it lying around the camps. It was used in powder form as the main elephant tonic.

The idea seemed impossible. But there was the pill. On such a matter Joseph and San Pyoo would not lie. I looked out at the curtain of rain which hung from the roof of the veranda and cursed the monsoon and the mud of the jungle.

I sent for Po Toke, told him the story and asked him what he thought the quickest way would be to get through to headquarters. "I am too old for such a journey," said Po Toke. "But I could take a messenger on Bandoola across the creek, after which there are no more rivers to cross."

He said that Saw Pa Soo, a Karen boy, was afraid of nothing, night or day. I scribbled a note to Susan warning her to accept no drinks from Po Lone, and saying I hoped to be back in headquarters in three days if I could negotiate the floods.

I handed the note to Saw Pa Soo and saw Bandoola, ridden by Po Toke, cross the river with the young Karen sitting behind him. It was dark when Po Toke reported back to me.

I tried to eat something. I certainly drank something. But the thought of Susan's danger and of the Karen boy struggling through the monsoon-laden jungle in the dark gave me no rest. If a Karen could do it, so could I.

I called a servant to prepare hot tea. This I laced with whisky, fifty-fifty, and filled two empty bottles with it. Those and a small tin of biscuits should see me through. I asked Aung Net if he would come with me. He agreed but added, "Why not take San Pyoo?"

"But he is sick."

"He is sick with worry, Thakin."

When San Pyoo knew I was going, he jumped at the suggestion. I placed Po Toke in charge of all I left behind: the only thing I took with me was my revolver.

Bandoola took us over the creek. We "camp-hopped", going, that is, from one camp to the next. It was the only time in all my years of forest life that I attempted night-marching off any beaten tracks. From that day to this I do not know how San Pyoo found his way.

We travelled night and day without a let-up. The third night was the worst. The tea-whisky was finished, the bottles were discarded, and I cursed the weight of my revolver. We were already nearly dead-beat when we embarked on five miles of elephant track, which in places was three feet deep in mud. Added to physical exhaustion was the anxiety of what we should find at the other end.

We reached the Tunbin Forest resthouse, from which a real forest road led the remaining four miles to headquarters. On the veranda we both nearly collapsed. Dawn was coming up fast. San Pyoo persuaded me to try to sleep while he went to a village about a mile away in the hope of hiring a pony. I lay back in a chair and closed my eyes.

Suddenly I became conscious of the beat of galloping hoofs. I opened my eyes and there around the bend of the forest road came Susan, followed by my servant.

I got to my feet and shouted to them, waving till I saw that they had noticed and were cantering over. There was no need to ask how she was.

She was blooming with health. Saw Pa Soo, so Susan told me, had arrived at headquarters the previous night with my note.

And yet there remained the mystery of the pills. We never discovered for certain what Po Lone was trying to do. The police theory was that, knowing what had happened to the other servants, he was afraid that he would be dismissed, and that he obtained from the priest in his village pills which would have the magical effect of winning him Susan's favour. If that was so, he was mistaken. He got the sack at once.

I sent orders for Po Toke to move my camp to headquarters. As happened so often after a tour of the jungle in the monsoon, I was in for a bad spell of malaria. I promoted Po Toke back to the position of Singaung in charge of the camp and promised him that if I could help it he would never lose charge of Bandoola.

Saw Pa Soo, on receiving his reward, asked for leave to go to Karenni and I never saw him again. San Pyoo continued for some years with his work as jungle messenger, which he combined with a remunerative traffic in opium to the camps. In the end, in an attempt to reach the main river and renew his supplies before he collapsed, he was drowned trying to shoot the Myittha Rapids on an empty kerosene oildrum, a quicker and less painful death, the Burmese said, than if he had died from want of his drug.

12

Not very long after my marriage I was transferred from the northwestern to the northeastern forests of Burma. I use the word "transfer", but I mean none of the comfortable things associated with that word. There was no question of getting onto a launch or a train and arriving at the new headquarters in a matter of a few days. We walked every foot of the way and the journey took five months, because my instructions were to inspect other large forest areas en route.

As it was the open season, I took Susan with me. I must confess that I was slightly apprehensive. But there was no need. Susan was not new to the jungle—she had often toured with her uncle, who spent every moment he could spare from conserving forests, stalking and shooting big game. Camp life to her was a familiar and enjoyable thing. But the sort of life which I had to lead added something to her experience which she had not found with the great hunter and fisherman. She came to enjoy all the living things of the jungle: the birds, the beasts and the flowers. She treated the jungle as another woman might treat her garden, the more delightful because it was full of surprises.

I had previously enjoyed my loneliness in the jungle, despite all my longing for companionship. I enjoyed it because it brought me private joys which I could not believe that anyone would ever share with me. The discovery that Susan could not only share my pleasures but also enlarge them was the perfection of my happiness.

And then there was Molly Mia, whom Susan had adopted, or rather who had adopted Susan, when I went off to the Andamans. I had been slightly jealous at the way Molly Mia transferred her affection to Susan when I left. But when we got married, she shared us, as children share their parents. She was fearless of forest and stream and all that lived therein. At night she would adjust her own mosquito net, which was the shape of a bell tent and slit at one side, and actually tuck herself in. Then she would snap at every mosquito which was inside, after which she would sit on her haunches and look about to see whether anything else remained which might disturb her; and finally she would roll into a ball and sleep.

Like all dogs she loved to retrieve a stick flung into a river, but best of all if it was from a ten- or twelve-foot bank, so that she could leap off into midair and land belly-flat with a resounding splash. One evening when I'd flung a stick for her and she was swimming towards it, I saw with alarm a large watersnake coming downriver, head well above the water like a cobra. I called to her, pointing in warning. Molly turned and with one snap gripped it just behind the head and neck and swam ashore. She never let it go, though it was lashing out like a whip; she just trotted over and dropped it at my feet with a broken neck.

On the occasions when, reluctantly, I had to leave her in camp I did not chain her. She would remain behind, though she made no effort to hide the fact that she felt hurt.

A curious thing arose out of this. When I left her in camp, she was never far from my thoughts; although there were plenty of other things to occupy my mind, the image of Molly Mia kept obtruding itself on me, a clear and distinct image of Molly Mia sitting on her haunches, watching me, listening either for the sound of my voice or some noise in the jungle, a sign that I had come back. There seemed to be some curious mental affinity between us.

I then discovered, quite separately, that I was able to make her obey me without my speaking. It happened one evening without my realizing that I had done it. She was shaking the bamboo floor of the jungle hut and I thought, "For goodness sake, lie down," and she lay down. But I couldn't be sure that I hadn't thought aloud, so I tried my first experiment. I went on with my work, but I willed Molly Mia to come to my side, and she immediately got up and came to my side.

I then began to will her from longer distances. I started about a hundred yards from camp, out of sight, and it was uncanny, because she came to me as fast as if I'd called her.

Having succeeded in calling her from distances as far away as two miles in dense jungle, I attempted what seemed to me the most arduous of all experiments.

At six am I set off on my forest work, first crossing the river and later re-crossing it. At noon, when I was at least four miles away, I withdrew from my Burmans and sat down and concentrated hard on Molly. Within half an hour I heard her ranging somewhere near me, and sure enough, she came bounding towards me in a minute or two.

It was because of this very strange bond between us that I had been so surprised at Molly Mia's instant change of allegiance to Susan.

THE LIFE-SPAN of a dog is sadly short, and in the jungle shorter still. Some years later I was alone in camp with Molly as my only companion. For the first time I noticed her in a mood. She looked through and beyond me. I tied her up. I had a horrible fear of rabies.

Yet I could not bear to see her tied up, a dog that had never been chained. That evening I let her loose to take her for a walk. In the moment I freed her, I knew that I had no control of her. She might never have seen me before.

At first I thought she would make for the jungle. But having got free, she kept circling the camp like a wild animal who had refound fear. She hid behind trees. But when I reached them, she was gone. I looked round and there she was, still watching me with staring eyes.

At last I gave up the attempt to control her and began to make my way back to camp. As I did so, I suddenly realized that the whole emphasis of the chase had altered. She was now the pursuer and I the pursued. Any moment, I thought, she'll really go mad and attack me. I had my gun and so I shot her dead.

She certainly had rabies. At first all I felt was grief for the dog. But then I realized that though Molly Mia had not bitten me, I might have been infected by her saliva entering a cut or slight abrasion. I knew that I had no chance of getting treatment. My grief gave way to anxiety. The incubation period for rabies is extraordinarily variable, so it was weeks and even months before the apprehension left me.

I FOUND THAT SUSAN shared my envy of the animals for something they have which man has lost, an understanding of their environment so acute that they seem able to foresee what is going to happen. How is it that the barking deer always barks that familiar call of the jungle when the river is going to reach full spate that night? I came to know it as a certain forecast. How did it know so surely?

Elephants were not so sensitive to the threat of water, but they certainly reacted quickly to the threat of fire. They knew even better than men that forest streams were God's firelines, and hearing the crackle of a forest fire they would put a stream between them and it as soon as possible.

When there were tropical storms brewing, elephants would wait without movement for the flash of lightning and the crack of thunder, their bodies drawn up in tension.

Once on a very close day I arrived ahead of my elephants at a dilapidated old forest resthouse. I was enjoying the stillness and eeriness of the place, when suddenly there was a terrific snort and a stampede of hooves. I had disturbed a full-grown bull bison in the tall grass inside the compound. He went at full gallop straight at the four-foot teak fence, a magnificent creature, quite seventeen hands at the withers, and with his short, stocky legs tucked under him he took the fence like a hunter.

"A strange place to find a bison," said my gunboy. I sat down and shortly afterwards the elephants arrived, chirping with joy at the prospect of being unloaded. They were halted, as usual, outside the compound while they relieved themselves, and then brought to the veranda, which had been built as high as an elephant's back to make unloading easy.

The pack saddlery was removed and arranged in line along the rails of the fence over which the bison had jumped. Heavy jungle grew up to within fifty yards of this fence, and the animals as they were released entered it, feeding at will. I settled in and had a meal myself. It was stifling hot, but I saw to my surprise that the elephants had returned from the jungle; and not only that, they had completely left the shade. They were standing out in the open under the blazing sun in what appeared to be the hottest spot they could have chosen. They were all standing perfectly still, as if lost in thought. I had never seen elephants look quite like that before and I wondered why.

But it was so hot I did not care. There had been a wind like the blast from an open furnace door scuffling the dry bamboo leaves. Then the wind dropped and the temperature rose still higher. There was a terrible silence. Not a leaf moved.

I stood up, as from very far away there came a low rumbling. Suddenly

the whole forest swayed before my eyes and the tree boles creaked and groaned. The six elephants swayed in time with each other, the old forest resthouse swayed with them, creaking on its rough-hewn posts, and I swayed too, like a sailor on a boat coming into a swell.

Then the earth shook like a wet spaniel shaking its coat. Millions of leaves and old dead branches showered to the ground, but there was no resounding crash. The trees and, more importantly, the resthouse were still standing. The Burmese belief is that the world is carried on the shoulders of four elephantine creatures, and when one of the monsters wants to change shoulders, the earth quakes.

The stillness that succeeded the quake was broken by the shouting of my camp men. The elephants, as though they had finished attending some solemn ceremony, left the clearing and re-entered the jungle to make up for lost time. "It won't come back," said my gunboy. "*They* know."

13

The last time that I saw Bandoola before I left the northern forests, he was dying; dying, what is more, from the most inglorious of complaints, colic brought on by over-eating.

I received a message from Po Toke urging me to come quickly, because Bandoola was "down". When a sick elephant goes down, it's the worst of signs. It means that he has given up hope of ever standing up again.

Luckily it was noon when I got the message. Bandoola was down half a mile from Po Toke's camp and I reached him in time to work on him in daylight. One look at the elephant was enough. His belly was distended to bursting point and he lay on his side, his eyes staring, his trunk spread out in front of him like some prehistoric reptile.

When I taxed him, Po Toke confessed that when tethered in camp the night before Bandoola had got at the paddy in the rice go-down. With his trunk he had broken off the bamboo matting wall until he had made a hole large enough for his tusk to puncture the rice bags. Then, inserting his trunk, he siphoned it out, surely and silently all night long. Next morning his oozie noticed the damage to the go-down; but kept quiet about it.

Within an hour Bandoola went to drink. The gases created by the mixture of water and paddy blew him out and in agony he had collapsed.

We all agreed that unless we could get him up, he would die. But the question remained, how? Po Toke had already tried putting green chilli-juice, the Burmese technique, into Bandoola's eyes. It had inflamed them but had made no difference to the elephant's position.

How, I asked myself, can one make an elephant belch or vomit? The belly was visibly distending before my eyes like a balloon being steadily inflated. But where you punctured an elephant to relieve him of superfluous gases was a mystery to me.

"Send for Poo Zone and Swai Zike with dragging gear," I ordered. "If we don't get him up, he'll be dead in half an hour." When I spoke of Bandoola dying, Po Toke was terrified. He set off for Poo Zone and Swai Zike, who were working near the camp, while we who stayed behind whacked Bandoola with bamboos; soused him with water from the creek; beat him on the most sensitive of his public parts, his toenails. But would he budge? No!

I had heard tales of two African elephants supporting a wounded comrade on either side to help it to escape so my idea, when the two tuskers arrived, was to use them to lift Bandoola up. But it was a hopeless failure. Both animals, head to head with their tusks below the barrel of Bandoola's back, could only move him a foot or so. There wasn't a hope of lifting him up.

In desperation I decided to roll him over. We attached Poo Zone's dragging chains to Bandoola's underneath foreleg and Swai Zike's to the underneath hindleg, and together the two tuskers took the strain, so even and so gentle in their combined action that I felt sure they understood the delicacy of the action.

Bandoola's legs gradually rose until they were pointing to the sky. Then, as his huge head turned, he groaned—the first sound I had heard from him, and encouraging. For a moment his trunk waved in the air. His mouth opened, gulping. Then the whole body rolled over and fell with a terrific thud on the near side. It was rather like turning a very heavy feather mattress, and I was afraid that he was going to be as limp and inanimate on the near side as he had been on the off. But something had shifted. He seemed to deflate on one side and then he struggled to his feet. He was up.

The effort of getting him up had forced some stringy undigested bamboo from his lower bowel. It hung from him in strands. I emptied it as far as I could, plunging in my arm a dozen times as far as the armpit. Then my job of elephantine plumbing was over. The stoppage was unblocked and nature relieved him of his inflated gas as if he had been punctured.

I gave orders for him to be secured and starved for twenty-four hours and then hand-fed. Within the day he had recovered.

KNOWING THAT I SHOULDN'T see Po Toke again for some years—if ever, because he was an ageing man—I had him up to say goodbye. I had learned so much from him about elephants and the jungle that I owed him a debt of gratitude. His ruling passion had been Bandoola. Though there had been a time when he had neglected Bandoola because of the second wife he had taken, that was all over. There had been no children in this case either and the girl went back to her village. Po Toke's adventures with women were ended. In the same way, his career as an elephant trainer was over, but he still remained the man who understood Bandoola better than any other man in the jungle.

His hair had turned grey, and was untidily knotted. His hands, however, were very clean and he took pains to draw my attention to the nail on the little finger of his left hand which he had grown to a length of at least half an inch, in a pathetic attempt to show himself a man of authority. He had also tried to grow a beard. It consisted of two hairs, which made up in length what they lacked in number. As he spoke, he continuously stroked and played with them. These little attempts to impress were really quite unnecessary, because the old man was still handsome.

We sat outside my tent as the evening sun dropped behind the western hills. Po Toke pointed to one escarpment they called Lovers' Leap, the tree line of which showed against the orange sky like the finest lace. He said that it was a story current with the oozies that a princess eloped with a Burman commoner, and because she was not allowed to marry him, they took refuge on the top of the peak; when they had finished all their food, they finished all their love as well and jumped over the precipice.

He laughed. "That's only an oozie's story," he said, "but they don't laugh at the story of Bo Gyi the old wild tusker and Ma Gyi the old wild female, because that story is true."

He hesitated, then resumed his narrative. "Bo Gyi and Ma Gyi," he said, "had been spoken of as inseparable companions all their lives and they did not live with a herd. Bo Gyi was a tusker of tuskers and he lived in this part for hundreds of years. And always with him went his mate, Ma Gyi.

"Their names were a legend. When our fathers and our forefathers came upon the footprints of Bo Gyi and Ma Gyi they pronounced the names of these great elephants with deep respect. For these two elephants, wild though they were, molested no one. They damaged no crops."

"Perhaps," I said, joking, "perhaps Bandoola was one of their descendants."

"It may very well be," Po Toke answered, and he looked towards the fading silhouette of Lovers' Leap. "But here is the fantastic part of the story. One evening some hunters were camped just where we are now. They had cooked their rice and were having their evening meal squatting in a circle, when an oozie said that he had found that evening the carcass of an old elephant dead and already beginning to stink. But nearby there was an old tusker grumbling and mumbling as if his heart was broken.

" 'If that's Ma Gyi,' said one of the others, 'mark my words, Bo Gyi won't last much longer.'

"They went on eating. All hands were busy, when suddenly an elephant trumpeted. They looked up, and there on the slope of Lovers' Leap they saw silhouetted a huge tusker, climbing towards the peak.

"It was Bo Gyi. The aged elephant moved very slowly. It must have taken him an hour to reach the top; and when he got there he stood on the peak looking over the dense forest spread out before him four hundred feet below. He was clearly silhouetted and he seemed to revive himself, because he lifted his head high."

I could see the whole thing, because Po Toke was acting it for me. His arm, as he told of Bo Gyi lifting his head, lifted like an elephant's trunk.

"The hunters were down here watching him, Thakin. And old Bo Gyi surveyed all below him, trunk in the air. Then suddenly he blew a terrific trumpet, his Last Post. And then slowly, this is what he did." Po Toke opened his mouth wide and with his arm still imitating the trunk he put his fingers like the end of the trunk into his mouth. "He blew his brains out and toppled over the precipice."

When I came to reflect on it, I laughed more and more, thinking of the way in which Po Toke had built up my credulity. He was an artist.

I DID NOT SEE Po Toke or Bandoola again for seven years; and then it was under circumstances which were to test all three of us. Po Toke, Bandoola and I had been curiously held together by our service to Bombine. We had worked together comparatively peaceably—in peacetime. But in April 1942, with the Japanese flooding into Burma and the British getting out just as fast as they could, I wondered what Po Toke's feelings would be towards the Japanese talk of co-prosperity spheres and the liberation of the oriental peoples.

I saw Po Toke during the retreat. He was still a headman and his elephants, including Bandoola, were bridge-building. Streams of women and children, weary and heartbroken, glanced towards the animals as they worked. A whole squadron of tanks was routed to cross by our bridges. Po Toke was superb. He talked to Bandoola, pacified him and kept him hard at work, handling the most massive tree-lengths. This was the tempo of war, working against time, oblivious of what lay ahead when this job was over. And when the job was finished—again a characteristic of war—no squadron arrived. One lone, lame tank crossed the bridge. Bandoola watched it from a respectful distance, prepared at any moment to bolt.

To those of us who had worked with elephants that retreat was a heartbreaking and humiliating thing. We had to leave behind us the men and animals with whom we had worked for years. The whole structure of Bombine had collapsed—and it must have seemed to Po Toke and hundreds of other oozies, seeing the straggling columns winding towards India, that it had collapsed for ever. I saw Po Toke before I left and I gave him some money. "Hide it if you can," I said. "I promise you that I will come back when this Dokha gyi (big trouble) has sorted itself out." I meant it, despite the evidence of what was passing before our eyes.

Po Toke took the money; but he did not look as if he believed me. In fact I don't think he believed in anything or anyone any more, except Bandoola. His wives had failed him, or he had failed them. The money which he had expected to receive from the Bombine Provident Fund had not materialized. The British dominion over Burma was being exchanged for a Japanese dominion. I think he felt as old and tired and bitter as he looked.

Bandoola's oozie ran away. And as the rearguard of the retreating army and the last straggling refugees departed towards Assam, Po Toke mounted Bandoola and rode him off. He had loved and tended and coveted this elephant as his own for forty-five years; and now in this moment of defeat Bandoola was his. He rode him by game tracks known only to himself, making for his native village, Witok.

When he reached Witok, he found it in sorry shape. It had been invaded by hordes of evacuees, and the villagers, afraid of cholera and other diseases, had fled into the jungle.

Po Toke took Bandoola up one of the headwater tributaries of the Witok Creek. He fettered him securely and attached to his forefetters two heavy chains twenty feet in length which would prevent him from wandering so far that he could not track him again. Then he went back to his village.

The Japanese, who were now in full occupation of Burma, sent out orders that all elephant riders should report with their animals. The penalty for disobedience was death.

Po Toke went to report. He said that Bandoola, who was a dangerous and savage tusker, had joined the wild elephant herds. No one would ever handle him again. In that case, they said, he could have an appointment mustering as many deserted elephants as he could find. He pleaded that he was old and sick, and he returned to his war-scarred village.

As far as he knew no one in the village knew that he had Bandoola hidden. During the 1942 monsoons Po Toke left the village half a dozen times. Each time he found Bandoola, but he knew that every visit was dangerous. His absences made people talk, and the time might come when he would be called on to explain them to the Japanese.

The money which I had given him lasted for six months. His sixth visit to Bandoola he knew would be his last. He would have to find a job with the invaders which would give him food, and Bandoola must be free to fend for himself. He took off the fetters and chains. "Keep clear of wild tuskers and don't fight," he said. "Buddha provided food for you in the jungle. But for me there is nowhere where life is easy. My life is at an end, but I shall not rob you of yours." He patted Bandoola's massive trunk, then made his way downstream towards his unhappy village. Bandoola watched him until he was out of sight and then went back to his eating.

In October there was the usual break in the monsoon, in peacetime a promise to the jungle Burman that the torrential rains would soon be over. But this year the promise turned to a threat. With the end of the rains, the villages would be at the mercy of enemy patrols; and for the Burmans, the soldiers of either side were the enemy.

One evening, a few days after his return from his last visit to Bandoola, Po Toke was lying in his hut. He had lost all pride. His few rags of clothes were dirty. His hair hung long and uncombed.

Suddenly he heard a sound which he had not heard for months, the laughter of children, and then a familiar voice. "He's come!" the children shouted. "He's come!"

Po Toke peeped through a hole in the matting wall and saw Harold Browne with six or seven children scrambling to hold his hands. Harold was more loved by the Burmans than anyone I ever knew. A young Burmese girl of twenty ran to him and hugged him round his waist, crying with joy.

Old Po Toke for the first time in months hurriedly tied his hair into a bunch and grabbed a piece of cloth and wound it round his head in respect. As he came out of his hut, Harold called to him, "Po Toke, I want to talk to you."

Harold took him on one side and told him that I was at Tamu and I wanted to see him. Coming to Witok when all the talk was of how the Japanese were going to sweep on into India, he must have brought heart to them as no one else could. "Of course, I will go to see Williams Thakin Gyi," Po Toke said, and he told him how he had kept Bandoola in hiding.

When Harold picked up Po Toke at dawn next day, they set out together to find Bandoola. Three days later Bandoola was marched back into camp. Po Toke made an occasion of it, and it was truly an occasion. For this was for all of us the first step in the fight back after that ignominious retreat. I did not recognize Po Toke at first. Months of near-starvation had taken a savage toll of his body. But it had quickened his spirits. Po Toke had no doubts now where his loyalties lay.

Bandoola was presented to me to be enrolled as No. 1 War Elephant, the first of the elephants to fight for the freedom of Burma from the Japanese, and worthy of his glorious name.

What a contrast he was to poor undernourished old Po Toke! I have never seen even a wild elephant in such magnificent condition. And it was just as well. Three gruelling years of war lay ahead, three years in which those careful considerations of elephant-management which we had built up in peacetime were flung to the winds.

In *Elephant Bill*, an earlier book of mine, I told part of Bandoola's wartime story, of the way when evacuating from Assam into India we came to an almost sheer cliff, and Bandoola led the elephant train up steps we cut in the rock and along a narrow path with a precipice on one side. It was a moment of greatness, a heroic moment in which Po Toke had his full share. Without Bandoola and Po Toke we should never have come through.

Coming down from the ridge, we descended into the valley of the Barak River, which was broad and open and swampy. That childhood experience of Bandoola's asserted itself. He who had walked beside the precipice was terrified of swamps. He wouldn't lead. We had to get a young female to lead, while Bandoola made a detour round the swampy ground. And so we waited a day for this timorous great elephant to catch up with us.

The last time I saw Bandoola was five months later when he was marched back to Burma as part of the great offensive. The god of war is a harsh god, who hates individuality more than anything. I myself became impersonal, a machine which was part of a greater machine. I had to think of elephants and their oozies in hundreds and then in thousands. I was part of a new army advancing.

But the elephants weren't and the oozies weren't. The oozies did not obey me because I had a crown and a pip stencilled on an old Bombine khaki shirt. They obeyed me because I was a Bombine man, and I knew about elephants. Po Toke left Witok and brought Bandoola with him to work for me. He had no idea that he would become part of the army. In his own mind he was probably still working for Bombine.

I must explain this because it is important, if one is to understand what happened. To Po Toke the whole thing was incomprehensible. We were accredited to the Royal Indian Engineers, and if there was anyone the good Burmese nationalist hated more than a Japanese it was an Indian. Indian engineers knew nothing about elephants. There was continual friction between what the military wanted and what elephants were able to do.

In *Elephant Bill*, I told part of the story of Bandoola's end. As the British army swept back into Burma, Po Toke was put in charge of an elephant camp, feeding two sawmill units with teak for boat-building. For the facts, let me quote from *Elephant Bill*:

"The camp was two miles away from the main military road, and in it one could only just hear the grind of the incessant stream of army lorries.

"Before I went forward to visit army headquarters, I visited Po Toke's camp, for I thought it would help to keep up the morale of the oozies, who were already becoming impatient for the war to be over.

"To my surprise, Bandoola was absent from the parade, and I naturally asked Po Toke where he was.

"He replied, 'He has been missing for three days, Thakin Gyi.'

"I said no more but, after inspecting the animals, went on into Po Toke's camp, where his men were quartered.

"'You all know the difficulties we have with elephants getting lost in peacetime, and how far worse it is in war. Have you all been on an organized tracking party, looking for Bandoola?'

"No one answered me so, looking at Po Toke, I asked him, 'Have you not organized one?'

"Old Po Toke looked pale and worried and replied in a low voice, 'There is no trace of his tracks anywhere.'

"I went back to camp with the feeling that what I had heard was no normal story of a missing elephant. I went on to army headquarters, and when I got back five days later, I heard that Po Toke had been taken ill, and there was still no trace of Bandoola.

"I went straight off, and blasted old Po Toke to hell. He burst into tears and said, 'Bandoola is dead within four hundred yards of camp. Go and see him. I am too ill to walk, Thakin Gyi.'

"Two of the oozies silently led me along a track leading from the camp towards the hills, and before long I could smell the frightful stench of a decomposing elephant. The two oozies stood aside, and I walked on into a cleared patch of short grass. There lay Bandoola, his enormous belly distended with decomposition—and his right tusk gone, sawn off at the lip. The left tusk, half imbedded in mud and earth, on the lower side, had not been taken.

"My feelings were a terrible mixture of grief and anger. I was determined to find out the truth. Bandoola had been shot. There was a bullet hole in his forehead and he had obviously dropped dead where he was standing. As far as I could see, there was no trace of the spot having been visited for several days by any living soul.

"All I could get out of poor old Po Toke was the pitiful statement that Bandoola's oozie had found him dead one evening, ten days before, and

on going with the oozie to the spot the next morning he had found that the right tusk had been sawn off. In his panic and grief, he had sworn all his men in camp to silence. He pleaded that he had been unable to face breaking such terrible news, as he knew that my grief would be as great as his own. It was useless calling him a bloody fool and cursing him because his prevarication made it far more difficult to discover the culprit. Such arguments meant nothing to Po Toke. Bandoola was dead, and his own interest in life was over. Nothing mattered to him any more. By noon next day a .303 bullet had been extracted from Bandoola's brain. The slenderness of this, my only bit of evidence, can be realized. Thousands of lorries passed nearby along the army's lines of communication every day. I had inquiries made at every unit in the neighbourhood, but it seemed most unlikely that any sepoy had been guilty, as most of them belonged to non-combatant units. Every check was reported to have been made on ammunition—with the negative results that might have been expected. I even made a search of their huts, hoping I might find the sawn-off tusk. But I drew a blank.

"I then gave orders to dismiss Po Toke and Bandoola's oozie, hoping this would produce some reaction. Once more I drew blank."

I DO NOT PRETEND to have an answer to the mystery of Bandoola's death. But I have a theory.

After I had sacked him, Po Toke went back to Witok and in due course he got the two to three thousand rupees owing to him from the Bombine Provident Fund. On that he could have settled down and lived comfortably for the rest of his life. But according to my informant, who went back to the chaos of Burma after the war was over, Po Toke did not settle down to a graceful old age. With the money he got from Bombine he started a band of dacoits—perhaps his hope for Burmese independence had gone sour on him when he discovered so many members of the new government were ex-Japanese collaborators—perhaps he'd always wanted to head a band of dacoits and had only been restrained from doing so by the need to look after Bandoola—perhaps the failure of all things in which he had believed had made him bitter. All that is certain is that Po Toke was one of the leaders of the dacoits making it difficult for the administration of New Burma.

I have always distrusted the statement that each man kills the thing he loves as being, if nothing else, too sweeping. But I suspect that it was true of Po Toke. The more I think of it, the more certain I am that his behaviour in the sawmill camp was inconsistent with his innocence. Why should he lie about the length of time that Bandoola had been lost? Why, when he knew exactly where the carcass was, should he conceal the fact?

Yet what could have induced Po Toke to kill the thing he loved? I have not a shred of evidence that would be accepted in a court of law, but I believe that working for the sawmills for long hours, often indeed far into the night, Po Toke became desperate. I was far away. There wasn't a man to whom he could turn, who would understand what a truly remarkable elephant Bandoola was. He was older than Bandoola; he would die before him. The only person to whom Po Toke might have trusted him was myself, and he had a shrewd suspicion that I would never go back.

So I think that with a curious mixture of possessiveness and conceit ("no one can manage Bandoola like me") he took a service rifle and shot the animal he had defended and protected from birth. Then he sawed off one of the tusks to make it appear as if Bandoola had been killed for ivory, and took this tusk as his memento. If I am right, this must be one of the very few *crimes passionels* committed against an animal.

J.H. Williams

J. H. Williams was born in England in 1897 and fought in World War I. In the early 1920s he joined the Bombay Burma Corporation and immediately became deeply interested in elephants and their welfare; then, when the Japanese overran Burma in World War II, "Elephant Bill" organized a rescue operation to move women and children to safety in India. He then returned to the hills, ran a refugee camp and helped many more people escape to India.

After the war Colonel Williams went back to England with his wife and children. Here he managed a Cornish market garden, and wrote his best selling reminiscences. He died in 1958.

AUSTRALIA:
THE WILD CONTINENT

A picture feature taken from the book by
MICHAEL MORCOMBE

Photographer and writer Michael Morcombe has travelled all over his native Australia—a continent where wilderness still reigns unchallenged despite encroaching civilization. He has photographed the whole vast array of Australian wildlife, seeking out the creatures of every region, from parched deserts to cool rain forests. Some animals are familiar, some exotic, some found nowhere else in the world; each is sensitively portrayed in its natural habitat in this superb photographic portrait of a magnificently untamed continent.

WILDERNESS CAN STILL BE found on the Australian continent. Here landscapes unchanged by man owe their every detail to the forces of nature acting over the ages. Thousands of miles of coastline remain which would show no sign of change, could their cliffs and beaches now be seen by the pioneer navigators who first sighted them nearly four hundred years ago. There are still extensive tracts of country where there are no roads or trails, and where there has probably never been the imprint of wheels upon the soil.

Even with the first arrival of man, there was insignificant change to Australia as a wild continent. As hunters and gatherers, the Aboriginal people lived in harmony with their environment, and did not try to reshape their surroundings. By contrast, mankind in many other parts of the world has modified his environment by grazing his flocks, and clearing land for crops. Because European man was late to arrive in Australia, many parts of the continent are still rich and varied wilderness areas.

The forbidding nature of these areas has itself protected them. The greater part of the population is crowded into the climatically pleasant southeastern and southwestern corners of the continent. Remote from these centres of population, the wild regions remaining offer great diversity of scenery, from rain forests to deserts and mountain ranges. Each region supports its own plants and animals, each is a whole new world.

Rain forests are dominated by huge trees that compete for all the life-giving light that is available. Under a dense canopy of foliage is a world of sunlit greenery, with brightly coloured butterflies and superbly plumaged birds. Below, at the level of the sodden rain-forest floor, the sunlight is filtered to a perpetually gloomy greenish twilight.

In total contrast is Australia's arid interior. In the summer the midday heat becomes stifling, and the glare of the sun hurts the eyes. The shimmering air above the sun-baked land distorts reality; mirages put reflecting pools of water into dry saltlakes, where hills and scrub appear mirrored with tantalizing reality.

Australia has some impressive mountain regions, too. Most ruggedly spectacular are those of Tasmania. Here is scenery of true alpine character, with glaciated landforms, ice-carved cliffs, jagged horizons and peaks.

Australia has through ages past been a lonely continent. Originating as part of a much larger land mass some forty million years ago, it drifted free, separating from other slabs of the earth's crust that were to be known as South America and Antarctica.

The underlying landforms of Australia, together with its climate, have produced in each region a unique and distinctive vegetation. These areas of vegetation in turn support an animal population, ranging from the smallest microbes and insects, through the whole spectrum of reptiles, birds and mammals. Each natural habitat, whether in rain forests, deserts or coasts, is a complete and self-sustaining ecosystem.

Most conspicuous among Australia's wealth of wildlife are the birds of which there are 775 species. Among these are some of the world's most distinctive creatures. Here are parrots and cockatoos displaying brilliant colours in the treetops, bowerbirds attending courtship arenas, honey eaters in great numbers probing the flowers, and huge flightless birds.

Among the furred animals are the well-known koala and kangaroo. But there is a host of others less well-known; most are shy, secretive creatures of the night. There are tiny but fierce marsupial mice, gliders, ring-tailed and brush-tailed possums, potoroos, dunnarts and mulgaras.

Almost 400 species of reptiles inhabit the Australian continent. In the arid regions they are one of the most common forms of animal life. Australian lizards include the startling Thorny Devil, which has an armour of sharp thick spines over head and body, and a group of burrowing lizards which are entirely legless. There are also the impressive monitors, or goannas, and although these reptiles are found outside Australia, on this continent they have evolved into their greatest variety.

My interest in the photography of Australia's wildlife began in the late 1950s when, still a student, I found a Splendid Wren's nest near my home. I was so enthused by its magnificent deep blue plumage that I tried, most unsuccessfully, to photograph it. Thereafter the photography of wildlife developed as a fascinating hobby until, in 1966, the publication of my first book, *Wild Australia,* encouraged me to begin a career as a full-time writer and photographer.

The photographs that follow are arranged according to Australia's distinct natural habitats which, as already mentioned, are classified according to type of vegetation. It is my hope that the pictures capture some of the variety and beauty of this continent's magnificent wildlife.

The Australian wilderness abounds with strange and fascinating animals, few more startling than this denizen of the rain forests. Despite its appearance, the Boyd's forest dragon is completely harmless and seems to rely on camouflage for protection.

Along the upper ranges of the arid spinifex regions, small eucalypts known as "ghost gums" grow precariously. The mulgara (inset), a carnivorous marsupial, survives such dry conditions by obtaining all the moisture it needs from its prey. Hunting by night, it spends the day in deep, cool burrows.

In Australia's heathlands and sandplains, strong winds can strip sand and vegetation from the ancient limestone beneath. A tremendous variety of flowering plants grows on the sandy soils, attracting nectar-sipping honeyeaters like the spinebill (above right) and also the diminutive splendid wren (below right).

Australia has relatively
few wetlands, but after
tropical cyclones, floods
can create vast areas of
temporary marshland. At
other times of year this
swamp is dry, but heavy
rain has now made it a
haven for black swans (far
right) and the green and
gold bell frog.

More than twenty per cent of the
Australian continent supports the
spiny grasses known as spinifex.
Softer, perennial grasses spring up
after the rains (left) but creatures
like the hairy-footed dunnart
(below right), a tiny insect-
eating marsupial, can survive
very arid conditions, as can the
black-headed monitor (above
right). This fast-moving goanna
lives in rock crevices or burrows.

Australia's lush rain forests extend down the eastern coast through tropical and temperate regions. This palm forest (below left) is typically dense and luxuriant and shelters many species of birds and mammals, including the spectacular regent bower bird (above left), and the mountain brushtail possum (right).

Mulga, or acacia scrub, is
well adapted to survive
long periods of drought,
but dead trees (left) show
the toll taken by the harsh
environment. These arid
central regions are the
home of Australia's largest
goanna, the $2\frac{1}{2}$m long
perentie (above), and of
the wolf spider. The
female (right) hunts at
night with her brood
clustered all over her body.

The emu (left) stands almost 2m tall and though flightless can run up to 30 mph. Emus inhabit remote semi-desert regions. The agile wallaby (right) is common in the northern tropical forests, while the bizarre thorny devil or moloch (left below) lives in the central and western part of the continent. The potoroo (right below), a very small member of the kangaroo family, is common only to Tasmania, depending on dense, moist vegetation for survival.

The rainbow lorikeet (above) inhabits the forests of the eastern coast. The flocks are nomadic and feed in flowering trees on nectar and insects. The tiny feathertail glider (left) lives in eucalyptus forests on a similar diet, leaping considerable distances from tree to tree.

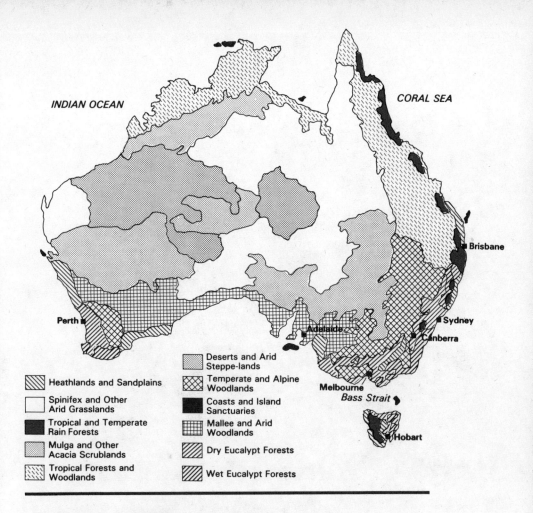

INDIAN OCEAN

CORAL SEA

■ Brisbane

Perth ■

Adelaide

■ Sydney

■ Canberra

Melbourne
Bass Strait

■ Hobart

	Deserts and Arid Steppe-lands
Heathlands and Sandplains	Temperate and Alpine Woodlands
Spinifex and Other Arid Grasslands	Coasts and Island Sanctuaries
Tropical and Temperate Rain Forests	Mallee and Arid Woodlands
Mulga and Other Acacia Scrublands	Dry Eucalypt Forests
Tropical Forests and Woodlands	Wet Eucalypt Forests

Michael Morcombe

Michael Morcombe's interest in wildlife photography began in the late 1950s when as a schoolboy he found a Splendid Wren near his home and tried, most unsuccessfully, to photograph it. Thereafter, wildlife and cameras claimed all his spare time; Morcombe won many important photography awards, and in 1966 the success of his first book, *Wild Australia*, encouraged him to become a full-time author. Since then he has published some 35 books, most of them about his native Australia. He lives with his wife Irene (who has co-authored many of the books) and their two daughters near Perth, Western Australia.

Never Cry Wolf

A CONDENSATION OF THE BOOK BY
Farley Mowat
ILLUSTRATED BY LIZ MOYES

Young Farley Mowat had only recently been recruited to the Canadian Wildlife Service—so he was a little alarmed to hear that he, and he alone, had been chosen to carry out an important and dangerous mission. Rumour had it that, up in Canada's desolate Barren Lands, vicious and insatiable wolves were ravaging the deer population: so serious was the problem that a full-scale investigation was called for. Mowat was sent to find out what was happening—to live alone amongst the wolves.

This is his account of the many months he spent in the wilderness, observing creatures who turned out to be very different from the fierce, blood-thirsty wolves he had been led to expect. Studying one wolf family in particular, he found them to be loyal, playful and affectionate animals, whose reputation had been falsified by hunters who were themselves slaughtering deer by the thousand.

Told with warmth, compassion and a refreshing wit, *Never Cry Wolf* is a fascinating story, in which the author effectively vindicates the noble beasts who so trustingly allowed him to share their lives.

Chapter 1

I T IS A LONG WAY from the bathroom of my Grandmother Mowat's house in Oakville, Ontario, to the bottom of a wolf den in the Barren Lands of central Keewatin, and I have no intention of retracing the entire road which lies between. Nevertheless, there must be a beginning to any tale, and the story of my sojourn amongst the wolves begins properly in Granny's bathroom.

When I was five years old, my parents took me to Oakville and left me in the care of my grandparents while they went off on a holiday. The Oakville house—"Greenhedges" it was called—was a genteel establishment, and I did not feel at home there. My cousin, who was some years older than myself, refused to have anything to do with me except under the most formal circumstances. Grandmother, an aristocratic lady of Welsh descent, tolerated me but terrified me too. She terrified most people, including Grandfather, who had long since sought surcease in assumed deafness. He used to while away the days as calm and unruffled as Buddha, ensconced in a great leather chair and oblivious to the storms which swirled through the corridors of Greenhedges.

Because there were no soulmates for me at Greenhedges, I took to roaming about by myself. One hot summer day I was meandering aimlessly beside a little local creek when I came upon a stagnant pool. In the bottom, only just covered with green scum, three catfish lay gasping out their lives. They interested me. I dragged them up onto the bank, found a tin can, put them in it along with some scum, and took them home.

I had begun to like them, in an abstract sort of way, and wished to know them better. But the problem of where to keep them was a major one. There were no washbasins in Greenhedges. There *was* a bath, but the plug did not fit and consequently it would not hold water for more than a few minutes. By bedtime I had still not resolved the problem and I was driven to the desperate expedient of finding temporary lodgings for them in the bowl of Granny's old-fashioned toilet.

I was too young at the time to appreciate the problems which old age brings. It was one of these problems which was responsible for the dramatic encounter between my grandmother and the catfish during the small hours of the night.

It was a traumatic experience for Granny and for me, and probably for the catfish too. Throughout the rest of her life Granny refused to eat fish of any kind and always carried a high-powered torch with her during her nocturnal peregrinations. I cannot be as certain about the effect on the catfish, for my unfeeling cousin—once the hoo-ha had died down a little—callously flushed the toilet. As for myself, the effect was to engender in me a lasting affinity for the lesser beasts of the animal kingdom. In a word, the affair of the catfish marked the beginning of my career, first as a naturalist and later as a biologist. I had started on my way to the wolf den.

MY EARLY YEARS as a naturalist were free and fascinating, and as I entered manhood I began my academic training in the hope of becoming a professional biologist. My personal predeliction lay towards studies of living animals in their own habitat. Being a literal fellow, I took the word *biology*—which means the study of life—at its face value. But during my time at the university it was becoming unfashionable to have *anything* to do with animals, even dead ones. The new biologists were concentrating on highly specialized statistical and analytical research, whereby the raw material of life became no more than fodder for calculating machines.

My inability to adjust to the new trends had an adverse effect upon my professional expectations. As graduation approached I found that the majority of my contemporaries were assured of excellent research jobs, while I seemed to have nothing in particular to offer in the biological marketplace. It was, therefore, inevitable that I should end up working for the government.

THE DIE WAS CAST one winter's day when I received a summons from the Dominion Wildlife Service in Ottawa, informing me that I had been hired at the munificent salary of one hundred and twenty dollars a month. Two days later I arrived in the windswept, grey-souled capital of Canada and found my way into the dingy labyrinth which housed the Wildlife Service. Here I presented myself to the chief mammalogist, and during the next several days I was subjected to something called "orientation"—a process which, so far as I could see, was designed to reduce me to a malleable state of hopeless depression.

Military titles were *de rigeur*. All memos were signed captain this or colonel that, and those who had not had the opportunity to acquire military status were reduced to the expedient of inventing suitable ranks. Levity was not looked upon with favour anywhere in those austere offices, as I discovered for myself while attending a conference concerning my first assignment.

A tentative list of the material requirements for this assignment lay on the conference table, surrounded by many grave countenances. It was a formidable document imposingly headed:

DESIDERATA FOR THE LUPINE PROJECT

Having already been unnerved by the gravity of the gathering, I lost my head completely when the assembly began to consider the twelfth item listed in this horrendous document: *Paper, toilet, government standard: 12 rolls.* An austere suggestion by the representative of the finance department that, in the interests of economy, the quantity of this item might be reduced, providing the field party (which was me) exercised all due restraint, sent me into an hysterical spasm of giggling. I mastered myself almost instantly, but it was too late. The two most senior men, both "majors", rose to their feet, bowed coldly, and left the room.

The Ottawa ordeal drew towards its end. One early spring morning I was called for a final interview before departing "into the field". My chief sat behind a massive desk whose dusty surface was littered with yellowing groundhog skulls (he had been studying rates of tooth decay in groundhogs ever since he joined the department). After a long silence, during which he toyed portentously with some of his skulls, he began his briefing.

"As you are aware, Lieutenant Mowat," he began, "the *Canis lupus* problem has become one of national importance. Within this past year alone this department has received no less than thirty-seven memoranda from members of the House of Commons, all expressing the deep concern of their constituents that we should do something about the wolf. Wolves are killing all the deer, and more and more of our fellow citizens are coming back from more and more hunts with fewer and fewer deer.

"As you may possibly have heard, my predecessor supplied the minister with an explanation contending that there were fewer deer because the hunters had increased to the point where they outnumbered the deer by about five to one. The minister, in all good faith, read this fallacious statement in the House of Commons, and he was promptly shouted down by members howling 'Liar!' and 'Wolf-lover!' Three days later my predecessor retired to civilian life, and the minister issued a press statement: 'The department of mines and resources is determined to do everything in its power to curb the carnage being wreaked upon the deer population by hordes of wolves. A full-scale investigation of this vital problem is to be launched at once.'"

At this juncture my chief seized a particularly robust groundhog skull and began rhythmically clacking its jaws together as if to emphasize his final words: "You, Lieutenant Mowat, have been chosen for this great task! It only remains for you to go out into the field at once and tackle this work in a manner worthy of the great traditions of this department. The wolf, Lieutenant Mowat, is *your* problem!"

Somehow I staggered to my feet, and involuntarily made a smart salute before fleeing from the room.

I fled from Ottawa too, that same night, aboard a Canadian airforce transport plane. My immediate destination was Churchill, on the western shore of Hudson Bay; but beyond that, somewhere in the desolate wastes of the subarctic Barren Lands, lay my ultimate objective—the wolf himself.

THE TRANSPORT WAS a twin-engined plane capable of carrying thirty passengers, but by the time all my "desiderata" were aboard there was barely room left for the crew and me. The pilot, an amiable flight lieutenant wearing a handlebar moustache, watched the load going aboard with honest bewilderment. His only information about me was that I was some sort of government man going on a special mission to the Arctic. His expression grew increasingly quizzical as we swung three great bundles of clanking wolf traps into the cabin, following these with the mid-section of a collapsible canoe which looked like nothing so much as a bathtub without ends. True to departmental precedent, the bow and stern sections of this canoe had been shipped to another biologist who was studying rattlesnakes in the south Saskatchewan desert.

My armament consisted of two rifles, a revolver complete with holster and cartridge belt, two shotguns, and a case of teargas grenades with which I was expected to persuade reluctant wolves to leave their dens so that they could be shot. There were also two large smoke generators prominently labelled DANGER, to be used for signalling to aircraft in case I got lost. A case of "wolf getters"—fiendish devices which fire a charge of potassium cyanide into the mouth of any animal which investigates them—completed my arsenal.

My scientific gear followed, including two five-gallon cans at the sight of which the pilot's eyebrows shot right up under his cap. They were marked: *100% Grain Alcohol for the Preservation of Specimen Stomachs.* Then there were tents, camp stoves, sleeping bags, and a bundle of seven axes (to this day I do not know why *seven*, for I was going to a treeless land where even one would have been superfluous), skis, snowshoes, dog harness, a radio transceiver and innumerable boxes and bales whose contents were as inscrutable to me as to the pilot.

When everything was in and securely roped down, the pilot, copilot and I crawled over the mass of gear and wedged ourselves into the cockpit. The pilot commented gloomily that he "doubted if the old crate would get airborne with all that lot aboard." Secretly, I doubted it too, but although the plane rattled and groaned dismally, she managed to take off.

The flight north was long and uneventful. Once we had landed in Churchill the pilot was unable to contain his curiosity any longer. "I know it's none of my damn business," he began apologetically as we walked towards one of the hangars, "but for heaven's sake, what's up?"

"Oh," I replied cheerfully, "I'm going off to spend a year or two living with a bunch of wolves, that's all."

The pilot grimaced like a small boy rebuked for an impertinence. "Sorry," he mumbled contritely. "Never should have asked."

THAT PILOT WAS NOT the only one who was curious. When I began trying to make arrangements in Churchill for a commercial bushplane to fly me on into the interior, my innocent explanation of my purpose, together with the admission that I hadn't the slightest idea where, in the almost untravelled wilderness, I wanted to be set down, drew either hostile stares of disbelief or conspiratorial winks. However, I was only trying to follow the operation order which had been laid down for me in Ottawa:

Para. 3, Sec.(C), Subpara. (iii)

You will, immediately upon reaching Churchill, proceed by chartered air transport in a suitable direction for the requisite distance and thereupon establish a base at a point where it has been ascertained there is an adequate wolf population and where conditions generally are optimal to the furtherance of your operations. ...

Most of the people I spoke to were unhelpful. After some delay I located the pilot of an ancient Fairchild ski plane, who made his precarious living flying Barren Lands trappers to their remote cabins. When I put my problem to him he was roused to exasperation.

"Listen, Mac!" he cried. "Only nuts hire planes to go somewhere they don't know where; and only nuts'd expect a guy to swallow a yarn about goin' off to keep house with a bunch of wolves. You go find yourself another plane jockey, see? I'm too busy to play games."

As it happened there *were* no other plane jockeys in the dismal shantytown of Churchill at that time. There was clearly nothing for it but to stay at the local hotel, a creaking barn through whose gaping walls a fine drift of snow used to whirl and settle on a windy day. There was no other kind of day in Churchill.

Nevertheless I was not idle. Churchill was then full of missionaries, prostitutes, mounted policemen, rum runners, trappers, fur smugglers, ordinary fur traders and other interesting characters, all of whom, so it developed, were authorities on wolves. From these sources I received some fascinating information. I discovered that, although wolves reputedly devour several hundred people in the Arctic zone every year, they will always refrain from attacking a pregnant Eskimo. (The missionary who provided me with this remarkable data was convinced that this encouraged a high birthrate among the Eskimos and a consequent lamentable concern with reproductive rather than spiritual matters.) I was told that every four years wolves are subject to a peculiar disease which causes them to shed their skins—and during the period when they are running about naked they are so modest they will curl up in a ball if closely approached. The trappers whom I interviewed informed me that wolves were rapidly destroying the caribou herds; that each wolf killed thousands of caribou a year just out of blood lust, while no trapper would think of shooting a caribou except under the most severe provocation.

Quite early in my inquiry I was asked by an old trapper if I would like some wolf juice. Since anything to do with wolves was grist to my mill, I was willing to have a go. The old man thereupon led me off to Churchill's only beer parlour and introduced me to wolf juice: a mixture of something called Moose Brand beer liberally adulterated with anti-freeze alcohol obtained from the soldiers at the air base.

Shortly after my baptism of wolf juice I submitted my first progress report. It was in longhand and fortunately proved completely indecipherable. No one in Ottawa could read a word of it; from which fact it was assumed that the report must be tremendously erudite. This report is, I believe, still on file with the department, and is still consulted by government specialists requiring expert data about wolves.

During my enforced stay in Churchill I also made a discovery of great importance. I found that when the laboratory alcohol with which I had been supplied was mixed sparingly with Moose Brand beer, a variety of wolf juice resulted which was positively ambrosial. Thoughtfully, I added fifteen cases of Moose Brand to my "desiderata". I also purchased several gallons of formaldehyde—as good a preservative of dead animal tissue as is grain alcohol.

Chapter 2

My stay in Churchill came to an end during the last week in May. For three days there had been a howling blizzard; then, during the third day, with visibility reduced to zero by blinding snow squalls, an aircraft came over the hotel at nought feet and with an expiring stutter flopped down on the ice of a nearby pond. The wind would have blown it away again had not several of us rushed out of the beer parlour and caught hold of its wings.

This plane was a decrepit bi-motor built as a military training aircraft. It had been discarded after long years of service, only to be resuscitated by a lanky, hollow-eyed ex-RAF pilot who had delusions about starting his own airline in the Canadian north. He had come, he said, from Yellowknife, some seven hundred miles to the northwest, and his destination was The Pas.... "was this The Pas?" Gently we informed him that The Pas lay some four hundred miles to the southwest. This news did not seem to dismay him. "Ah, well, any old port in a storm," he said gaily, and having been joined by his sluggish mechanic he accompanied us back to the beer parlour. Here, somewhat later in the day, I found myself confessing my difficulty to him.

"No problem," he said, after he had heard me out. "Gas up the old kite tomorrow and take you anywhere. Fly northwest—best course for us. Can't trust compass on any other course. Fly nice and low. Find lots of wolves; then put you down, and Happy Landings!"

ALTHOUGH THE NEXT three days proved inauspicious for the flight, on the morning of the fourth we prepared to depart. Because the plane could carry only a small load, I was forced to jettison some of my "desiderata", including the. useless canoe-cum-bath. I was able, however, to trade a gallon of alcohol for a seventeen-foot canvas-covered canoe, and this—so the pilot assured me—we could carry with us, lashed under the belly of the aircraft.

At this point I played a somewhat underhanded trick. My Moose Brand had been amongst the gear set aside as nonessential; but one evening, by torchlight, I discovered that the whole fifteen cases would fit nicely into the canoe which, when tied tightly up against the plane, betrayed nothing of the vital cargo it carried.

It was a beautiful day when we departed. The wind had sunk to about forty miles an hour from the east, and there was no snow falling as we took off through a black sea fog, promptly lost sight of Churchill, and circled into the northwest. Flying in the midst of an opaque grey cloud, we droned on for nearly three hours, during which we might as well have been submerged in a barrel of molasses for all we could see of the world below. Then the pilot put the aircraft into a steep dive and at the same time yelled to me: "Going down now! Only enough petrol to get home. Good wolf country around here, though. Best kind of wolves!"

We emerged under the cloud at an altitude of something over thirty feet, and discovered we were flying up a mile-wide valley between high rocky hills, and over a frozen lake. Without an instant's hesitation the pilot landed. He did not cut the engines.

"This is it, chum," he said merrily. "Out you go now. Got to be quick. Be dark before we raise Churchill."

The lethargic mechanic sprang to life and in moments my mountain of supplies was on the ice and the canoe had been cut loose.

After a glance at its contents, the pilot bent a sorrowful look upon me. "Not quite cricket, eh?" he asked. "Ah well, suppose you'll need it. Cheery-bob. Come back for you in the fall sometime if the old kite hasn't pranged. Not to worry, though. Sure to be lots of Eskimos around. They'll take you back to Churchill any time."

"Thanks," I said meekly. "But just for my records, do you mind telling me where I am?"

"Sorry about that. Don't quite know myself. Say about three hundred miles northwest of Churchill? Close enough. No maps of this country anyway.... Toodle-oo."

The cabin door slammed shut, and the plane went bumping across the ice, lifted off unwillingly, and vanished into the overcast.

I had arrived safely at my base.

As I LOOKED ABOUT ME at the stark and cloud-topped hills, the waste of pressure-rippled ice and, beyond the valley, the desolate and treeless tundra, I had no doubt that this was excellent wolf country. But it did not seem very prepossessing. True, I had apparently penetrated to the heart of the Keewatin Barren Lands. And I had established a kind of base, although its location—on the lake ice, far from land—left much to be desired. So far, I had adhered strictly to my instructions; but the next paragraph in my operation order was a stickler.

Para. 3, Sec.(C), Subpara. (iv)

Immediately after establishing a permanent base you will proceed, by means of canoe and waterways, to make an extensive general survey of the surrounding country, in order to determine the range/population ratio of Canis lupus *and in order to establish contact with the study species. . . .*

I was willing enough to carry on as per instructions, but the ice underfoot had a solidity about it which suggested that canoeing would have to be deferred for several weeks. Furthermore, without some alternative means of transport, I did not see how I could even begin the task of moving my mountain of gear to a permanent location on dry land. As to establishing contact with the study species—this seemed out of the question at the moment, unless the wolves themselves decided to take the initiative. Under the circumstances there was only one thing I could do: seek new orders from Ottawa.

Briskly I went to work, uncovering the portable radio and setting it up on top of a pile of boxes. On opening the instruction manual I was a little taken aback to find that my model was intended for the use of forest rangers, and could not normally work over ranges of more than twenty miles. Nevertheless I connected the batteries, rigged the aerial, turned knobs and pressed buttons according to the instructions—and went on the air.

For some reason known only to the department of transport, which licenses such mobile transmitters as mine, my call sign was "Daisy Mae". For the next hour Daisy Mae cried plaintively into the darkening subarctic skies without raising a whisper of a reply. I was ready to give up when I caught the faint echo of a human voice above the rustle of static in the earphones. Hastily I tuned the set until I could make out a gabble of words which it took me some time to identify as Spanish.

Since I realize that what I must now recount may strain the credulity of some of my readers, and since I have no technical knowledge whatsoever about radio, I can do no more than put forward an explanation given to me later by an expert. It embraces a mysterious phenomenon known as "wave skip", whereby it is sometimes possible (particularly in the north) for low-powered transmitters to span great distances. My set outdid itself. The station I raised belonged to an amateur operator in Peru.

His English was easily as imperfect as my Spanish, so that it was some time before we began to get through to each other, and even then he seemed convinced I was calling from somewhere near Tierra del Fuego. I was beginning to feel exceedingly frustrated before the Peruvian finally agreed to take down the substance of my message and forward it by commercial means to my chief in Ottawa. It caused something of a crisis—as I was to learn many months later.

Perhaps because of its South American origin the message was delivered, not to my own department, but to the department of external affairs. External could make nothing of it, except that it seemed to come from Tierra del Fuego and appeared to be in code. The ministry of defence failed to penetrate the code, or to identify any known Canadian agent in the Cape Horn region.

It was only through fortuitous circumstances that the mystery was ever resolved. Some weeks later one of the secretaries at external affairs who was in the habit of lunching with a senior man in my department told him the story and, in the telling, casually mentioned that the inscrutable message was signed, "Varley Monfat". With commendable and rather surprising acumen, the senior man identified me as the probable originator of the message; but this only led to the posing of a new and even more disturbing mystery, since no one could be found who would admit to having authorized me to go to Tierra del Fuego in the first place. The upshot was that a series of urgent messages were dispatched to me through the Canadian consul in Chile, instructing me to report to Ottawa.

None of these messages ever reached me, nor could they have done so even if they had been sent by a more direct route, for the battery in my radio was good for only six hours' use, and the only station I was ever again able to raise before the batteries went dead was broadcasting a light-music programme from Moscow.

But to return to my narrative. By the time I had finished my business with Peru, it had begun to grow dark. I had as yet seen no sign of wolves; but they were understandably very much on my mind when I glimpsed a flicker of distant movement near the valley mouth and detected a faint but electrifying sound—one that I instantly recognized, for, though I had never before heard it in the wild, I *had* heard it several times in cowboy films. It was unmistakably the howling of a wolf pack in full cry, and the pack was crying full in my direction. At least one of my problems appeared to have been solved. I was about to establish contact with the study species.

The solution of this problem led directly to the discovery of several new ones, not the least of which was that I had only six rounds in my pistol and couldn't for the life of me remember where I had stowed the reserve ammunition. This was a matter of some moment. I therefore decided to retire underneath the upturned canoe.

Honesty compels me to admit that I now found it difficult to maintain an attitude of correct scientific concentration. I was particularly worried about my canoe. Being lightly built of canvas over thin cedar staves, it might, I suspected, be easily damaged, in which case I would be completely immobilized in the future. The second thing which was bothering me was so unusual that I must give it special emphasis. I found myself fervently wishing I were a pregnant Eskimo.

Since I could no longer see what was happening, my ears kept me informed as the pack swept up at full speed, circled my pile of equipment once, and then rushed straight for the canoe. A terrific chorus of howls, barks and yelps very nearly deafened me, and so confusing was the noise that I began to experience hallucinations, imagining I could hear the deep-throated roar of an almost human voice above the general tumult. The roar sounded rather like: FURGODSAKESTOPYOUSONSABITCHES!

At this point there was much scuffling, an outburst of pained yelping, and then, miraculously, total silence.

Very cautiously I put one eye to the narrow slit between the gunwale of the canoe and the ice below. At first I could see nothing but wolf feet—scores of them; but then my glance fastened on another pair of feet—a *single* pair—which could have belonged to no wolf. I lifted the side of the canoe, stuck out my head, and peered upwards into the bewildered

and rather apprehensive face of a young man clad all in caribou furs.

Scattered around him, and staring at me with deep suspicion, were the fourteen large and formidable huskies which made up his team. But of wolves there was no sign.

Chapter 3

Naturally I was disappointed that my first encounter with wolves should turn out to be an encounter with nonwolves; but there were compensations. The young man who owned the dogs was, so it developed, a trapper of mixed Eskimo and white parentage who possessed a cabin a few miles away. It was ideally suited to serve me as a permanent base camp. Apart from a small band of Eskimos including his mother's family, living seventy miles away to the north, this young man, whose name was Mike, was the only human inhabitant of an area of some ten thousand square miles.

Mike was at first inclined to treat me with suspicion. During his eighteen years of life he had never known an aircraft land in his part of the Barren Lands, and indeed had only seen two or three planes before, and those had been passing high overhead. Probably because he could not think what else to do with me, he led me off to his cabin that first night. Although it was hardly a palatial affair, being built of poles and roofed with decaying caribou hides, I saw at once that it would serve my purposes.

Having been empowered by the department to hire native assistance, so long as expenditure did not exceed three dollars a month, I promptly made a deal with Mike, giving him an official IOU for ten dollars to cover three months' accommodation in his cabin, as well as his services as guide and general factotum. I suspect, from the nature of subsequent events, that the bargain I struck with Mike was rather one-sided and that he may not have fully grasped its implications; but in any event he provided the services of his dog team to help me move my supplies and equipment to his cabin.

During the next days I was extremely busy unpacking my equipment and setting up my field laboratory—being obliged to usurp most of the limited space in the tiny cabin in the process. I had little time to spare for Mike, and he seemed to be naturally taciturn—except with his dogs. Nevertheless I did occasionally try to divert him by offering demonstrations of some of my scientific equipment.

Although these demonstrations seemed to fascinate him, his attitude, if anything, got worse. Shortly after I showed him the cyanide "wolf getters" and the four gross of mousetraps with which I intended to collect small mammals to be used in determining the identification of animal remains found in wolf stomachs, he departed the cabin without a word and refused to take his meals with me from that time forward. Then one evening I inveigled him over to the corner where I had set up my portable laboratory and proudly showed him my collection of glittering scalpels, bone shears, brain spoons and other intricate instruments which I would use in conducting autopsies on wolves, caribou and other beasts. With a two-page colour diagram of a human abdomen under dissection I was well into my explanation of what was meant by an autopsy, when I realized that Mike was backing slowly towards the door, his black eyes fixed on me with an expression of horror. I sprang up to reassure him, but at my movement he turned and fled through the door.

I did not see him again until the following afternoon when, returning from setting out a trapline for mice, I found him in the cabin packing his equipment. In a voice so low and rapid that I had difficulty in understanding him, he explained that he had been urgently called away to visit his sick mother at the camp of the Eskimos, and would probably be gone for some time. With that he rushed out to where his team stood ready harnessed, and departed at a furious pace into the north.

I was sorry to see him go, for the knowledge that I was now entirely alone with the local wolves seemed to intensify the desolate atmosphere of the stormswept lands around me. However, a sick mother took precedence—though I am still at a loss to understand how Mike knew his mother was ill.

BY THE END OF THE WEEK I decided that it was time to get out and about. As a newcomer to the Barrens, it behoved me to familiarize myself with the country in a cautious manner. Hence, on my first expedition afield I contented myself with making a circular tour on a radius of about three hundred yards from the cabin.

This expedition revealed little except the presence of four or five hundred caribou skeletons surrounding the cabin. Since I knew from my researches in Churchill that trappers never shot caribou, I could only assume that these animals had been killed by wolves. This was a sobering conclusion, indicating that wolves must kill, on the average, about twenty million caribou a year in Keewatin alone.

After this dismaying tour of the boneyard it was three days before I found time for another trip afield. Carrying a rifle and wearing my revolver, I went a quarter of a mile on this second expedition—but saw no wolves. However, to my surprise I observed that the density of caribou remains decreased in an almost geometric ratio to the distance from the cabin. I resolved to question Mike about it if or when I saw him again.

MEANTIME SPRING had come to the Barrens with volcanic violence. The snows melted so fast that the frozen rivers could not carry the melted water, which flowed six feet deep on top of the ice. Finally the ice let go, with a thunderous explosion; then it promptly jammed, and in short order the river beside which I was living entered into the cabin, bringing with it the accumulated refuse left by fourteen huskies during a long winter.

Eventually the jam broke and the waters subsided; but the cabin had lost its charm, for the repellent debris on the floor was a foot thick. I decided to pitch my tent on a gravel ridge above the cabin, and here I was vainly trying to go to sleep that evening, when I became aware of unfamiliar sounds. They were coming from just across the river, to the north, and they were a weird medley of whines, whimpers and howls.

I was not to be fooled twice. The cries were obviously those of a husky, probably a young one. Mike owned three half-grown pups not yet trained to harness, which ran loose after the team, and I deduced that one of these had got lost, retraced its way to the cabin, and was now begging for someone to come and be nice to it.

I was delighted. If that pup needed a friend, I was its man! I climbed into my clothes, ran down to the riverbank, launched the canoe, and paddled lustily for the far bank.

I assumed the dog was only a few yards away from the far bank, but as I made my way in the dim half-light over broken boulders and across gravel ridges, I appeared to be getting no closer. The pup was retreating, perhaps out of shyness, and when the whimpering wail stopped I was uncertain which direction to pursue. However, I saw a steep ridge ahead of me; from its summit, I would be able to locate the lost animal. As I neared the crest I got down on my stomach and cautiously inched my way the last few feet.

My head came slowly over the crest—and there was my quarry. He was lying down, evidently resting after his mournful singsong, and his nose was about six feet from mine. We stared at one another in silence. I do not know what went on in his massive skull, but my head was full of the most disturbing thoughts. I was peering straight into the amber gaze of a fully grown arctic wolf.

For some seconds neither of us moved, but continued to stare hypnotically into one another's eyes. The wolf was the first to break the spell. With a spring which would have done justice to a Russian dancer, he leaped about a yard straight into the air and came down running. The textbooks say a wolf can run twenty-five miles an hour, but this one did not appear to be running, so much as flying low. Within seconds he had vanished.

My own reaction was not so dramatic, although I may very well have set some sort of a record for a cross-country traverse myself. My return over the river was accomplished with such verve that I paddled the canoe almost her full length up on the beach on the other side. I entered the cabin, barred the door, and made myself as comfortable as I could for the balance of the short-lived night.

It had been a very strenuous interlude, but I could congratulate myself that I had at last established contact—no matter how briefly—with the study species.

WHAT WITH ONE THING and another I found it difficult to get to sleep, so finally I lit Mike's oil lantern, and resigned myself to waiting for the dawn.

I allowed my thoughts to return to the events of the evening. The more I thought about them, the more I realized that I had not cut a very courageous figure. My withdrawal from the scene had been hasty and devoid of dignity. But then the compensating thought occurred to me that the wolf had not stood upon the order of his (her) going either, and I began to feel better: a state of mind which may have coincided with the rising of the sun, now illuminating the bleak world outside my window with a grey and pallid light. As the light grew stronger I began to wish that I had followed the wolf and endeavoured to gain his confidence, or at least tried to convince him that I harboured no ill will towards his kind.

The Canada jays who came each day to scavenge the debris in the cabin were now becoming active. I lit the stove and cooked my breakfast. Then, filled with resolution, I packed some grub in a haversack, loaded my rifle and revolver, slung my binoculars round my neck, and set out to make good my failure of the previous evening. My plan was straightforward: I intended to go directly to the spot where I had seen the wolf disappear, pick up his trail, and follow until I found him.

The going was rough and rocky, but eventually I scaled the low crest where I had last seen him (or her). Ahead of me a vast expanse of boggy muskeg promised well for tracks; and indeed I found a set of footprints

almost immediately, leading off across a patch of chocolate-coloured bog.

I should have felt overjoyed, yet somehow I did not. The truth is that my first sight of the wolf's pawprints was a revelation for which I was quite unprepared. It is one thing to read in a textbook that the prints of an arctic wolf measure six inches in diameter; but it is quite another thing to see them laid out before you in all their bald immensity. The mammoth prints before me, combined as they were with a forty-inch stride, suggested that the beast I was proposing to pursue was built on the scale of a grizzly bear.

I studied those prints for quite a long time, until I discovered I had neglected to bring my pocket compass with me. Since it would have been foolhardy to proceed without it, I decided to return to the cabin.

When I got back the compass was not where I had left it. In fact I couldn't remember where I *had* left it, or even if I had seen it since leaving Ottawa. It was an impasse; but in order not to waste time I got down one of the standard works with which the department had equipped me, and reread the section on wolves.

Arctic wolves, the author informed me, were the largest of the many subspecies or races of *Canis lupus*. Specimens had been examined which weighed one hundred and seventy pounds; which measured eight feet seven inches from tip of nose to tip of tail; and which stood forty-two inches high at the shoulders. An adult of the arctic race could eat (and presumably did, on favourable occasions) thirty pounds of raw meat at a sitting. The teeth were "massive in construction and capable of both rending and grinding action, which enables the owner to dismember the largest mammals with ease, and crush even the strongest bones." The section closed with the following succinct remarks: "The wolf is a savage, powerful killer. It is one of the most feared and hated animals known to man, and with excellent reason."

I was very thoughtful for the balance of the day, and wondered if my hopes of gaining the confidence of the wolves might not be overly optimistic. As to demonstrating that I bore them no ill will—this I felt would be of little value unless the wolves felt like reciprocating.

THE NEXT MORNING, in the process of cleaning up the mess in the cabin, I uncovered my compass. I resigned myself to making another effort to contact the wolves.

My progress on this second safari was even slower, since I was carrying my rifle, shotgun, pistol and pistol belt, a small hatchet and my hunting knife, together with a flask of wolf juice in case I fell into one of the icy streams. It was a hot day, and spring days in the subarctic can be nearly as hot as in the tropics. The first mosquitoes were already heralding the approach of the sky-filling swarms which would soon make travel on the Barrens a veritable trip through hell. I located the wolf tracks and resolutely set out upon the trail.

It led directly across the muskeg for several miles; but although the wolf had sunk in only three or four inches, my steps sank in until I reached solid ice a foot beneath the surface. It was with great relief that I finally breasted another gravel ridge and lost all trace of the tracks.

My attempts to find them again were perfunctory. As I gazed around me at the morose world of rolling muskeg and frost-shattered stone that stretched uninterruptedly to a horizon so distant it might as well have been the horizon of the sea, I felt lonelier than I had ever felt in all my life. No friendly sound of aircraft engines, no distant rumble of traffic—only the whistling of an unseen plover gave an indication that life existed anywhere in all this lunar land, where no tree grew.

I found a niche amongst some lichen-covered rocks and, firmly jammed into it, ate and drank my lunch. Then I picked up the binoculars and began to scan the barren landscape for some signs of life.

Directly in front of me was the ice-covered bay of a great lake, and on the far side was a yellow sand esker, rising to a height of fifty feet and winding sinuously away into the distance like a gigantic snake. These eskers are the inverted beds of long-vanished rivers which once flowed through and over the glaciers that, ten thousand years ago, covered the Keewatin Barrens to a depth of several thousand feet. When the ice melted, sandy riverbeds were deposited on the land below, where they now provide almost the sole visual relief in the bleak monotony of the tundra plains.

I studied this one closely; and as I swept it with my glasses I saw something move at last. The impression I had was of someone, just the other side of the esker crest, waving his arm above his head. Much excited, I stumbled to my feet, trotted along the ridge to within three hundred yards of the esker, and took another look.

The object now looked like a white feather boa being vehemently waved by persons or person unseen. As I stared in perplexity, the first boa was joined by a second one, also waving furiously, and both boas began to move slowly along, parallel to the crest.

I felt uneasy. In fact I was on the point of abandoning the spectacle when, without warning, both boas turned towards me, rising higher and higher, and finally revealed themselves as the tails of two wolves proceeding to the top of the esker.

Hunkering down, I did my best to be unobtrusive. But the wolves paid no attention to me, if indeed they even saw me. They were far too engrossed in their own affairs which, as I slowly and incredulously realized, were at that moment the playing of a game of tag.

They were romping like a pair of month-old pups! The smaller wolf, a female, took the initiative. Putting her head down on her forepaws and elevating her posterior in a most undignified manner, she suddenly pounced towards the much larger male, whom I now recognized as my acquaintance of two days earlier. He, in his attempt to evade her, tripped and went sprawling. Instantly she was upon him, nipping him smartly in the backside, before leaping away to run round him in frenzied circles. The male scrambled to his feet and gave chase, but only by the most strenuous efforts was he able to nip *her* backside. Thereupon the roles were again reversed, and the female began to pursue the male, who led her on a wild scrabble up, over, down and back across the esker, until finally both wolves lost their footing on a steep slope and went skidding down it, inextricably locked together.

When they reached the bottom they separated, shook the sand out of their hair, and stood panting heavily, almost nose to nose. Then the female reared up and quite literally embraced the male with both forepaws while she proceeded to smother him in long-tongued kisses.

The male appeared to endure this with stoicism until the female tired. Turning away from him, she climbed halfway up the esker slope and ... disappeared.

Not until I swung the glasses towards a dark shadow in a fold of the esker did I understand. The shadow was the mouth of a cave or den, and the female wolf had almost certainly gone into it. I was so elated by the realization that I had not only located a pair of wolves, but by an incredible stroke of fortune had found their den as well, that I forgot all caution and ran to a nearby knoll in order to gain a better view of the den mouth.

The male wolf, who had been loafing about at the foot of the esker, saw me. In three or four bounds he reached the ridge, where he stood facing me in an attitude of tense and threatening vigilance. No longer like a playful pup, he had metamorphosed into a magnificent engine of destruction which impressed me so much that the neck of my flask positively rattled against my teeth.

I decided I had better not disturb the wolf family any more that day, so I withdrew. It was not an easy withdrawal, for one of the most difficult things I know of is to walk backwards up a broken rocky slope for three quarters of a mile encumbered, as I was, by the complex hardware of a scientist's trade.

When I reached the ridge, I took a last quick look through the binoculars. The female was still invisible, and the male was lying down on the crest of the esker, with the evident intention of having a nap. It was a great relief to see he was no longer interested in me.

I VISITED THE DEN again the next morning with a high-powered periscopic telescope and tripod.

It was a fine sunny morning with enough breeze to keep the mosquito vanguard down. When I reached the bay, I chose a rock some four hundred yards from the den, and set up my telescope so that its lenses peered over the crest, but left me in hiding. The wolves could not possibly have seen me and, since the wind was from them to me, they would have had no suspicion of my arrival.

When all was in order, I focused the telescope; but to my chagrin I could see no wolves, though I searched every inch of the esker for a distance of a mile on each side of the den. By noon, I had a bad case of eyestrain and a worse one of cramp, and I had almost concluded that the "den" was just a fortuitous hole in the sand. This was discouraging, for if this was not the wolves' den, I had about as much chance of locating it in this faceless wilderness as I had of finding a diamond mine.

Glumly I went back to my telescope. The esker remained deserted. The hot sand sent up heat waves which increased my eyestrain. By 2:00 pm I gave up hope, got stiffly to my feet and prepared to relieve myself, first surreptitiously glancing around to reassure myself that I was alone.

I was *not*. Standing directly behind me, and not twenty yards away, were the missing wolves.

They appeared to be quite relaxed, as if they had been standing there behind my back for hours. The big male seemed a trifle bored; but the female's gaze was fixed on me with what I took to be an expression of unabashed and even prurient curiosity.

My reaction was one of violent indignation. Outraged, I turned my back and with fingers shaking with vexation, hurriedly did up my buttons. When decency, if not my dignity, had been restored, I rounded on those wolves with a virulence which surprised even me. "Shoo!" I screamed at them. "What do you think you're playing at, you ... you ... peeping Toms! Go away, for heaven's sake!"

The wolves were startled. They glanced at each other with a wild surmise, and then trotted off in the direction of the esker. They did not once look back.

With their departure I experienced a reaction of another kind. The realization that they had been sitting almost within jumping distance of my unprotected back for God knows how long set up such a turmoil of the spirit that I gave up all thought of following them. Suffering from both mental and physical strain, I hurriedly packed my gear and set off for the cabin.

MY THOUGHTS THAT EVENING were confused. I was becoming prey to a small but nagging doubt as to just *who* was watching *whom*. In order to establish my ascendancy once and for all, I determined to visit the wolf esker again the following morning and make a detailed examination of the presumed den. I decided to go by canoe, since the rivers were now clear and the rafting lake ice was being driven offshore by a stiff northerly breeze.

It was a fine, leisurely trip to Wolf House Bay, as I had now named it. The annual spring caribou migration, north from the forested areas of Manitoba towards the distant tundra plains near Dubawnt Lake, was under way, and from my canoe I could see countless skeins of caribou crisscrossing the muskegs and the rolling hills in all directions. No wolves were in evidence as I neared the esker, and I assumed they were away hunting caribou for lunch.

I ran the canoe ashore and, fearfully laden with cameras, guns, binoculars and other gear, laboriously climbed the shifting sands of the esker to the shadowy place where the female wolf had disappeared. The den was located in a small wadi in the esker, and was so well concealed that I was on the point of walking past it when a series of small squeaks attracted my attention. I stopped and turned, and there, not fifteen feet below me, were four small, grey beasties engaged in a free-for-all wrestling match.

At first I did not recognize them for what they were. The fat, fox faces with pinprick ears; the butterball bodies, as round as pumpkins; the short, bowed legs and the tiny upthrust sprigs of tails were so far from my conception of a wolf that my brain refused to make the logical connection.

Suddenly, one of the pups caught my scent. He stopped in the midst of attempting to bite off a brother's tail and turned smoke-blue eyes up towards me. What he saw evidently intrigued him. Lurching free of the scrimmage, he padded towards me with a rolling, wobbly gait; but a flea bit him unexpectedly before he had gone far, and he had to sit down to scratch. At this instant an adult wolf let loose a full-throated howl, vibrant with alarm and warning, not more than fifty yards from me.

The idyllic scene exploded into frenzied action.

The pups became grey streaks which vanished into the darkness of the den mouth. I spun round to face the adult wolf, lost my footing, and started to skid down the loose slope towards the den. In trying to regain

my balance I thrust the muzzle of the rifle deep into the sand, where it stuck fast until the carrying strap dragged it free as I slid rapidly away from it. I fumbled wildly at my revolver, but so cluttered was I with cameras and equipment straps that I did not succeed in getting the weapon clear as, accompanied by a growing avalanche of sand, I shot past the den mouth, over the lip of the main ridge and down the full length of the esker slope. Miraculously, I kept my feet; but only by dint of superhuman contortions during which I was alternately bent forward like a skier going over a jump, or leaning backwards at such an acute angle I thought my backbone was going to snap.

It must have been quite a show. When I got myself straightened out and glanced back up the esker, it was to see *three* adult wolves ranged side by side, like spectators in the royal box, all peering down at me with expressions of incredulous delight.

I lost my temper. My scientific detachment was no longer equal to the strain. With a snarl of exasperation I raised the rifle but, fortunately, the thing was so clogged with sand that when I pressed the trigger nothing happened.

The wolves did not appear alarmed until they saw me begin to dance up and down in helpless fury, waving the useless rifle and hurling imprecations at their cocked ears; whereupon they exchanged quizzical looks and silently withdrew.

I too withdrew. To tell the truth, I was in no fit state to do anything except hurry home and seek solace for my tattered nerves and frayed vanity in the bottom of a jar of wolf juice.

I had a long and salutary session with the stuff that night, and under its healing influence I reviewed the incidents of the past few days. Inescapably, the realization was being borne in upon my preconditioned mind that the centuries-old concept of wolf character was a palpable lie. On three separate occasions in less than a week I had been completely at the mercy of these "savage killers"; but far from attempting to tear me limb from limb, they had displayed a restraint verging on contempt, even when I invaded their home and appeared to be posing a direct threat to the young pups.

When I emerged from my session with the wolf juice the following morning I was somewhat the worse for wear physically; but I was purified spiritually. I had made my decision that, from this hour onwards, I would go forward open-minded into the lupine world and learn to see and know the wolves, not for what they were supposed to be, but for what they actually were.

Chapter 4

During the next weeks I put my decision into effect with notable thoroughness. I went completely to the wolves. Abandoning Mike's cabin (with considerable relief, since as the days warmed up so did the smell), I set up a tiny tent on the shore of the bay immediately opposite the den esker. I kept my camping gear to the barest minimum—a small primus stove, a saucepan, a kettle and a sleeping bag. I took no weapons of any kind. The big telescope was set up in the mouth of the tent in such a way that I could observe the den by day or night without even getting out of my sleeping bag.

During the first few days I stayed inside the tent to allow the animals to get used to it. But my precautions against disturbing the wolves were superfluous. They managed to ignore my presence with a thoroughness which was somehow disconcerting.

Quite by accident I had pitched my tent within ten yards of one of the major paths used by the wolves on their way to, or from, their hunting grounds to the west; and only a few hours after I had taken up residence one of the wolves discovered me and my tent. He was at the end of a hard night's work and was clearly tired, and anxious to go home to bed. He came over a small rise straight on to within fifteen yards of me, and might have gone right past the tent without seeing it at all, had I not banged my elbow resoundingly against the kettle. The wolf's head came up and his eyes opened wide, but he did not stop. One brief, sidelong glance was all he vouchsafed me as he continued on his way.

It was true I wanted to be inconspicuous, but I felt uncomfortable at being so totally ignored. Nevertheless, during the two weeks which followed, one or more wolves used the track past my tent almost every night—and never did they show the slightest interest in me.

I was learning a good deal about my neighbours, and one of the facts was that they were not nomadic roamers, as is almost universally believed, but were settled beasts and the possessors of a large permanent estate. The territory owned by my wolf family comprised more than a hundred square miles, bounded on one side by a river but otherwise not delimited by geographical features. Nevertheless, there were very definite boundaries, clearly indicated in wolfish fashion.

Anyone who has observed a dog doing his neighbourhood rounds and leaving his personal mark on each convenient post will have already guessed how the wolves marked out *their* property. Once a week, more or

less, the clan made the rounds of the family lands and freshened up the boundary markers—a sort of lupine beating of the bounds.

I decided to use this system to make them at least recognize my existence. One evening after they had gone off for their nightly hunt I staked out a property claim of my own, embracing perhaps three acres, with the tent at the middle, and including a hundred-yard-long section of the wolves' path.

Staking the land turned out to be rather more difficult than I had anticipated. In order to ensure that my claim would not be overlooked, I felt obliged to make a property mark on stones, clumps of moss, and patches of vegetation at intervals of not more than fifteen feet around the circumference of my claim. This took most of the night and required frequent returns to the tent to consume copious quantities of tea; but before dawn the task was done, and I retired somewhat exhausted to observe results.

I had not long to wait. At 0814 hours, according to my wolf log, the leading male of the clan appeared over the ridge behind me, padding homewards with his usual air of preoccupation. As usual, he did not deign to glance at the tent; but when he reached the point where my property line intersected the trail, he stopped as abruptly as if he had run into an invisible wall. He was only fifty yards from me, and with my binoculars I could see his expression clearly.

His attitude of fatigue vanished and was replaced by a look of bewilderment. Cautiously he sniffed at one of my marked bushes. After a minute he backed away a few yards and sat down. And then, finally, he looked directly at the tent and at me. It was a long, thoughtful, considering sort of look.

As the look became yet more thoughtful I began to grow fidgety, for I dislike staring matches. In an effort to break the impasse I loudly cleared my throat and turned my back on the wolf (for a tenth of a second) to indicate as clearly as possible that I found his continued scrutiny impolite, if not actually offensive.

He appeared to take the hint. Getting to his feet he had another sniff at my marker, and then briskly began a systematic tour of the area I had staked out as my own. As he came to each boundary marker he sniffed it once or twice, then carefully placed *his* mark on the outside of each clump of grass or stone. He made his mark with such economy that he was able to complete the entire circuit without having to reload once or, to change the metaphor slightly, on one tank of fuel. The task completed—and it had taken him no longer than fifteen minutes—he rejoined the path at the point where it left my property and trotted off towards his home—leaving me with a good deal to occupy my thoughts.

ONCE IT HAD BEEN formally established and its existence ratified by the wolves themselves, my little enclave in their territory remained inviolate. Never again did a wolf trespass on my domain. Any lingering doubts I might have had as to my personal safety dissolved, and I was free to devote all my attention to the study of the beasts themselves.

Very early in my observations I discovered that they led a well-regulated life. Early in the evenings the males went on the nightly hunt, always—as far as I could tell—staying within the limits of the family territory. I estimated that during a normal hunt they covered thirty or forty miles before dawn. During the daylight hours they slept—but in their own peculiarly wolfish way, which consisted of curling up for short wolf naps of five or ten minutes' duration. After each they would take a quick look about, and then turn once or twice before dozing off again.

The females and the pups led a more diurnal life. Once the males had departed in the evening, the female usually went into the den and stayed there, emerging only occasionally for a breath of air, a drink, or sometimes for a visit to the meat cache for a snack. This cache was located in a jumble of boulders half a mile from the den. No food was ever stored or left close to the den; any surplus from a hunt was carried to the cache and stuffed into rock crevices, primarily for the use of the nursing female who, of course, could not join the male wolves on extended hunting trips.

During the day, while the male wolves took it easy, the female would be reasonably active about her household chores. Emerging boisterously from the close confines of the den, the pups also became active—to the point of total exhaustion. Thus, throughout the entire twenty-four-hour period, there was usually something going on, or at least the expectation of something, to keep me glued to the telescope.

After the first two days and nights of nearly continuous observing I had about reached the limits of my endurance. I did not dare go to sleep for fear of missing something vital. On the other hand, I became so sleepy that I was seeing double, if not triple on occasion; and I saw that something drastic would have to be done or my whole study programme would founder. I could think of nothing adequate until, watching one of the males dozing comfortably on a hillock near the den, I recognized the solution to my problem. It was simply to learn to nap like a wolf.

It took some time to get the knack of it. As I eventually discovered, the business of curling up to start with, and spinning about after each nap, was vital to success. I don't know why this is so. Perhaps changing the position of the body helps to keep the circulation stimulated. I *do* know, however, that a series of properly conducted wolf naps is infinitely more refreshing than the unconscious coma of seven or eight hours' duration which represents the human answer to the need for rest.

As I grew more attuned to their daily round, I found it increasingly difficult to resist the impact of the wolves' individual personalities. Because he reminded me irresistibly of a royal gentleman for whom I had worked as a simple soldier during the war, I found myself calling the father of the family George, even though in my notebooks he was austerely identified only as wolf "A".

George was a massive and regal beast whose coat was silver-white. He was about a third larger than his mate, but he hardly needed this extra bulk to emphasize his air of masterful certainty. George had presence. His dignity was unassailable, yet he was by no means aloof. Conscientious to a fault, thoughtful of others, and affectionate within reasonable bounds, George was the kind of father every son longs to acknowledge as his own.

His wife was equally memorable. A slim, almost pure-white wolf with a thick ruff round her face and wide-spaced, slightly slanted eyes, she was a real minx and devilish when the mood was on her; yet there could have been no better mother anywhere. I found myself calling her Angeline. I became deeply fond of her and still live in hopes that I can somewhere find a human female who embodies all her virtues.

Angeline and George seemed as devoted a mated pair as one could hope to find but, alas, the many pages in my notebook which had been hopefully reserved for describing the sexual activities of wolves remained obstinately blank as far as they were concerned. I discovered that physical lovemaking enters into the lives of mated wolves only during a period of two or three weeks early in the spring, usually in March. Virgin females (and they are all virginal until their second year) then mate; they take only a single male, and for life.

Whereas the phrase "till death us do part" is one of the more amusing mockeries in the nuptial arrangements of a large proportion of the human race, with wolves it is a simple fact. Wolves are also strict monogamists and quite undeserving of the reputation for unbridled promiscuity which we have bestowed on them.

While it was not possible for me to know with exact certainty how long George and Angeline had been mated, I was later able to discover from Mike that they had been together for at least five years—or the equivalent of thirty years in terms of men.

One factor concerning the organization of the family mystified me very much at first. During my early visit to the den I had seen *three* adult wolves. Whoever the third wolf was, he was definitely a character: smaller than George, not so lithe and vigorous, and with a grey overcast to his otherwise white coat. He became Uncle Albert to me after the first time I saw him with the pups.

The sixth morning of my vigil had dawned bright and sunny, and Angeline and the pups took advantage of the good weather. Hardly was the sun risen (at three am) then they all left the den and adjourned to a nearby sandy knoll. Here the pups worked over their mother with an enthusiasm which would certainly have driven any human female into hysterics. They were hungry; but they were also full to the ears with mischief. Two of them did their best to chew off Angeline's tail, worrying it and fighting over it until I thought I could actually see her fur flying like spindrift, while the other two did what they could to remove her ears.

Angeline stood it with noble stoicism for about an hour and then, sadly dishevelled, she attempted to protect herself by sitting on her tail and tucking her mauled head down between her legs. This was a fruitless effort. The pups went for her feet, one to each paw, and I was treated to the spectacle of the demon killer of the wilds trying at once to cover her paws, her tail and her head.

Eventually she gave up. Harassed beyond endurance she raced to the top of a high sand ridge behind the den. The four pups rolled cheerfully off in pursuit, but before they could reach her she gave a most peculiar cry, a high-pitched and yearning whine-cum-howl.

Within seconds a saviour appeared: it was the third wolf. He had been sleeping in a bed hollowed in the sand at the southern end of the esker, where it dipped down towards the waters of the bay. I had not known he was there until I saw his head come up. He jumped to his feet, shook himself, and trotted straight towards the den—intercepting the pups as they prepared to scale the last slope to reach their mother.

I watched, fascinated, as he used his shoulder to bowl the leading pup over on its back and send it skidding down the lower slope towards the den. Having broken the charge, he nipped another pup lightly on its fat behind; then he shepherded the lot of them back to what I later came to recognize as the playground area.

I hesitate to put human words into a wolf's mouth, but the effect of what followed was crystal clear. "If it's a workout you kids want," he might have been saying, "then I'm your wolf!"

And so he was. For the next hour he played with the pups with as much energy as if he were still one himself. Leaping, rolling and weaving, he never left the area of the nursery knoll, while at the same time leading the youngsters such a chase that they eventually collapsed into complete somnolence. Only then did he disengage himself and settle on the edge of the nursery knoll, where he began wolf-napping, taking a quick look at the pups every few minutes to make sure they were still safely near at hand.

His true relationship to the rest of the family was still uncertain; but to me he had become "good old Uncle Albert".

Chapter 5

After some weeks of study I still seemed to be as far as ever from solving the salient problem of how the wolves made a living.

Caribou are the only large herbivores to be found in any numbers in the Arctic. They had shown a catastrophic decrease during the three or four

decades preceding my trip to the Barrens. Evidence obtained by various government agencies from hunters, trappers and traders seemed to prove that the plunge of the caribou towards extinction was primarily due to the depredations of the wolf. It therefore must have seemed a safe bet, to the politicians-cum-scientists who employed me, that a research study of wolf-caribou relationships in the Barrens would uncover incontrovertible proof with which to damn the wolf and justify a general campaign for his extirpation.

But although I had searched diligently for evidence which would please my superiors, I had so far found none.

Towards the end of June the last of the migrating herds had passed Wolf House Bay, heading for the high Barrens some two or three hundred miles to the north, where they would spend the summer. Whatever my wolves were going to eat during those long months, it would not be caribou. What *was* it to be? Arctic hares were present; but they were very scarce and fleet of foot. Ptarmigan and other birds were numerous; but they could fly. Lake trout, arctic grayling and whitefish filled the lakes and rivers; but wolves are not otters.

The days passed and the mystery deepened. To make the problem even more inscrutable, the wolves seemed reasonably well fed; and the two male wolves went off hunting every night and returned every morning, but never appeared to bring anything home.

As far as I could tell, the whole lot of them seemed to be existing on a diet of air and water.

About this time I began having trouble with mice. As June waned into July the country seemed to become alive with little rodents. Red-backed mice and meadow mice began invading Mike's cabin in such numbers that it looked as if *I* would soon be starving, unless I could thwart their appetite for my supplies. And when I awoke one morning to find that a meadow mouse had given birth to eleven naked offspring inside the pillow of my sleeping bag, I began to know how Pharaoh must have felt when he antagonized the God of the Israelites.

Late one afternoon, while the male wolves were still resting, Angeline emerged from the den and, leaving Albert to do duty as a babysitter, went down to the bay for a drink. I pointed my telescope on her.

She went directly to the rocky foreshore, waded out until the icy water was up to her shoulders, and had a long drink. As she was doing so, a small flock of Old Squaw ducks flew round the point and alighted a hundred yards or so away from her. She raised her head and eyed them speculatively for a moment, then waded back to shore, where she suddenly became demented.

Yipping like a puppy, she began to chase her tail; to roll over and over among the rocks; to lie on her back; to wave all four feet furiously in the air; and in general to behave as if she were clean out of her mind. It was an awe-inspiring sight, and so interested were the ducks that they swam in for a closer view. Closer and closer they came, necks outstretched and gabbling incredulously. And the closer they came, the crazier grew Angeline's behaviour.

When the leading duck was not more than fifteen feet from shore, Angeline gave one gigantic leap towards it. There was a vast splash, a panic-stricken whacking of wings, and all the ducks were up and away. Angeline had missed dinner by no more than inches.

This incident was an eye-opener, since it suggested a versatility at food-getting which I would hardly have credited to a human being, let alone to a mere wolf. However, Angeline soon demonstrated that the charming of ducks was a mere sideline. Having dried herself with a series of energetic shakes, she padded back across the grassy swale. But now her movements were quite different; by stretching herself so that she literally seemed to be walking on tiptoe, and by elevating her neck like a camel she seemed to gain several inches in height. She began to move slowly upwind, her nose wrinkling as she sifted the breeze for the most ephemeral scents.

Suddenly she pounced. Flinging herself up on her hind legs like a horse trying to throw its rider, she came down again with driving force, both forelegs held stiffly out in front of her. Instantly her head dropped; she snapped once, swallowed, and returned to her peculiar mincing ballet across the swale. Six times in ten minutes she repeated the straight-armed pounce, and six times she swallowed—without my having caught a glimpse of what she had eaten. The seventh time she missed her aim, spun round and began snapping frenziedly in a tangle of cotton grasses. This time when she raised her head I saw, quite unmistakably, the tail and hindquarters of a mouse quivering in her jaws. One gulp, and it too was gone.

Although I was much entertained by the spectacle of one of this continent's most powerful carnivores hunting mice, I did not really take it seriously. I thought Angeline was only having fun; snacking, as it were. But when she had eaten some twenty-three mice I began to wonder. Mice are small, but twenty-three of them adds up to a fair-sized meal, even for a wolf.

It was only later, by putting two and two together, that I was able to bring myself to an acceptance of the obvious. The wolves of Wolf House Bay and, by inference at least, all the Barren Lands wolves who were raising families outside the summer caribou range, were living largely, if not almost entirely, on mice.

Only one point remained obscure, and that was how they transported the catch of mice (which in the course of an entire night must have amounted to a formidable number) back to the dens to feed the pups. I never did solve this problem until I met some of Mike's relations. One of them, a charming fellow named Ootek, who became a close friend (and who was a first-rate, if untrained, naturalist), explained the mystery. Since it was impossible for the wolves to carry the mice home externally, they did the next best thing and brought them home in their bellies. I had already noticed that when either George or Albert returned from a hunt they went straight to the den and crawled into it. Though I did not suspect it at the time, they were regurgitating the day's rations, already partially digested.

The discovery that mice constituted the major item in the wolves' diet gave me a new interest in the mice themselves. I at once began a mouse-survey, by setting some hundred and fifty mousetraps in a nearby bog in order to obtain a representative sample of the mouse population. The second day my trap line was set, George happened in that direction, and I saw to my horror that he was heading straight for a cluster of ten traps set near the burrows of a lemming colony. Without thought I leaped to my feet and yelled: "George! For God's sake *hold it!*"

It was too late. My shout only startled him and he broke into a trot. He went about ten paces on the level and then, for the first and only time that I knew him, George lost his dignity. Yipping like a dog who has caught his tail in a door, he began climbing an unseen ladder to the skies, shedding mousetraps like confetti. Then he streaked for home.

I went over to examine the site. I found he had scored six traps out of the possible ten. They could have done him no real harm, of course, but the shock of having a number of his toes nipped simultaneously by an unknown antagonist must have been considerable.

I felt badly about the incident. It might easily have resulted in a serious rupture in our relations. That it did not do so I can only attribute to the fact that George's sense of humour, which was well-developed, led him to accept the affair as a crude practical joke—of the kind to be expected from a human being.

The mouse-wolf relationship was, I realized, a revolutionary discovery which would be treated with suspicion unless it could be thoroughly substantiated. I had already established two major points: that wolves caught and ate mice; and that the small rodents were sufficiently numerous to support the wolf population. There remained, however, a third vital point. It was imperative to prove that a diet of small rodents would suffice to maintain a large carnivore in good condition.

For some days I pondered the problem and then, one morning, while I was preparing some lemmings and meadow mice as specimens, inspiration struck me. Why not use myself as a test subject? While not absolutely conclusive, evidence that *my* metabolic functions remained unimpaired under a mouse regimen would strongly indicate that wolves, too, could survive and function normally on the same diet.

I began the experiment at once. Having cleaned the basinful of small corpses which remained from my morning session of mouse skinning and gutting, I placed them in a pot with some water and hung it over my primus stove. The pot gave off a most delicious odour as the water boiled, and I was in excellent appetite by the time the stew was done.

Eating these small mammals presented something of a problem at first because of the numerous minute bones; however, I found that the bones could be chewed and swallowed without much difficulty. The taste of the mice was pleasing, if rather bland.

During the first week of the diet I found that my vigour remained unimpaired, and that I suffered no apparent ill effects. However, I did begin to develop a craving for fats. It was this that made me remember that the wolves *ate the whole mouse*; and my dissections had shown that these small rodents stored most of their fat in the abdominal cavity, adhering to the intestines, rather than subcutaneously or in the muscular tissue. So from this time to the end of the experimental period I too ate the whole mouse, without the skin of course, and I found that my fat-craving was considerably eased.

It was during the final stages of my mouse diet that Mike returned to his cabin. He brought his cousin Ootek with him. This young Eskimo was to become my boon companion and prove invaluable to me in my wolf researches.

I had made a trip back to the cabin to fetch some additional supplies, and the sight of smoke rising from the chimney cheered me greatly, for, to tell the truth, there had been times when I had missed human companionship.

Though I never did manage to make Mike understand the importance and nature of my scientific work, I had no such difficulty with Ootek: though he may not have understood it, he seemed from the first to share my conviction that it was important. Much later I discovered that Ootek was a minor shaman, or magic priest, in his own tribe; and he had assumed, from the tales told him by Mike, that I must be a shaman too, if of a somewhat unfamiliar variety.

In any event, Ootek decided to attach himself to me; and the very next day he appeared at the wolf observation tent, bringing with him his sleeping robe, and obviously prepared for a long visit. He had been taught some English by Mike, and I was gradually picking up quite a lot of Eskimo, so we were soon able to establish rudimentary communications. He showed no surprise when he understood that I was studying wolves. In fact, he conveyed to me the information that he too was keenly interested in wolves, partly because his personal totem, or helping spirit, was Amarok, the Wolf Being.

He had a great deal to add to my knowledge of wolves' food habits, and told me that wolves ate, as well as mice, great numbers of ground squirrels. At times they even seemed to prefer them to caribou, for they are easy prey and a wolf can often kill enough of them to make a good meal with only a fraction of the energy expended in hunting caribou.

I had assumed that fish could hardly enter largely into the wolves' diet, but Ootek told me he had several times watched wolves fishing for jackfish or northern pike. At spawning time in the spring these big fish, which sometimes weigh as much as forty pounds, invade the intricate network of narrow channels in boggy marshes along the lake shores. When a wolf decides to go after them he jumps into one of the larger channels and wades upstream, splashing mightily as he goes, and driving the pike ahead of him into progressively narrower and shallower channels. Eventually the fish realizes its danger and turns to make a dash for open water; but the wolf stands in its way, and one quick chop of those great jaws is enough to break the back of even the largest pike. Ootek told me he once watched a wolf catch seven pike in less than an hour.

Wolves also caught suckers, when these sluggish fish were making their spawning runs up the tundra streams, he said; but the wolf's technique in this case was to crouch on a rock in a shallow section of the stream and snatch up the suckers as they passed—a method similar to that employed by bears when they are catching salmon.

These revelations were fascinating, but it was when we came to discuss the caribou that Ootek really opened my eyes. The wolf and the caribou were so closely linked, he told me, that they were almost a single entity. He explained what he meant by telling me a story which was a part of the semi-religious folklore of the inland Eskimos. Here it is.

"In the beginning there was a Woman and a Man, and nothing else walked or swam or flew in the world, until one day the Woman dug a great hole in the ground and began fishing in it. One by one she pulled out all the animals, and the last one was the caribou. Then Kaila, who is the God of the Sky, told the woman that the caribou was the greatest gift of all, for the caribou would be the sustenance of man.

"The Woman set the caribou free and ordered it to go out over the land and multiply; and in time the land was filled with caribou, so the sons of the Woman hunted well, and they were fed and clothed and had good skin tents to live in. The sons of the Woman hunted only the big, fat caribou, for they had no wish to kill the weak and the small and the sick, since these were no good to eat, nor were their skins much good. And, after a time, it happened that the sick and the weak came to outnumber the fat and the strong, and when the sons saw this they were dismayed and they complained to the Woman.

"Then the Woman made magic and spoke to Kaila and said: 'Your work is no good, for the caribou grow weak and sick, and if we eat them we must grow weak and sick also.'

"Kaila heard, and he said: 'My work is good. I shall tell Amarok (the Spirit of the Wolf), and he shall tell his children, and they will eat the sick and the weak and the small caribou, so that the land will be left for the fat and the good ones.'

"And this is what happened, and this is why the caribou and the wolf are one; for the caribou feeds the wolf, but it is the wolf who keeps the caribou strong."

I was slightly stunned by this story. I could hardly believe that the powerful wolf would limit himself to culling the sick and infirm from the caribou herds when he could, presumably, take his choice of the fattest and most succulent individuals. Furthermore, I had excellent ammunition with which to demolish Ootek's thesis.

"Ask him then," I told Mike, "how come there are so many skeletons of big and evidently healthy caribou scattered around the cabin and all over the tundra for miles to the north of here."

"Don't need to ask him that," Mike replied with unabashed candour. "It was me killed those deer. I got myself and fourteen dogs to feed and it takes maybe two, three caribou a week for that. Skinny caribou are no use, what I got to have is the big fat ones."

I was staggered. "How many do you think you kill in a year?" I asked.

Mike grinned proudly. "I'm pretty damn good shot. Kill maybe two, three hundred, maybe more. Every trapper got to do the same. Indians, white men, all the way down south far as caribou go in the wintertime. Of course they not all the time lucky to get *enough* caribou; then they got to feed the dogs on fish. But dogs can't work good on fish—get weak and can't haul no loads. Caribou is better."

I knew from having studied the files at Ottawa that there were eighteen hundred trappers in those portions of Saskatchewan, Manitoba and southern Keewatin which composed the winter range of the Keewatin caribou herd. I also knew that these trappers, to a man, denied that they killed more than one or two caribou a year; and they all insisted that wolves slaughtered the deer in untold thousands.

Although mathematics have never been my strong point, I tried to work out some totals and came up with the fantastic figure of 112,000 animals killed in this area alone every year. I realized, however, that it was not a figure I could use in my reports—not unless I wished to be posted to the

Galápagos Islands to conduct a ten-year study on tortoise ticks. In any event, what Mike and Ootek had told me was largely hearsay evidence, and this was not what I was employed to gather. Resolutely I put these disturbing revelations out of my mind, and went back to learning the truth the hard way.

Chapter 6

Ootek had many singular attributes as a naturalist, not the least of which was his apparent ability to understand wolf language. I had already noted the variety and range of the vocal noises made by George, Angeline and Uncle Albert: howls, wails, quavers, whines, grunts, growls, yips and barks, with innumerable variations; but my real education in lupine linguistics began a few days after Ootek's arrival. The two of us had been observing the wolf den for several hours without seeing anything of note. It was a dead-calm day, so that the flies had reached plague proportions, and Angeline and the pups had retired to the den to escape, while both males, exhausted after a hunt which had lasted into mid-morning, were sleeping nearby. I was getting bored and sleepy myself when Ootek suddenly cupped his hands to his ears and began to listen intently.

I could hear nothing, and I had no idea what had caught his attention until he said: "Listen, the wolves are talking!" and pointed towards a range of hills some five miles to the north of us.

I listened, but heard nothing except the baleful buzzing of mosquitoes. But George, who had been sleeping on the crest of the esker, suddenly sat up, cocked his ears forward and pointed his long muzzle towards the north. After a minute or two he threw back his head and howled; a long, quavering howl which started low and ended on the highest note my ears could register.

Ootek grabbed my arm and broke into a delighted grin. "Caribou are coming; the wolf says so!"

It was not until we returned to the cabin and I had Mike's services as an interpreter that I learned the full story. According to Ootek, a wolf living in the next territory to the north had not only informed our wolves that the long-awaited caribou had started to move south, but had even indicated where they were at the moment. This wolf had not actually seen the caribou himself, but had simply been passing on a report received from a still-more-distant wolf. George, having heard and understood, had then passed on the good news in his turn.

I made no secret of my amusement at Ootek's attempt to impress me with this fantastic yarn. But if I was incredulous, Mike was not. Without more ado he began packing for a hunting trip. I was amazed that he should be willing to make a two- or three-day hike over the tundra on such improbable evidence, but when I said as much Mike went taciturn and left without another word.

Three days later, when I saw him again, he offered me a haunch of venison and a pot of caribou tongues. He also told me he had found the caribou exactly where Ootek had said they would be—on the shores of a lake called Kooiak some forty miles northeast of the cabin. He explained that the wolves not only possessed the ability to communicate over great distances but, so he insisted, could "talk" almost as well as we could. He admitted that he himself could neither hear all the sounds they made, nor understand most of them, but he said some Eskimos, and Ootek in particular, could hear and understand so well that they could quite literally converse with wolves.

I mulled this information over for a while and concluded that anything this pair told me from then on would have to be recorded with a heavy sprinkling of question marks.

FOR TWO MORE DAYS my scepticism ruled—until the afternoon when once again George appeared on the crest and cocked his ears towards the north. Whatever he heard, if he heard anything, did not interest him much this time, for he did not howl, but went off to the den to sniff noses with Angeline.

Ootek, on the other hand, was definitely interested. Excitement filled his face. He fairly gabbled at me, but I caught only a few words, *Innuit* (Eskimos) and *kiyai* (come). When I still looked dense Ootek gave me an exasperated glance and headed off across the tundra in a northwesterly direction.

I was a little annoyed by his cavalier departure, but I soon forgot about it, for it was now late afternoon and the time was approaching for the males to set off on the evening hunt.

There was a definite ritual about their preparations. George usually began by making a visit to the den. If Angeline and the pups were inside, his visit brought them out. If they were already outside, Angeline's behaviour changed from that of domestic boredom to one of excitement. She would begin to romp and George would respond by engaging in a mock battle with his mate. Alerted by the sounds of play, Uncle Albert would appear on the scene and join the group.

After anywhere from twenty minutes to an hour of conviviality—in which the pups took part, getting under everyone's feet—the three adults would adjourn to the crest of the den, usually led by Angeline. Once more they would form a circle and then, lifting their heads high, would "sing" for a few minutes.

This was one of the high points of their day, and it was certainly *the* high point of mine. The first few times the three wolves sang, the old ingrained fear set my back hairs tingling. However, with the passage of time I not only came to enjoy the chorus, but to anticipate it with acute pleasure. And yet I find it almost impossible to describe. The best I can do is to say that this full-throated and great-hearted chorus moved me as I have very occasionally been moved by the bowel-shaking throb and thunder of a superb organ.

The impassionata never lasted long enough for me. In three or four minutes it would come to an end and the circle would break up. Angeline would move towards the den as George and Albert trotted off along one of the hunting trails.

On this particular night the male wolves, instead of taking one of the trails leading north, or northwest, headed off towards the east, in the opposite direction from Mike's cabin and me. I thought no more about this variation until some time later when a human shout made me turn round. Ootek had returned—with three bashful friends, all grinning, and all shy at this first meeting with the strange *kablunak* who was interested in wolves.

I joined the four Eskimos in the trek to the cabin. Mike was home, and greeted the new visitors as old friends. Eventually I found a chance to ask him a few questions.

Yes, he told me, Ootek had indeed known that these men were on their way, and would soon arrive. How did he know? He knew because he had heard the wolf on the Five Mile Hills reporting the passage of the Eskimos through his territory. He had tried to tell me about it; but then, when I failed to understand, he had felt obliged to leave me in order to intercept and greet his friends.

And that was that.

DURING THE THIRD WEEK in June, Angeline began to show increasing signs of restlessness. She gave the distinct impression that her domestic life was beginning to pall. When George and Albert departed of an evening for the hunt, she took to accompanying them on the first part of their journey. At first she went no further than a hundred yards from the den;

but on one occasion she covered a quarter of a mile before returning slowly home.

George had been trying for weeks to persuade her to join him, and he was clearly delighted with her changing mood. The desire to have a night out together was obviously mutual, but the welfare of the pups remained paramount with Angeline, even though they seemed large enough to need far less attention.

On the evening of 23 June I was alone at the tent when the wolves gathered for their pre-hunt ritual singsong. Angeline surpassed herself on this occasion, lifting her voice in such an untrammelled paean of longing that I wished there were some way I could volunteer to look after the kids while she went off with George. I need not have bothered. Uncle Albert also got the message, for when the song was done Angeline and George trotted buoyantly off together, while Albert mooched morosely down to the den and settled himself in for an all-night siege of pups.

A few hours later a driving rain began and I had to give up my observations. There were no wolves in sight the next morning when the rain ceased and the mist lifted; but shortly before nine o'clock George and Uncle Albert appeared on the crest of the esker.

Both seemed nervous. After a good deal of restless pacing and nose sniffing they split up. George took himself off to the highest point of the esker, where he sat down in full view and began to scan the country to the east and south. Uncle Albert trotted off along the ridge to the north, and lay down on a rocky knoll, staring intently out over the western plains.

There was still no sign of Angeline, and this, together with the unusual actions of the male wolves, began to make me uneasy too. The thought that something might have happened to Angeline struck me with surprising pain.

I was on the point of climbing the ridge to have a look for her myself, when I saw her emerge from the den with something in her mouth. For a moment I could not make out what she was carrying, then with a start of surprise I recognized it as one of the pups. The pup must have weighed ten or fifteen pounds, but despite her burden Angeline trotted briskly up the esker slope and disappeared into a small stand of spruce. Fifteen minutes later she was back at the den for another pup, and by ten o'clock she had moved the last of them.

After she disappeared for the final time both male wolves, who had evidently been keeping guard over the move, gave up their vigils and followed her; leaving me to stare bleakly over an empty landscape. I was greatly perturbed. Had I somehow disturbed the wolves so seriously that they felt impelled to abandon their den? I hurried back to the cabin to consult Ootek.

The Eskimo set my fears at rest. He explained that this shifting of the pups occurred with every wolf family at about this time of year. The pups had now been weaned and, since there was no water supply near the den, it was necessary to move them to where they could slake their thirst elsewhere than at their mother's teats.

"They are too old to live in a hole in the ground, but still too young to follow their parents," Mike interpreted, as Ootek explained. "So the old wolves take them to a new place where there is room for the pups to move around and learn about the world, but where they are still safe."

As it happened both Ootek and Mike were familiar with the location of the new "summer den", and the next day we moved the observation tent to a position overlooking it. The pups' new home, half a mile from the old den, was a narrow, truncated ravine filled with gigantic boulders split off the cliff walls by frost action. A small stream ran through it. It also embraced an area of grassy marsh alive with meadow mice: an ideal place for the pups to learn the first principles of hunting. Leaving the ravine

involved a stiff climb which was too much for the youngsters, so they could be left in their new home with little danger of straying; and since they were now big enough to hold their own with the only other local carnivores of any stature—the foxes and hawks—they had nothing to fear.

Chapter 7

The new summer den was ideal from the wolves' point of view, but not from mine, for the clutter of boulders made it difficult to see what was happening. In addition, caribou were now trickling back into the country, and the pleasures of the hunt were siren calls to all three adult wolves. During the day they were usually so tired from their nightly excursions that they did little but sleep.

I was beginning to find time hanging heavy on my hands when Uncle Albert rescued me from boredom by falling in love.

Throughout June Mike's team of dogs had remained with the Eskimos because the absence of caribou made it impossible to feed them; but now that the deer were returning south they were brought back to the cabin. They were magnificent beasts. Smaller in stature than wolves, true huskies are of a much heavier build, with broad chests, shorter necks, and bushy tails which curl over their rumps like plumes. They differ from wolves in other ways too: husky bitches come into heat at any time of the year.

When Mike's team returned one of the bitches was just coming into heat: hot-blooded by nature and amorous by inclination, she soon had the rest of the team in an uproar, causing Mike no end of trouble. He was just complaining about the problem one evening when inspiration came to me.

My study of the wolves had so far revealed nothing about their sexual life, and I knew that unless I was prepared to follow them during the brief mating season in March, when they wander with the caribou herds, I stood no chance of filling this vital gap in my knowledge. But I also knew, from Mike and Ootek, that wolves will mate with dogs, and vice versa. The opportunity does not arise often, because the dogs are almost invariably tied up except when working, but it *does* happen.

To my delight Mike agreed to my proposition. In fact he seemed quite pleased, for he had long wished to discover for himself what kind of sled dogs a wolf-husky cross would make.

I decided to do the experiment in stages, firstly taking the bitch, whose name was Kooa, for a walk round my new observation site, in order to make her existence and condition known to the wolves. Kooa was more than willing. In fact, when we crossed one of the wolf trails, she became so enthusiastic it was all I could do to restrain her by a heavy chain leash. With great difficulty I dragged her back to the cabin where, once firmly tethered, she reacted by howling her frustration the whole night through.

Or perhaps it was not frustration that made her sing; for when I got up next morning the tracks of a big wolf were plainly visible in the wet sand of the riverbank not a hundred yards from the dog lines. Probably it was only the presence of the jealous male huskies which had prevented the romance from being consummated that very night.

I now had to rush the second phase of my plan into execution. A hundred yards beyond the observation tent in the direction of the summer den, Ootek and I strung a length of heavy wire between two rocks about fifty feet from one another.

The next morning we led Kooa—or more properly were led *by* Kooa—to the site, and managed to shackle her chain to the wire. Rather to my surprise she settled down and spent most of the afternoon sleeping. No adult wolves were in evidence, but about 8:30 pm they suddenly broke into their pre-hunting song, although they themselves remained invisible behind a rock ridge.

The first sounds had barely reached me when Kooa leaped to her feet and joined the chorus. And *how* she howled! Although there is not, as far as I am aware, any canine or lupine blood in my veins, the seductive quality of Kooa's siren song was enough to set me thinking longingly of other days and other joys.

The wolves' song stopped in mid-swing, and seconds later all three of them came surging over the crest of the ridge into view. Although she was a quarter of a mile away, Kooa was clearly visible to them, and after only a moment's hesitation both George and Uncle Albert started towards her at a gallop.

George did not get very far. Before he had gone fifty yards Angeline had overtaken him and, while I am not prepared to swear to this, I had the distinct impression that she tripped him. At any rate he went sprawling in the muskeg, and when he picked himself up his interest in Kooa seemed to have evaporated. He and Angeline withdrew to the summer den, where they lay down and watched proceedings.

I do not know how long Albert had been celibate, but it had clearly been too long. When he reached the area where Kooa was tethered he was moving so fast he overshot, but he turned somehow, and his wild rush slowed. Then, when he was within ten feet of Kooa, Albert's manner suddenly changed. He stopped dead, lowered his great head and turned into a buffoon.

It was an embarrassing spectacle. Laying his ears back until they were flush with his broad skull, he began to wiggle like a pup, while at the same time wrinkling his lips in a frightful grimace which may have been intended to register infatuation, but which looked to me more like a symptom of senile decay. He also began to whine in a disgusting wheedling falsetto. Belly to earth, he grovelled towards Kooa, while his grimace widened into an expression of sheer idiocy.

Thinking the wolf had taken complete leave of his senses I was about to intervene, but Ootek restrained me. He was grinning, and made it clear that things were progressing quite normally from a wolfish point of view.

At this point Albert shifted gears with bewildering rapidity. Scrambling to his feet he suddenly became the lordly male. His ruff expanded until it made a huge silvery aura framing his face. His body stiffened until he seemed to be made of white steel. His tail rose until it was as high, and almost as tightly curled, as a true husky's. Then, pace by delicate pace, he closed the gap.

Kooa, who at first had seemed nonplussed by his behaviour, was no longer in doubt. *This* was something she could understand. She turned her back and as he stretched out his great nose to offer his first caress she spun about and nipped him coyly on the shoulder. . . .

My notes on the rest of this incident are, I fear, too technical to deserve a place in this book. I shall therefore content myself with the observation that Albert certainly knew how to make love.

My scientific curiosity had been satisfied, but Uncle Albert's passion hadn't, and a most difficult situation now developed. Although we waited for two hours, Albert showed not the slightest indication of ever departing from his new-found love. Ootek and I wished to return to the cabin with Kooa, and in some desperation we eventually made a sally towards the enamoured pair, but Albert ignored us totally. It was a stalemate which was only broken when I, with much reluctance, fired a shot into the ground.

Albert leaped high into the air and bounded off a dozen yards. We untied the chain, and while Ootek dragged the sullenly reluctant Kooa off towards home, I covered the rear with the rifle. Albert stayed right with us, fifteen to twenty yards away. Back at the cabin we again tried to cool his ardour by firing a volley in the air, but this had no effect except to make him withdraw a few yards further off. There was nothing for it but to take Kooa into the cabin for the night.

It was a frightful night. The moment the door closed, Albert broke into a lament. He wailed and whooped and yammered without pause for hours. The dogs responded with a cacophony of shrill insults and counterwails. Kooa joined in by screaming messages of undying love. It was an intolerable situation. By morning Mike was threatening to do some more shooting, and in real earnest.

It was Ootek who saved the day, and possibly Albert's life as well. He convinced Mike that if he released Kooa she would not run away, but would stay in the vicinity with the wolf. When her period of heat was over she would return, and the wolf would go back to his own kind.

He was perfectly right, as usual. During the next week we sometimes caught glimpses of the lovers walking shoulder to shoulder across some distant ridge. They never went near the den esker, nor the cabin. Then, one morning, we found Kooa lying at her old place in the dog line, looking exhausted but satiated.

The next evening Uncle Albert once more joined in the evening chorus at the wolf esker. However, there was now a mellow, self-satisfied quality to his voice that I had never heard before, and it set my teeth on edge. Braggadocio is something which I have never been able to tolerate—not even in wolves.

It was now well into July, and the rapidly growing pups needed increasing quantities of food. George, Angeline and Albert were forced to devote most of their energy and time to hunting far afield, but one day they killed a caribou close to home and this convenient food supply gave them an opportunity to take a holiday. That night they stayed near the den and rested.

The next morning dawned fine and warm. Angeline lay at her ease on the rocks overlooking the summer den, while George and Albert rested in sandy beds on the esker ridge. Towards noon, Albert roused himself and meandered down to the bay to get a drink. Then for an hour or two he fished in a desultory fashion, after which he started back towards his bed. Halfway there he gave up the idea of going on and sprawled out where he was instead. He was soon asleep.

George had been lying with his head on his forepaws, casually watching his friend's fishing expedition. When Albert collapsed in sleep, George got up, stretched, yawned hugely, and with an appearance of idle insouciance ambled off towards him. He seemed quite aimless, stopping to scratch himself and to sniff at shrubs and mouseholes, but when he had drifted to within fifty feet of the sleeping wolf his demeanour changed dramatically.

Lowering himself into an almost catlike crouch he began to inch towards Albert with every appearance of serious intent. The tension began to build up as he slithered closer and closer. Had the perfect harmony of the family broken down at last? When he was ten feet from Albert—who was still dead to the world—George drew his hindquarters up under him and launched himself in a tremendous leap, while at the same time letting loose a terrifying roar.

The impact of a hundred-and-fifty-odd pounds of pouncing wolf ought to have knocked the wind clean out of Albert; but he had some breath left, for he produced a brand-new sound for my catalogue of wolf noises. It was a high-pitched snarl of shock and outrage—not entirely unlike the sound I have heard an angry woman make when, in a crowded subway, someone pinched her bottom.

George leaped away, while Albert struggled to his feet. The chase which followed appeared to be in deadly earnest. George shot up the slope of the esker as if the hounds of hell were after him, while Albert followed grimly. As they swept past the summer den, Angeline bobbed up, took a quick look, and enthusiastically joined in. The odds were now two-to-one against George, and he was forced down off the esker, across the muskeg, and along the shore of the bay.

There was a huge split rock on the shore near the head of the bay, and George shot through the narrow gap, swerved so abruptly that sand and stones flew from under his feet, then circled sharply back round the rock just in time to catch Angeline broadside on, bowling her over and sending her slithering on her side. One of his pursuers was now out of action temporarily, but before he could be off again Albert was upon him and they went down together, locked in combat. Meanwhile Angeline picked herself up and joined the fray.

The melee ended as suddenly as it had begun, and the three wolves separated, shook themselves, sniffed noses, wagged their tails hard, and trotted back towards the den with every indication that a good time had been had by all.

Practical jokes such as this were rare amongst the wolves.

ANOTHER EVENT which took place in July gave me much to think about. Although Angeline now frequently went hunting with the males, there were nights when she did not go, and during one of these she had visitors.

It was well after midnight and I was dozing in my tent when a wolf howled from somewhere south of me. It was an unusual call, rather muted. Sleepily I picked up my binoculars and eventually found two wolves, both strangers, sitting on a point of land on my side of the bay and directly opposite the wolf esker.

This discovery brought me fully awake, for I had assumed that the territory of each family was sacrosanct as far as other wolves were concerned. I was curious to see how Angeline would react to this intrusion.

When I trained my glasses on the gully, she had already emerged and was standing facing the strangers. She was keenly alert, with head thrust forward, ears cocked, and her tail stretched out astern like that of a setter. None of the wolves moved for several minutes; then one of the strangers again essayed the rather tentative howl. Angeline reacted at once. She began slowly wagging her tail, and her tense attitude relaxed visibly; then she trotted forward to the edge of the ravine and barked sharply. At this the two strange wolves got to their feet and began trotting round the shore of the bay.

Angeline met them about a quarter of a mile from the den. Standing stock-still, she waited for them to approach, and when they were five or ten yards from her they too stopped. The tails of all three wolves began to wave slowly back and forth. Angeline stepped gingerly forward and sniffed noses. Whoever the strangers were, they were evidently welcome. When the greeting ceremonies had been concluded, all three wolves trotted towards the summer den, where one of the strangers began to romp with Angeline, and the second went down into the ravine where the four pups were. After twenty minutes the one in the ravine re-emerged; there was further nose-smelling among all three wolves, and then the strangers set off back the way they had come.

When I told Ootek what I had seen he was not at all surprised. After all, he pointed out, people do visit other people; so what was odd about wolves visiting other wolves?

Mike nodded. "I guess they come from the bunch in Hidden Valley," he said. "It is maybe three, four miles south of here. I seen them many times. Two bitches and one dog wolf, and some pups. I guess one of them's the mother of the bitch you call Angeline; the other's Angeline's sister, maybe. Anyhow in the fall they all join up with your bunch and go south together."

I considered this information in silence for a few minutes and then asked: "Since only one of these two bitches has a mate, the other must still be a spinster—which one would it be, do you think?"

Mike gave me a long and thoughtful stare. "Listen," he said, "how soon you figure to leave this country and go home, eh? I guess you been here too long already."

Chapter 8

In mid-July I decided it was time to begin seriously studying the hunting activities of wolves.

This decision was hastened by the accidental uncovering of my long-neglected operation order from under a pile of dirty socks which had been accumulating on top of it for several weeks. I had almost forgotten, not only about the order, but about Ottawa itself; but now I remembered that my first task should have been to conduct a census and general survey of wolves, followed by an intensive study of "wolf-caribou predator-prey relationships". One morning I struck my little tent, packed up the telescope, and closed down my observation post. Ootek and I loaded a camping outfit aboard the canoe, and set out on a prolonged cruise northwards through the tundra plains.

We covered a good many hundreds of miles during the succeeding weeks, and gathered much information concerning wolf population and wolf-caribou predator-prey relationships; together with a lot of associated information which, though it was unrelated to the department's aims, could not be entirely ignored.

A semi-official estimate of the wolf population of Keewatin, from the usual trapper-trader sources, was thirty thousand wolves. I was able to work this out as an approximate average of one wolf for every two square miles, which seemed pretty dense. Indeed, had it been true, Ootek and I might have had trouble making progress due to the sheer pressure of wolves.

Unhappily for the theoreticians we found the wolves widely scattered, in family groups—each family occupying a territory of one to three hundred square miles, although this dispersal was by no means uniform. Reluctantly, and recognizing that it was not going to endear me to my employers, I was forced to revise the population estimate downwards to three thousand, and that was probably a gross exaggeration.

The families we encountered were of all sizes from a single pair of adults with three pups to a group of seven adults and ten pups. Once again I resorted to Ootek for information about the relative status of these extra adults.

Female wolves do not breed until they are two years old, and males not until they are three, Ootek told me. Until they are of breeding age most of the adolescents remain with their parents; but even when they are of an age to start a family they are often prevented from doing so by a shortage of homesteads. There is simply not enough hunting territory available to provide the wherewithal for every bitch to raise a litter. So, they are forced to practise what amounts to birth control through abstinence, and some adult wolves may have to remain celibate for years before a territory becomes available. However, because the period of urgent amorous appetite is short—only about three weeks out of the year—these bachelors and spinsters probably do not suffer any great feeling of sexual deprivation. Moreover, their desire for domesticity and the companionship of other adults, as well as pups, is apparently met by the communal nature of the family group. Indeed, Ootek believed some wolves actually preferred the "uncle" or "aunt" status, since it gave them the pleasures of being involved in rearing a family without incurring the full responsibilities of parenthood.

Breeding among the wolves is apparently further restricted by a built-in birth-control mechanism. Thus it happens that when food species are abundant (or the wolf population is scanty) bitches give birth to large litters—sometimes as many as eight pups. But if the wolves are too numerous, or food is scarce, the number of pups in a litter may fall to as few as one or two.

Epidemic disease is the overriding factor which ensures that, even if other controlling factors fail to operate, the wolf population will not become too large. On those rare occasions when the general balance is upset (often as a result of man's interference) and wolves become too abundant, they soon begin to weaken physically as food grows scarce. At times such as these, devastating epidemics of rabies, distemper or mange invariably appear among the wolves, and their numbers are quickly reduced to a bare survival level.

Nineteen forty-six was a disastrous season for Eskimos, foxes and wolves alike. Hunger lay heavy on the land. The latent rabies virus flared up among the starving foxes, and the wolves soon began to contract the disease too.

Now, animals stricken with rabies do not "go mad" in the usual sense of the word. Their nervous systems are affected so that they become erratic and unpredictable, and they lose the protection of a sense of fear. Rabid wolves sometimes walk blindly into speeding automobiles and trains; they have come stumbling in among entire teams of huskies and have been torn to pieces as a result; and not infrequently they have wandered into village streets and have even entered tents or houses occupied by men. Such wolves are pitiable objects; but the human reaction to them is usually one of unbridled terror—not of the disease, for it is seldom recognized as rabies, but of the wolves themselves. Grotesque incidents occur which help to sustain the general myth about the vicious and dangerous nature of the wolf.

One such dying wolf appeared in Churchill during the 1946 epidemic. It was first encountered by a Canadian army corporal wending his way back to barracks after a session at the Churchill beer hall. According to the corporal's account, a gigantic wolf leaped at him, and he barely escaped with his life by running to the shelter of the guardhouse. He could exhibit no physical evidence of his ordeal, but his warning sent the whole army camp into a panic. Squads of grim-faced men armed with rifles, carbines and spotlights were soon scouring the surrounding country intent on dealing with a menace which, in a matter of hours, had grown into several packs of starving wolves.

During the ensuing excitement eleven husky dogs, one American private and a Chippewayan Indian coming home late became casualties—not of the wolf, but of the vigilantes.

For two days children and women stayed indoors. A wolf was glimpsed on the second day by a light army aircraft which had joined the hunt, and an intrepid detachment of Mounted Police sallied forth to deal with it. The wolf turned out to be a cocker spaniel belonging to the Hudson Bay Company's manager.

Not until the third day did the panic ease. Late that afternoon the driver of a six-ton army truck, returning to the camp from the airport, suddenly saw a bundle of fur on the road ahead of him. He jammed on the brakes but was unable to stop in time, and the wolf—by then so sick it could no longer move—was mercifully killed.

The aftermath was interesting. To this day there are residents of Churchill who will, at the drop of a hat, describe the invasion of the town by wolves in 1946. They will tell you of desperate personal encounters; of women and children savaged; of dog teams torn to ribbons; and of an entire human community living in a state of siege. All that is lacking is the final dramatic description of the North American equivalent of a Russian troika fleeing across the frozen plains, inevitably to be overwhelmed by a wave of wolves, while the polar night resounds to the crunching sound of human bones being cracked by wolfish jaws.

THE WEEKS WHICH Ootek and I spent cruising the tundra plains were idyllic. The weather was good, and the sensation of freedom which we derived from the limitless land was as invigorating as the wide-ranging life we led. This country belonged to the deer, the wolves, the birds and the smaller beasts. We two were no more than casual and insignificant intruders. Man had never dominated the Barrens. Even the Eskimos, whose territory it had once been, had all but vanished.

We encountered other human beings only on a single occasion. One morning, shortly after starting on our journey, we rounded a bend in a river and saw a squat skin tent on the foreshore. Ootek gave a shout, and two men, a woman and three half-grown boys piled out of the tent and ran to the water's edge to watch us approach.

We landed, and Ootek introduced me to one of the families of his tribe. All that afternoon we sat about drinking tea, gossiping, laughing and singing, and eating mountains of boiled caribou meat. Ootek told me that the men of the family had pitched their camp at this spot so they could intercept the caribou which crossed the river at a narrows a few miles further downstream. Paddling one-man kayaks and armed with short stabbing spears, they hoped to be able to kill enough fat animals at the crossing to last them through the winter. Ootek was anxious to join in their hunt, and he hoped I would not mind waiting a few days so that he could help his friends.

I had no objection, and the next morning the three Eskimo men departed, leaving me to bask in a magnificent August day.

The fly season was over. It was hot and there was no wind. I decided to get some sun on my pallid skin, so I went off a few hundred yards from the Eskimo camp (modesty is the last of the civilized vices which a man sheds in the wilds), stripped, swam, and then climbed a nearby ridge and lay down to sunbathe.

Wolflike, I occasionally raised my head and glanced around me, and about noon I saw a group of three wolves crossing the crest of the next ridge to the north. One of them was white but the other two were almost black—a rare colour phase.

I was in a quandary. I had only my rubber shoes and my binoculars with me on the ridge; but if I went back for my clothes, I knew I might lose track of these wolves. Still, I thought, who needed clothes on a day like this? The wolves had by now disappeared over the next crest, so I seized my binoculars and hared off in pursuit.

The countryside was a maze of low ridges separated by small, grassy valleys where small groups of caribou slowly grazed their way southwards. Sweating with excitement and exertion I breasted the first ridge, expecting to see some frenzied action as the three wolves came suddenly upon the unsuspecting caribou below. But I was disconcerted to find myself looking out over a completely peaceful scene. There were about fifty bucks in view, scattered in groups of three to ten animals, and all were busy grazing. The wolves were sauntering across the valley like three familiar dogs crossing a farm pasture.

The scene was all wrong. Incredulously, I watched the three wolves trot by within fifty yards of a pair of young bucks who were lying down chewing their cuds. The bucks turned their heads to watch the wolves go by, but they did not rise to their feet, nor did their jaws stop working. My bewilderment increased when, as the wolves disappeared over the next crest, I jumped up to follow and the two bucks leaped to their feet, staring at me in wild-eyed astonishment.

As I sprinted past them they spun on their heels and went galloping off as if pursued by devils. It seemed completely unjust that they should have been so terrified of *me*, while remaining so blasé about the wolves. However, I solaced myself with the thought that their panic might have been caused by the unfamiliar spectacle of a white man, slightly pink and clad only in boots and binoculars, racing madly across the landscape.

Within the space of an hour the wolves and I had covered three or four miles and passed within close range of perhaps four hundred caribou. In every case the deer had shown no interest while the wolves remained at a reasonable distance; casual interest if the wolves came very close; and avoiding-tactics only when a collision seemed imminent. There had been no stampeding and no panic.

Up to this time most of the deer we had encountered had been bucks; but now we began to meet numbers of does and fawns, and the behaviour of the wolves underwent a change. One of them flushed a lone fawn from a hiding place in a willow clump. The fawn leaped into view not twenty feet ahead of the wolf, who paused to watch it for an instant, then raced off in pursuit. My heart began to thud with excitement as I anticipated seeing a kill at last.

It was not to be. The wolf ran hard for fifty yards without gaining perceptibly on the fawn, then suddenly broke off the chase and trotted back to rejoin his fellows.

I could hardly believe my eyes. That fawn should have been doomed if even a tenth of the wolfish reputation was in fact deserved; yet during the next hour at least twelve separate rushes were made by all three wolves against single fawns, or groups of does and fawns, and in every case the chase was broken off almost before it was well begun.

I was becoming thoroughly exasperated. I had not run six miles across country and exhausted myself just to watch a pack of wolves playing the fool; and when the wolves began to leave the next valley I went charging

after them with blood in my eye. In the event I shot over the far crest—straight into the middle of the band.

They had probably halted for a breather, and as I burst in among them the group exploded. Wolves went tearing off at top speed in all directions—ears back, tails stretching straight behind them. They ran scared, and as they fled through the dispersed caribou herds the deer finally reacted, and the stampede of frightened animals which I had been expecting to witness all that afternoon became something of a reality. Only, and I realized the fact with bitterness, it was not the wolves who had been responsible—it was I.

I gave up then, and turned for home. When I was still some miles from camp I saw several figures running towards me and I recognized them as the Eskimo woman and her three youngsters. They were all screaming, and the woman was waving a two-foot-long snowknife while her three offspring were brandishing spears and skinning knives.

I stopped in some perplexity. For the first time I became uncomfortably aware of my condition. Not only was I unarmed, but I was stark naked. I was in no condition to ward off an attack—and one seemed imminent. Discretion seemed the better part of valour, so I sprinted hard to bypass the Eskimos.

But they were still game, and the chase continued back to the camp, where I scrambled into my trousers, seized my rifle, and prepared to sell my life dearly. Fortunately Ootek and the men arrived back just as the woman and her crew of furies swept down upon me, and battle was averted.

Somewhat later, when things had quieted down, Ootek explained the situation. One of the children had been picking berries when he had seen me go galloping naked across the hills after the wolves. Round-eyed with wonder, he had hastened back to report to his mother. She, brave soul, assumed that I had gone out of my mind (Eskimos believe that no white man has very far to go in this direction), and was attempting to assault a pack of wolves bare-handed and bare everything else. Calling up the rest of her brood, and snatching what weapons were at hand, she had set out at top speed to rescue me.

During the remainder of our stay, this good woman treated me with such a wary mixture of solicitude and distrust that I was relieved to say farewell to her. Nor was I much amused by Ootek's comment as we swept down the river and passed out of sight of the little camp. "Too bad," he said gravely, "that you take off your pants. I think she like you better if you left them on."

I ASKED OOTEK about the apparently inexplicable behaviour of the band of wolves I had seen at the Eskimo camp, and in his patient and kindly fashion he once more endeavoured to put me straight.

To begin with, he told me that a healthy adult caribou can outrun a wolf with ease, and even a three-week-old fawn can outrun all but the swiftest wolf. The wolves were fully aware of this and, being highly intelligent, they seldom even attempted to run down a healthy caribou. What they did instead was to adopt a technique of systematically testing the state of health and general condition of the deer in an effort to find one which was not up to par. When caribou were abundant this testing was accomplished by rushing each band and putting it to flight for just long enough to expose a sick, wounded or otherwise inferior beast.

When caribou were hard to find, different techniques were used. Several wolves acting in concert would sometimes drive a small herd of deer into an ambush where other wolves were waiting; or if caribou were very scarce, the wolves might use a relay system whereby one wolf would drive the deer towards another wolf posted some distance away, who would then take up the chase in his turn. Techniques such as these decreased the caribou's natural advantages, but it was usually still the weakest deer which fell victim to the pursuing wolves.

"It is as I told you," Ootek said. "The caribou feeds the wolf, but it is the wolf who keeps the caribou strong. We know that if it were not for the wolf there would soon be no caribou at all, for they would die as weakness spread among them."

Ootek also stressed the fact that, once a kill had been made, the wolves did no more hunting until the supply of food had been completely used up. These were novel concepts to one who had been taught that wolves were not only capable of catching almost anything but, actuated by an insatiable blood lust, would slaughter everything which came within their range.

Of the hunts I subsequently watched, almost all followed the pattern of the first one I had seen. Economy of effort seemed to be a guiding principle—and an eminently sensible one too, for the testing process often had to be continued for many hours before the wolves encountered a caribou sufficiently infirm to be captured. When the testing finally exposed such a beast, the attacking wolf would go for his prey in a glorious surge of speed and power which would bring him close behind the fleeing deer.

Drawing upon all his strength, the wolf would forge up alongside the caribou and leap for its shoulder. The impact was usually enough to send the deer off balance and, before it could recover, the wolf would seize it by the back of the neck and bring it down, taking care to avoid the wildly thrashing hoofs, a blow from any one of which could cave in the wolf's rib cage like so much brittle candy. The kill was quickly, and usually cleanly, made and I doubt very much if the deer suffered any more than a pig suffers when it is being butchered for human consumption.

Unlike man, the wolf never kills for fun. It is hard work for a wolf to catch and kill a big game animal, and he may hunt all night and cover fifty or sixty miles of country before he is successful. This is his business, his job, and once he has obtained enough meat for his own and his family's needs he prefers to spend the rest of his time resting, being sociable, or playing.

Contrary to yet another misconception, I found no evidence that wolves kill more than they can use, even when the rare opportunity to do so arises. A kill made during the denning season is revisited time and again until the last ounce of meat has been stripped from it. Of sixty-seven wolf-killed caribou which I examined after the wolves were finished with them, few consisted of anything except bones, ligaments, hair and offal.

Another point of interest is that what little remained of most of these carcasses showed evidence of disease, old age or serious debility. Fresh kills, where the whole carcass was available for examination, were hard to come by; but on a number of occasions I reached a deer almost as soon as the wolves had killed it and, with inexcusable gall, shooed the wolves away. Several of these deer were so heavily infested with external and internal parasites that they were doomed to die soon in any case.

As THE WEEKS WORE on towards the summer's end, the validity of Ootek's thesis became more and more obvious. The vital importance of the part played by the wolf in preserving rather than in destroying the caribou seemed irrefutable to me, although I was by no means sure it would appear in the same light to my employers. I needed overwhelming proof if I was to convince them.

With this in mind, I began making collections of the parasites found in wolf-killed caribou and, as usual, Ootek took a keen interest in this new aspect of my work. Through all of recorded time his people had been caribou eaters, living largely on raw or only partly cooked meat, because of the shortage of fuel for fires. Ootek himself was weaned on caribou meat, pre-chewed for him by his mother, and it had been his staple food ever since he gave up mother's milk. It had never occurred to him to turn an analytical eye upon his daily bread, and when he saw me producing thousands of worms and cysts from various parts of caribou anatomy, he was greatly surprised.

One morning he was watching in sombre fascination as I dissected a particularly pest-ridden old buck. Hauling a bladder cyst about the size of a golfball out of the caribou's liver, I explained that this was the inactive form of a tapeworm and that, if eaten by a carnivore, it would eventually develop into several segmented creatures about thirty feet in length, coiled neatly in the new host's intestines.

Ootek looked sick. "You mean when it is eaten by a wolf?" he asked hopefully.

"*Nahk*," I replied, exercising my growing Eskimo vocabulary. "Foxes, wolves, even people will do. It will grow in any of them."

Ootek shuddered and scratched his stomach. "I do not like liver, fortunately," he said, relieved to remember this fact.

"Oh, these worms are found all through the caribou," I explained, with the enthusiasm of an expert enlightening a layman. "Look here"— and I deftly extracted some threadlike nematode worms from the dissected lungs—"these have been found in men; in fact enough of them will choke a man to death in a very little while."

Ootek coughed convulsively and his mahogany-dark face grew wan again. "Tell me no more!" he pleaded, when he had got his breath back. "I go now, back to the camp, and I will forget what you have told me. You are not kind. For if these things be true, then surely I will have to eat fish like an otter, or else starve to death. But perhaps this is a white man's joke?"

There was a pathetic note of hope in his question, and I belatedly realized what I was doing to the man. I laughed, if in a somewhat artificial manner. "*Eema*, Ootek. It is a joke on you. Only a joke. Now go you back and cook our supper of big steaks. But," and in spite of myself I could not restrain the adjuration, "make damn sure you cook them well!"

Chapter 9

By mid-September the tundra plains burned in the subdued glow of russet and umber, where the early frosts had touched the ground cover of low scrub. The muskeg pastures about Wolf House Bay were fretted with fresh roads made by the southbound herds of caribou, and the pattern of the wolves' lives had changed again.

When Ootek and I returned to Wolf House Bay after our travels through the central plains, we found that our wolf family was ranging widely through its territory and spending the days wherever the hunt might take it.

The pups had left the summer den and begun to explore their world, and though they could not keep up with the adults on prolonged hunts, they went along on shorter expeditions. Those autumnal months must have been among the happiest of their lives.

I tried to share that wandering life, and I too enjoyed it immensely. The flies were all gone. Though there were sometimes frosts at night, the days were usually warm under a clear sun.

On one such warm and sunlit day I made my way north from the den esker, along the crest of a range of hills which overlooked a great valley, rich in forage, and much used by the caribou as a highway south. A soot-flecking of black specks hung in the pallid sky above the valley—flocks of ravens following the deer herds. Families of ptarmigan cackled at me from clumps of dwarf shrub. Flocks of Old Squaw ducks, almost ready to be off for distant places, swirled in the tundra ponds. Below me in the valley rolled a sluggish stream of caribou, herd after herd grazing towards the south unconsciously, yet driven by a knowledge that was old before we ever knew what knowledge was.

Some miles from the den esker I found a niche at the top of a high cliff overlooking the valley, and here I settled myself in comfort, my binoculars levelled at the living stream below me.

I was hoping to see the wolves, and they did not disappoint me. Shortly before noon two of them came into sight on the crest of a transverse ridge some distance to the north.

A few moments later two more adult wolves and the four pups appeared. I easily recognized Angeline and George. One of the other two adults looked like Uncle Albert; but the fourth, a rangy dark-grey beast, was a total stranger to me. I never did learn where he came from, but for the rest of the time I was in the country he remained a member of the band.

Only George seemed to feel any desire to be active. While the rest of us sprawled blissfully in the sun, he began to wander restlessly back and forth along the top of the ridge. Once or twice he stopped in front of Angeline but she paid him no attention other than to flop her tail lazily a few times.

Time slipped past, the river of deer continued to flow. I guessed that the wolves had already fed, and that this was the usual after-dinner siesta. I was wrong, for George had something on his mind. A third time he went over to Angeline, and this time he would not take "no" for an answer, for she scrambled to her feet, shook herself, and bounced amiably after him as he went to sniff at the slumbering forms of Uncle Albert and the Stranger. They too rose to their feet and the pups, never slow to join in something new, galloped over to join their elders. Standing in a rough circle, the whole group of wolves now raised their muzzles and began to howl, exactly as they used to do at the den esker before starting a hunt.

I was surprised that they should be preparing for a hunt so early in the day, but I was more surprised by the deer's lack of reaction: hardly a caribou within hearing even bothered to lift its head. I had no time to ponder the matter, for Angeline, Albert and the Stranger now started off, leaving the pups sitting disconsolately in a row on the crest, with George standing just ahead of them. When one of the youngsters made an attempt to follow the three adults, George turned on him, and the pup hurriedly rejoined his brother and sisters.

What little wind there was blew from the south and the three wolves moved off upwind in a tight little group, trotting easily through the groups of caribou until they were almost abreast of the niche where I was sitting.

At this point Angeline and the other two stopped, and then turned towards the ridge where George and the pups still sat. There were at least two hundred deer between the two groups of wolves, and more were coming into view round the eastern shoulder of the transverse ridge as Angeline and her companions, spreading out to form a line abreast, began to run north.

They were not running hard, but there was a new purposefulness to their movements which the deer seemed to recognize. Herd after herd began to turn about and move north, until most of the caribou in the valley were driven back the way they had come.

Three wolves could not sweep the whole width of the valley; and some of the deer soon discovered that they could swing around the open wings and so resume their southerly progress. Nevertheless, by the time the wolves were nearing the ridge, they were herding at least a hundred deer ahead of them.

Now for the first time the deer showed real signs of nervousness. What had become an almost solid mass of animals broke up into its constituent small bands again, and each went galloping off on its own course. Group after group began to swerve aside but the wolves no longer attempted to prevent them, and I was beginning to see what they were up to: they were now concentrating on one band of a dozen does and seven fawns, and every attempt which this little herd made to turn either left or right was promptly foiled. The deer gave up after a while, and settled down simply to outrun their pursuers.

They would have done it, too, but as they swept past the clump of willows at the end of the ridge a perfect flood of wolves seemed to take them in the flank.

I could not follow events well because of the distance, but I saw George racing towards a doe accompanied by two fawns. Then, just as he reached them, I saw him swerve away. He was passed by two pups going like grey bullets. These two went for the nearest of the two fawns, which promptly began jinking. One of the pups, attempting too sharp a turn, missed his footing and tumbled head over heels, but he was up on the instant and away again.

Then as the herd drew away at full gallop the other pups appeared in the rear, running flat out, although they no longer had a chance of overtaking the deer.

What of the adult wolves meanwhile? When I swung my glasses back to look for them I found George standing exactly where I had seen him last, his tail wagging slowly as he watched the progress of the chase. The other three wolves had by now returned to the crest of the ridge. Albert and the Stranger had lain down to rest, but Angeline was standing up and watching the rapidly retreating caribou.

It was half an hour before the pups came back. They were so weary they could hardly climb the ridge to join their elders, all of whom were now lying down relaxing. The pups joined the group and flopped, panting heavily; but none of the adults paid them any heed.

School was over for the day.

As September slipped into October and the white nights hardened the muskegs and skimmed the lakes with ice, I would have been glad to spend all my time afield, but an immense backlog of scientific trivia awaited my attention at the cabin.

Having chosen to spend my time observing living wolves I had deliberately neglected the innumerable peripheral studies which had been ordained for me by Ottawa, and now, as time grew short, I felt I should at least make a gesture of compliance with authority.

One of the sideshows with which I had been saddled was a vegetation study, a collection of all the species of plants in the area. This involved the use of a Raunkiaer's Circle, a big metal hoop which was a devilish mechanism. To use it, one stood on a stretch of muskeg, shut one's eyes, spun round several times like a top, and then flung the circle as far away as possible. This complicated procedure was designed to ensure a truly "random" throw but, in the event, it inevitably resulted in my losing sight of the hoop entirely, and having to spend an unconscionable time searching for it.

Once the hoop was found, misery began in earnest. I was then expected to pluck every plant, no matter how minute, which lay within its charmed circle; identify and count the number of species; and then count *individuals* belonging to each species.

It sounds easy? It is not. Barren Lands plants are small in any case, and many of them are almost microscopic. My first attempt with the circle cost me the best part of a day, most of which I spent crouched like a demented rabbit over the circle, plucking plantlets with a pair of tweezers. This resulted in severe eyestrain, and a seizure in the lumbar region.

Then I was faced with another distasteful duty—the completion of my scatalogical studies.

Because of the importance Ottawa attached to scatology—the study of animals' excretory droppings—I had been ordered to devote part of my time to collecting and analysing wolf scats. This was not a task with which I was enraptured, but as I went about the Barrens I had kept a casual eye open: using forceps I had picked up those I found and placed them in small canvas bags which I kept in the cabin. By the end of September I had amassed a formidable collection.

For a variety of reasons, not least of which was imagining how Ootek and Mike would react to what I was doing, I postponed the analytical work until one October morning when they went away together on a hunting trip, leaving me in sole possession of the camp. Due to prolonged storage, the scats had become as hard as rocks and had to be softened before I could work on them. I therefore carted them down to the riverbank and put them to soak in two galvanized pails filled with water. While the softening process was taking place I laid out my tools, notebooks and other equipment on a large flat rock.

The next step was to don my gas mask. I am not trying to be funny when I record this fact. I had been supplied with the gas mask, along with a case of teargas grenades with which I was supposed to drive wolves out of their dens so they could be shot as autopsy specimens. Naturally I had long since dumped the bombs into the nearby lake; but I had retained the mask. It now became useful, because wolf scats sometimes carry the eggs of a particularly baneful parasite which, if inhaled by man, hatch into

minute worms that bore their way into his brain, with fatal results. So I donned the mask, placed a scat on a white enamel plate which I had borrowed from the cabin, and began dissecting it with forceps and scalpel. As I identified its constituents through a hand lens, I noted the information in my record book.

It was a laborious process, and I soon became so wrapped up in my work that I ceased to be aware of my surroundings. Consequently when I stood up an hour or two later to stretch my muscles, I was intensely surprised to find myself confronted by a semicircle of a dozen unfamiliar Eskimos who were staring at me with expressions of incredulity mingled with revulsion.

It was a disconcerting moment. I was so startled that I forgot about the gas mask, with its elephantine snout and goggle eyes; and when I tried to greet these strangers my voice, filtered through two inches of charcoal and a foot of rubber pipe, had the muffled and lugubrious quality of wind blowing through a tomb—an effect which filled the Eskimos with consternation.

Hastily I tore off the mask and stepped briskly forward—whereupon the Eskimos, with the precision of a musical comedy chorus line, stepped briskly backwards, some of them shifting their gaze apprehensively to the shining scalpel clutched in my right hand.

They were clearly poised for flight; but I saved what was left of the situation by recalling appropriate Innuit words and blurting out a more or less formal welcome.

After a long pause one of them ventured a timid reply, and the stilted conversation which followed revealed that these people formed a part of Ootek's tribe which had spent the summer further east and had only just returned to the home camps, where they had been told of the presence of a strange white man at Mike's cabin. They had thereupon decided to come and see this phenomenon for themselves; but nothing they had heard in advance had prepared them for the spectacle which met their eyes when they arrived.

Since in Mike's absence I was the host, and since hospitality is the greatest of virtues in the North, I invited the Eskimos to join me in the cabin for a meal that evening. They seemed to understand and to accept my offer and, leaving me to complete my work on the last few scats, they withdrew to a nearby ridge to pitch their camp.

The results of the analysis were most interesting. Some forty-eight per cent of the scats contained rodent remains, largely incisor teeth and fur. The balance of the identifiable food items included fragments of caribou bones, caribou hair, a few bird feathers and, surprisingly, a brass button much corroded but still bearing a recognizable anchor-and-cable motif such as is used in various merchant navy services. I have no idea how this button happened to end up where it did, but its presence cannot be taken as evidence of a wolf having eaten some wandering sailor. In fact, there is no authentic report of wolves ever having killed a human being in the Canadian North; although there must have been times when the temptation was well-nigh irresistible.

Watched by two solemn little Eskimo boys, I now washed out the pails, then filled them with fresh water with which to make the several gallons of tea I knew would be required. As I walked back to the cabin I noted that the little boys were haring up the ridge as if filled with great tidings which they were anxious to impart to their elders, and I smiled at their enthusiasm.

My cheerful mood did not survive for long. Three hours later dinner was ready (it consisted of fish balls cooked Polynesian style with a sweet-and-sour sauce of my own devising), and there was no sign of my guests.

Indeed, I never saw them again. Their campsite was abandoned, and the people had vanished as totally as if the great plains had swallowed them up.

I was puzzled, and somewhat offended. When Ootek returned the next day I told him the story and demanded an explanation. He asked a number of searching questions about pails, scats, and other things—questions which did not seem to me to be particularly relevant. And in the end, he failed me—for the first time in our association. He insisted that he could not possibly explain why my kind hospitality had been so rudely spurned . . . and he never did.

Chapter 10

The time was drawing near when I would have to leave Wolf House Bay—not because I wished to, but because the wolves would soon be departing to their wintering grounds.

During late October, when winter begins to savage the bleak plains, the caribou begin working their way down into the alien but sheltered world of forests. And where they go, the wolves must follow; for in winter there is nothing left upon the frozen plains for the wolves to eat. From early November until April the wolves and caribou travel together through the *taiga*, the sparse borderline forests of stunted spruce and jackpine lying below the timberline. In years when the snowshoe rabbits are abundant, the wolves prey heavily upon them; but always they stay close to the deer, since, in time of famine, only deer can save them.

Each wolf family travels as a group, but it is not uncommon for two or three small groups to come together into a single band. Winter hunting requires close cooperation between several wolves if the hunt is to be successful; but if there are too many wolves they will not all get enough to eat from a given kill. A band of from five to ten individuals seems to be about the ideal size.

They do not appear to have fixed territories in winter. Each band hunts where and as it pleases. But the fact remains that, unless outright starvation sweeps the land, the nomadic winter wolf bands, moving at the whim of the equally nomadic caribou herds, somehow manage to avoid treading on one another's toes.

For the Barren Lands wolves, winter is the time of death.

Once they have entered timber they are exposed to a concentrated, highly skilled and furious assault from men. Trappers cannot bear them, for wolves not only compete for caribou but can wreak havoc with a trapline, springing the light traps used for foxes without getting caught themselves.

The war against wolves is kept at white heat by provincial and federal governments, almost all of which offer wolf bounties ranging from ten to thirty dollars per wolf; furthermore, most white trappers are afraid of wolves, and there is nothing like the whip of fear to lash men into a fury of destruction.

Much is said and written about the number of deer reputedly slaughtered by wolves. Very little is said about the actual numbers of wolves slaughtered by men. Traps and poison are the commonest wolf-killers; but there are other methods as well. One is the aeroplane, a favourite of those civic-minded sportsmen who serve society by sacrificing their time and money to the destruction of vermin. The crew of a high-flying aircraft keeps watch for wolves in the open, preferably on the ice of a lake. When one is found the aircraft is flown low over him and the beast is pursued so long and hard that he frequently collapses and sometimes dies even before a blast of buckshot strikes him.

However, I know of one occasion when this method failed. Two men in their own light aircraft had flown out from a large city; during previous hunts they had killed many wolves, and the pilot had become so adept at chasing the beasts that his skis would almost strike them. This day he came too close. The harassed wolf turned, leaped high into the air, and snapped at one of the skis.

He died in the ensuing crash; but so did the two men. The incident was described in a widely distributed sportsman's magazine as an example of the cunning and dangerous nature of the wolf, and of the boundless courage of the men who match themselves against him.

At Brochet, the northern Manitoba base for my winter studies, at which I was eventually to arrive from Wolf House Bay, anti-wolf feelings were strong and bitter. The local game warden aggrievedly described the situation to me: as recently as two decades before the local people had been able to kill fifty thousand caribou each winter, whereas now they were lucky if they could kill a couple of thousand. Caribou were becoming scarce to the point of rarity, and wolves were unanimously blamed. My rather meek remonstrance to the effect that wolves had been preying on caribou without depleting the herds for some tens of thousands of years before the white men came to Brochet, either fell on deaf ears or roused my listeners to fury.

One day early in the winter a trader burst into my cabin in a state of great excitement.

"Listen," he said challengingly, "you've been screaming for proof that wolves butcher the herds. Well, hitch up your team and get out to Fishduck Lake. You'll get your proof! One of my trappers came in an hour ago and he seen fifty deer down on the ice, all of 'em killed by wolves—and hardly a mouthful of the meat been touched!"

Accompanied by a Cree Indian companion, I did as I was bid, and late that afternoon we reached Fishduck Lake. We found a sickening scene of slaughter.

Scattered on the ice were the carcasses of twenty-three caribou, and the blood had turned great patches of snow into crimson slush. All but three of the animals were untouched. Two of those three were bucks—minus their heads; while the third, a young and pregnant doe, was minus both hindquarters.

There were no wolf tracks anywhere on the lake. But there were other tracks: the unmistakable triple trail left by the skis and tail-skid of a plane which had taxied all over the place. These deer had not been pulled down by wolves, they had been shot—some of them several times. One had run a hundred yards with its intestines dragging on the ice as a result of a gut wound. Several of the others had two or more bullet-broken limbs.

The explanation of what had actually happened was not far to seek. Two years earlier, the tourist bureau of the provincial government concerned had decided that Barren Lands caribou would make an irresistible bait with which to lure rich trophy hunters up from the United States.

Accordingly a scheme was developed for the provision of fully organized "safaris" in which parties of sportsmen would be flown into the subarctic, sometimes in government-owned planes and, for a thousand dollars each, would be guaranteed a first-rate set of caribou antlers.

During the winter sojourn of the caribou inside the timberline, they feed in the woods at dawn and dusk and spend the daylight hours on the ice of the open lakes. The pilot of the safari aircraft, therefore, had only to choose a lake with a large band of caribou on it and, by circling for a while at low altitude, bunch all the deer into one tight and milling mob. Then the aircraft landed, but kept under way, taxiing round and round the panic-stricken herd to prevent it from breaking up. Through open doors and windows of the aircraft the hunters could maintain a steady fire until they had killed enough deer to ensure a number of good trophies. When the shooting was over the carcasses were examined and the best available head taken by each hunter, whose permit entitled him to "the possession of" only a single caribou. If the hunters were also fond of venison a few quarters would be cut off and thrown aboard the plane, which would then depart southwards. Two days later the sportsmen would be home again, victorious.

The Cree who accompanied me had observed this sequence of events for himself the previous winter while acting as a guide. He did not like it; but he knew enough of the status of the Indian in the white man's world to realize he might just as well keep his indignation to himself.

I was more naive. The next day I radioed a full report of the incident to the proper authorities. I received no reply—unless the fact that the provincial government raised the bounty on wolves to twenty dollars some weeks afterwards could be considered a reply.

BUT MEANWHILE MY TIME AT Wolf House Bay was not quite over, and as winter approached I faced the problem of how I was to make my way south to Brochet. I had long since given up hope that the pilot who had brought me would ever return, so I was amazed when Ootek burst into the cabin one morning, announcing that he had seen an aircraft. Sure enough, a Norseman plane on floats was lazily circling over the tundra to the west of us.

The sight sent me into a dither of excitement. Remembering the smoke generators with which I had been supplied, I ran to get them. To my surprise they worked. A mighty coil of black and oily smoke went soaring into the skies and the Norseman (which had disappeared to the west) reappeared, homing in on my signal column. It landed in the bay, and I went out by canoe to greet the pilot, a narrow-faced and unprepossessing young man chewing a wad of gum. He had much to tell me.

As the months had passed without any word from me, my department had grown increasingly disturbed. Not only had they received no wolf reports, but some four thousand dollars' worth of government equipment had vanished into the tundra void. This was serious. The Royal Canadian Mounted Police were therefore asked to find me, but clues were scarce. The pilot who had taken me into the Barrens had since gone missing on a flight over the Mackenzie district and the police couldn't find any trace of him, let alone discover what he had done with me. Eventually they got hold of a rumour circulating in Churchill to the effect that I was a secret service agent who had been sent to spy on the floating Russian bases at the Pole, and they reported this to Ottawa, adding that the next time the department wanted something found, it had better be honest with them.

The pilot who had landed to investigate my smoke signal was engaged in a prospecting survey, and his discovery of me was purely fortuitous. However, he agreed to carry a message back to his base informing the department where its equipment was, and suggesting that a plane be sent immediately, before the freeze-up came. Meanwhile, I departed to complete some unfinished business at the wolf-den esker.

In order to round off my study of wolf family life, I needed to know what the den was like inside. For obvious reasons I had not been able to make this investigation while it was occupied, and since that time I had been too busy with other work to get around to it. Now, with time running out, I was in a hurry.

I trotted across country towards the den and was within half a mile of it when there was a thunderous roar behind me. I involuntarily flung myself down on the moss as the Norseman came over at about fifty feet, waggled its wings gaily, then lifted to skim the crest of the wolf esker, sending a blast of sand down the slope with its propeller wash. I picked myself up, thinking black thoughts about the humorist in the now rapidly vanishing aircraft.

The den ridge was, as I had expected, wolfless. Reaching the entrance to the burrow I shed my heavy trousers, tunic and sweater, and taking a torch and tape measure from my pack, I began the difficult task of wiggling down the entrance tunnel.

The tunnel was only just big enough to admit me. My mouth and eyes were soon full of sand, and the torch's dim orange glow barely enabled me to read the marks on the tape measure. I squirmed onwards, descending at a forty-five-degree angle for about eight feet, at which point the tunnel took a sharp upward bend and swung to the left. I pointed the torch in the new direction and pressed the switch.

Four green lights in the murk ahead reflected back the dim torch beam. At least two wolves were with me in the den.

Despite my close familiarity with these wolves, whom I had come to know and respect as friends, this was the kind of situation where irrational but deeply ingrained prejudices completely overmaster reason and experience. To be honest, I was so frightened that paralysis gripped me. I had no weapon of any sort, and in my awkward posture I could barely have got one hand free with which to ward off an attack. It seemed

inevitable that the wolves would attack me, for even a gopher will make a fierce defence when he is cornered in his den.

The wolves did not even growl. Save for the two faintly glowing pairs of eyes, they might not have been there at all.

The paralysis began to ease and sweat broke out all over my body. In a fit of blind bravado, I shoved the torch forward as far as my arm would reach.

It gave just sufficient light for me to recognize Angeline and one of the pups. They were scrunched hard against the back wall of the den, and they were as motionless as death.

The shock was wearing off by this time, and the instinct for self-preservation was regaining command. As quickly as I could I began wiggling back up the slanting tunnel, tense with the expectation that at any instant the wolves would charge. But by the time I reached the entrance and had scrambled well clear of it, I had still not heard nor seen the slightest sign of movement.

I sat down on a stone and shakily lit a cigarette, becoming aware as I did so that I was no longer frightened. Instead, an irrational rage possessed me. If I had had my rifle I believe I might have reacted in brute fury and tried to kill both wolves.

The cigarette burned down, and a wind began to blow out of the sombre northern skies. I began to shiver again, this time from cold instead of rage. My anger was passing and I was limp in the aftermath. Mine had been the fury of resentment born of fear: resentment against the beasts who had engendered naked terror in me and who, by so doing, had intolerably affronted my human ego.

I was appalled at the realization of how easily I had forgotten all that the summer sojourn with the wolves had taught me about them ... and about myself. I thought of Angeline and her pup cowering at the bottom of the den where they had taken refuge from the thundering apparition of the aircraft, and I was ashamed.

Somewhere to the east a wolf howled: lightly, questioningly. I knew the voice, for I had heard it many times before. It was George, sounding the wasteland for an echo from the missing members of his family. But for me it was a voice which spoke of the lost world which once was ours before we chose the alien role; a world which I had glimpsed and almost entered.

Farley Mowat

Farley Mowat was born in Ontario in 1921 and served with the Canadian Army during World War II. While still a student at the University of Toronto, he spent two years in the Arctic, where he studied wolves and caribou and also became deeply concerned with the problems of the Eskimos. The Eskimos were the subject of his first book, *People of the Deer;* since its publication in 1952 Farley Mowat has been a full-time writer, and today he is one of Canada's most respected authors, with over twenty-five books to his credit. He has travelled extensively all over Canada and now lives with his wife Claire in Port Hope, Ontario.

BORN
FREE

A condensation of the book by
Joy Adamson

with additional material from
her book LIVING FREE

What does a woman do when her husband brings home three orphaned lion cubs?

Joy Adamson, living in Kenya with her game warden husband, George, decided to rear the cubs until they were old enough to go to a zoo—but in the end the smallest cub, called Elsa, was allowed to stay. Playful and loving, she became their constant companion, but she was more than just a pet—for the Adamsons were determined to bring her up so that one day she would be able to go back to her own kind. When they went on safari Elsa went too, sharing their tent and even their camp beds; then, as she approached maturity, she was encouraged to hunt and kill for herself.

The story of Elsa's return to the wild is a unique testament to the mutual love and respect that can exist between men and animals. For even after she had become a free-roaming lioness with a mate and cubs of her own, Elsa still came back to visit her old friends, rewarding their patience and affection with a touching loyalty. Joy Adamson's portrait of this remarkable lioness is deservedly one of the most popular books ever written.

Cub Life

FOR MANY YEARS my home has been in the northern frontier province of Kenya, that vast stretch of semi-arid thornbush, covering some hundred and twenty thousand square miles, which extends from Mount Kenya to the Ethiopian border.

Civilization has made little impact on this part of Africa. There are no white settlers; the local tribes live very much as their forefathers did, and the place abounds in wildlife of every description.

My husband, George, is senior game warden of this huge territory and our home is on the southern border of the province, near Isiolo, a small township of about thirty Europeans, all of whom are government officials engaged in the task of administering the territory.

George has many duties, such as enforcing the game laws, preventing poaching, and dealing with dangerous animals that have molested the tribesmen. His work causes him to travel on safari over tremendous distances, and whenever possible I accompany him. In this way I have had unique opportunities of coming to grips with this wild, unchanged land.

This story has its beginning on one of those safaris. A Boran tribesman had been killed by a man-eating lion. It was reported to George that this animal, accompanied by two lionesses, was living in some nearby hills and so it became his duty to track them down.

Early on the morning of the 1st of February 1956, I found myself far to the north of Isiolo, in camp alone with Pati, a rock hyrax who had been living with us as a pet for six and a half years. She looked like a guinea pig, though zoologists believe that the hyrax's bone structure shows it to be most nearly related to rhinos and elephants.

Suddenly I heard the vibrations of a car; this could only mean that George was returning much earlier than expected. Soon our Land-Rover broke through the thornbush and stopped near our tents, and I heard George shout: "Joy, where are you? Quick, I have something for you . . . ."

I rushed out with Pati on my shoulder and saw the skin of a lion. But before I could ask about the hunt, George pointed to the back of the car.

There were three lion cubs, tiny balls of spotted fur, only a few weeks old and with their eyes still covered with a bluish film. They could hardly crawl, nevertheless they tried to creep away. I took them on my lap to comfort them, while George, who was most distressed, told me what had happened. Towards dawn, he and another game warden, Ken, had been guided near to the place where the man-eater was said to lie up. When first light broke they were charged by a lioness who rushed out from behind some rocks. Though they had no wish to kill her, she was very close and the way back was hazardous, so George signalled to Ken to shoot; he hit and wounded her, causing the animal to swerve; then George was able to kill her. She was a big lioness in the prime of life, her teats swollen with milk. When he saw this George realized she had been so angry because she was defending her litter.

He ordered a search to be made for the cubs; presently he and Ken heard infantile growls and snarls coming out of a crack in the rock face. They put their arms down the crevice as far as they could reach, and after a lot of probing managed to drag the cubs out; they could not have been more than two or three weeks old. They were carried to the car where the two biggest growled and spat during the whole of the journey back to camp. The third and smallest, however, offered no resistance and seemed quite unconcerned.

Now the three cubs lay in my lap, and to my amazement Pati, who was usually very jealous of any rival, soon came to nestle among them. From that day onwards, the four became inseparable. During these early days Pati was the biggest of the company and also, being six years old, was very dignified compared with the clumsy little velvet bags who couldn't walk without losing their balance.

It was two days before the cubs accepted their first milk—I had tried every trick I knew to make them swallow diluted unsweetened tinned milk, but they only pulled up their tiny noses and protested. Once they had accepted the milk, however, they could not get enough of it, and every two hours I had to warm it and clean the flexible rubber tube which served as a teat until we were able to get a proper baby's bottle. We had sent at once to the nearest African market, which was about fifty miles away, not only for the teat but also for cod-liver oil, glucose and cases of unsweetened milk. At the same time we sent an SOS to the district commissioner at Isiolo, announcing the arrival there within a fortnight of three Royal Babies, and asking him to be good enough to have a comfortable wooden home made in time for our return.

Within a few days the cubs had settled down and were everybody's pet.

190

Pati, their self-appointed nanny, remained in charge; she was devoted to them, and never minded being pulled and trodden on by the three fast-growing little bullies. All the cubs were females. Even at this age each had a definite character; the big one had a benevolent superiority, the second was a clown, and the third cub, although the weakling in size, was the pluckiest in spirit. She pioneered all round, and was always sent by the others to reconnoitre when something looked suspicious to them. I called her Elsa, because she reminded me of someone of that name.

In the natural course of events Elsa would probably have been the throw-out of the pride. The average number of cubs in a litter is four, of which one usually dies soon after birth and another is often too weak to be reared. It is for this reason that one usually sees only two cubs with a lioness. Their mother looks after them till they are two years old. For the first year she provides their food, giving milk to begin with and then regurgitating meat. During the second year the cubs are allowed to take part in the hunting, but they get severely disciplined if they lose their self-control. Since at this time they are unable to kill on their own, they have to rely on what may be left over from a kill by the full-grown lions of the pride. Often very little remains for them, so they are usually in a bad, scruffy condition at this age. Nature's law is harsh and lions have to learn the hard way from the beginning.

The quartet—Pati and the three cubs—spent most of the day in the tent under my camp bed. They were by nature house-trained and always took great care to reach the sand outside. In every way they were wonderfully clean and had no smell. Their tongues were already as rough as sandpaper; as they grew older we could feel them, even through our khaki clothes, when they licked us.

When after two weeks we returned to Isiolo, our Royal Babies had a palace awaiting them, and we appointed our garden boy, a young Somali called Nuru, as guardian and lionkeeper in chief. The post pleased him, for it raised his social status.

For twelve weeks we kept them on a diet of unsweetened milk mixed with cod-liver oil, glucose, bone meal and a little salt. Soon they only required three-hourly feeds, and then gradually the intervals became longer.

By now their eyes were fully opened, and they were romping all over the house and its surroundings. We gave them rubber balls and old inner tubes to play with—the latter were perfect for tug-of-war games. Indeed anything that was soft and flexible fascinated them. They would try to take the inner tube from each other, pulling with all their might. Then, when the battle had been won, the victor would parade with the trophy in front of the others and deliberately provoke another attack.

Surprise was the most important element in all their games. They stalked each other—and us—from the earliest age, and instinctively knew how to do it properly. They always attacked from the rear: keeping under cover, they crouched, then crept slowly until the final rush was made at flying speed and the attacker landed with all her weight on the back of her quarry. When we were the object of such an attack we always pretended to be unaware of what was going on; obligingly we crouched down and looked the other way until the final onslaught took place. This delighted the cubs.

Pati always wanted to be in the game, though, as the cubs were soon three times her size, she took good care to avoid being squashed by her charges. In all other circumstances she retained her authority by sheer character; small as she was, if the cubs became too aggressive she put them in their places by just turning round and facing them.

Pati had come to us when she was newly born, and had entirely adapted her life to ours; at night she would sleep round my neck like a fur. She was a vegetarian but had a craving for alcohol, especially strong spirits: whenever the opportunity arose she would pull the bottle over, extract the cork and swig the liquor. As this was very bad for Pati's health we took every precaution to prevent her indulging in whisky or gin, but we were not always successful.

As the lions became increasingly aware of their strength, they tested it on everything they could find. For instance, a groundsheet, however large, *had* to be dragged about, and they would set to work in proper feline fashion, placing it under their bodies and pulling it between their front legs, as in later life they would drag a kill. Another favourite game was "king of the castle". A cub would jump onto a potato sack and keep her attacker at bay until she was suddenly dethroned by the other sister coming up from behind.

Our few banana trees were also regarded as delightful toys, and very soon their luxuriant leaves hung in tattered fringes. Tree climbing was another favourite game. The little lions were born acrobats, but often they ventured so high that we felt obliged to rescue them.

When at dawn Nuru let them out of their pen, they shot out of doors with a whole night's pent-up energy, and on one such occasion they spotted a tent in which two men who had come to visit us were staying. Within five minutes it was a wreck and our guests were vainly trying to rescue their belongings while the cubs, wild with excitement, dived into the wreckage and reappeared with a variety of trophies—slippers, pyjamas, shreds of mosquito nets. We had to enforce discipline that time with a small stick.

Putting them to bed was also no mean task. Imagine three very naughty little girls who, like all children, hated bedtime, but who could run twice as fast as those who were in charge of them and had the added advantage of being able to see in the dark.

Outdoor games were all very well, but the cubs also developed a fancy for books and cushions. So, to save our library and other possessions, we were eventually obliged to ban them from the house. The cubs resented this very much, so to compensate them for their lost playground, we hung a tyre from a tree, and this proved to be grand for chewing and also as a swing. But best of all was a hessian bag, which we filled with old inner tubes and tied to a branch, from which it dangled invitingly. It had another rope attached to it, and when the cubs hung on to the bag we pulled and swung them high up into the air; the more we laughed the better they enjoyed the game.

When the cubs were three months old they had teeth big enough to enable them to eat meat. So now I gave them raw minced meat, which was the nearest we could get to their mother's regurgitated food. For several days they refused to touch it and pulled grimaces of disgust. Then they made the experiment, found it to their taste, and soon there was a fight at every meal. This meant that poor Elsa, who was still weaker than the others, had little chance of getting her fair share, so I used to take her onto my lap for her meals. She loved this and at these times she would suck my thumbs and massage my thighs with her front paws as though she were kneading her mother's belly in order to get more milk. It was during these hours that the bond between us developed. We combined playing with feeding, and my days were happily spent with these charming creatures.

They were lazy by nature and it needed a lot of persuasion to get them to move from a comfortable position. Even the most desirable marrow-bone was not worth the effort of getting up, and they would roll into position to get at it by the easiest way. But best of all they liked me to hold their bone for them while they lay on their backs, paws in the air, and sucked at it.

When the cubs went into the bush they often had adventures. One morning five donkeys approached them. This was the first time they had seen such big animals, and they certainly showed the proverbial courage of a lion, for they all charged simultaneously. This put them into such good heart that when, a few days later, our forty pack donkeys and mules came near the house, the three little lions fearlessly put the whole cavalcade to flight.

At five months they were in splendid condition and getting stronger every day. They were quite free except at night, when they slept in an enclosure of rock and sand which led off from their wooden shelter. This was a necessary precaution, for wild lions, hyenas, jackals and elephants frequently roam round our house and any of these might have killed them.

The more we grew to know the cubs the more we loved them, so it was hard to accept the fact that we could not keep three fast-growing lions for ever. Regretfully we decided that two must go and that it would be better that the two big ones should leave, since they were always together and less dependent on us than Elsa. Our African servants agreed with our choice of which to keep; when asked their opinion they unanimously chose the smallest. Perhaps they were impressed by visions of the future and thought: "If there must be a lion in the household, then let it be as small as possible."

As to Elsa, we felt that if she had only ourselves as friends she would be easy to train, not only for life at Isiolo but also as a travelling companion on our safaris.

As a home for the big ones, we chose the Rotterdam Blydorp Zoo and made arrangements for them to make the journey by air.

Since they would have to leave from the Nairobi airfield, which was one hundred and eighty miles away, we decided to get them accustomed to motoring, and took them for short daily trips in my one-and-a-half-ton truck, which had a wired box-body.

On the last day, when we drove off, Elsa ran a short way down the drive and then stood with the most mournful expression watching the car in which her two sisters were disappearing. I travelled in the back with the cubs and had armed myself with a small first-aid kit, fully expecting to be scratched during the long journey. However, my medical precautions were put to shame for, after an hour of restlessness, the cubs lay on the bags beside me, embracing me with their paws. We travelled like this for eleven hours, delayed by two blowouts. The lions could not have been more trusting. When we reached Nairobi they were puzzled to know what to make of all the strange noises and smells. Then the plane carried them off for ever from their native land.

After a few days we received a cable announcing the safe arrival of our cubs in Holland. When I visited them, about three years later, they accepted me as a friendly person and allowed me to stroke them, but they did not recognize me. They were living in splendid conditions but nevertheless I was glad to know that almost certainly they had no recollection of a freer life.

Elsa Meets Other Wild Animals

George told me that, while I was absent in Nairobi, Elsa was very much upset; she followed him around, sat under his office desk when he was working, and at night slept on his bed. Each evening he took her for a walk but, on the day of my return, she refused to accompany him and sat herself down expectantly in the middle of the drive. Nothing would move her. Could it have been that she knew I was coming back? If so, to what animal instinct can one attribute such foreknowledge? Behaviour of this kind is difficult to explain.

When I arrived alone she gave me a great welcome, but it was heart-breaking to see her searching for her sisters. For many days she gazed into the bush and called for them. To comfort her we kept her in the house; she slept on our bed and we were often woken by her rough tongue licking our faces.

As soon as we could make the necessary arrangements we took her on safari in order to break this atmosphere of waiting and distress. Luckily she loved it: my truck, packed with soft luggage and bedding rolls, was ideal for her to travel in, since, from this comfortable couch, she could watch all that was going on.

We camped by the Uaso Nyiro River, whose banks are lined with doum palms and acacia bush. Near our camp there were rocky ridges; Elsa explored their clefts, sniffed among the rocks and usually ended by settling herself on the top of some rock from which she could survey the surrounding bush. In the late afternoon the sun turned the country into a blaze of warm colours, and then she blended into the reddish stone as though she were a part of it.

This was the most enjoyable part of the day: everything and everyone relaxed after the great heat; the shadows lengthened and became a deep purple; the world grew silent and all was in suspense, awaiting the darkness and the awakening of the bush.

I remember one particular evening: I secured Elsa to a tree in front of the tents and she started to chew her dinner while I sat in the darkness. Pati hopped onto my lap and, nestling comfortably, began to grind her teeth, a sure sign that she was happy. A cicada chirruped near the river where rippling waters reflected the rising moon. In the soft darkness above, the stars sparkled brilliantly—and suddenly, the unmistakable grunts of lion became audible!

Gradually they grew louder and louder. What could Elsa be thinking about all this? In fact, she seemed utterly unconcerned. She tore at her meat, then she rolled on her back with all four paws in the air and dozed off, while I sat listening to the magnificent chorus of the lions.

It is very hot at that season, so Elsa spent part of the day in the water; then, when the sun made this uncomfortable for her, she would rest in the reeds, at intervals rolling lazily into the river, where she landed with a great splash. As we knew that crocodiles were plentiful in the Uaso Nyiro this caused us some concern, but none ever approached her.

Elsa was always full of mischief; she would splash us whenever she found us off our guard, or she would jump quickly out of the water, pounce on us, wet as she was, and we would find ourselves rolling in the sand.

Elsa was very particular about her claws; certain trees with a rough bark provided her with the means of stretching her retractile claw muscles and she scratched away, leaving deep lines, until she was satisfied with the result of the operation.

Elsa was not afraid of the sound of a shot and she grew to know that "bang" meant a dead bird. She loved retrieving, especially guinea fowl, whose quills she crunched, though she very rarely ate the flesh and never the feathers.

Whenever she discovered some elephant droppings, she at once rolled in them; indeed it seemed that she regarded them as an ideal bath powder. Rhino droppings she also found attractive; in fact, she liked the droppings of most herbivorous animals. We often wondered about this behaviour— could it come from an instinct to disguise her own scent from the animals that, in a natural state, she would kill and eat? The habit, common to the domestic cat and dog, of rolling in excrement is no doubt a degenerate form of the same instinct. We never saw her roll in the droppings of carnivorous animals.

One afternoon Elsa rushed off into the bush attracted by the noise of elephant. Soon we heard loud trumpetings and screams and the cackling of guinea fowl as well. In great anxiety we waited the outcome of this meeting, for poor Elsa had no mother to warn her against these big animals who regard lion as the only enemies of their young and therefore sometimes kill them. After a while the elephant noises ceased, but to make up for it the guinea fowl raised a most alarming clatter. Then, to our amazement, Elsa emerged from a thicket closely followed by a flock of vulturine guinea fowl who seemed determined to chase her away, for, whenever she made an attempt to sit down, they chuckled and cackled, so that she just had to keep going. Only after these bold birds became aware of our presence was she allowed some peace.

When we returned to Isiolo the rains had started. The country was covered with little rivulets and pools. This provided fine fun for Elsa, she splashed in every one of them and, greatly invigorated, proceeded with pouncing leaps to cover us with what she evidently considered to be heavenly mud. This was beyond a joke; we had to make her realize that she had grown too heavy for such light-hearted flying jumps. We explained the situation to her by the judicious use of a small stick and she understood at once. By now Elsa also understood the meaning of "No", and she would obey even when tempted by an antelope. She had plenty of opportunity of seeing wild animals, but as we were usually with her when this happened, she gave chase merely in play and always came back to us after a short time.

We had animals of all kinds around our house. A herd of waterbuck and impala antelope and about sixty reticulated giraffes had been our neighbours for many years; Elsa met them on every walk and they got to know her very well, and a family of timid bat-eared foxes got so used to her that we were able to approach to within a few paces of their burrows while their cubs rolled in the sand in front of the entrance holes, guarded by the parent foxes.

But, if the foxes were fun, the baboons were infuriating. They were in the habit of spending the night on a sheer cliff near our house, where they were safe from leopards; before sunset they always retired to this refuge, and the cliff appeared to be covered with black spots. From their safe position they barked and shrieked at Elsa, who could do nothing in retaliation.

The beginning of the elephant season meant an annual invasion by herds numbering several hundred animals. The great beasts seemed to be very familiar with the geography of Isiolo and always went to the places where the best maize and brussels sprouts grew. Apart from this they behaved very well and gave little trouble. As our home, which is three miles distant from Isiolo, is surrounded by the best browsing, a large number of the invaders come to visit us, and an old rifle range in front of the house has become their favourite playground.

One day at noon Nuru and Elsa returned home followed by a large number of elephant; from our dining-room window we could see them in the bush. We tried to divert her attention but she was determined to meet the advancing herd. She watched them as they walked in single file across the rifle range, waiting until the last of about twenty elephant had crossed. Then she followed them slowly, her head held in a straight line with her shoulders, her tail outstretched. Suddenly the big bull in the rear turned and, jerking his massive head at Elsa, screamed with a high-pitched trumpeting sound. This war cry did not intimidate her, and she walked determinedly on; so did the big elephant. We went out and, following cautiously, saw glimpses of Elsa and the elephants mingling together in the undergrowth. There were no screams nor any sound of breaking branches, which would have indicated trouble. All the same, we waited anxiously until eventually the cub reappeared, looking rather bored with the whole business.

But not all the elephants which Elsa met were so amiable as these. On another occasion she succeeded in starting a colossal stampede. The first thing we heard was tremendous thundering on the rifle range, and when we reached the scene we saw a herd of elephant racing downhill with Elsa close behind them. Finally she was charged by a single bull, but she was much too quick for him. In time he gave up the attack and she returned to us; apparently she had had great fun and certainly did not understand why I was a nervous wreck.

To add to the excitement of Elsa's life there was now a rhino living close to our house. One evening at dark, when we were returning from a walk, the cub suddenly darted behind the servants' quarters. A tremendous commotion ensued. We went to find out what it was about and saw Elsa and the rhino facing each other. After a few moments of indecision, the rhino, snorting angrily, retreated with the cub in hot pursuit.

The following evening I was walking with Elsa and Nuru. We were late and it was getting dark, when suddenly the Somali grabbed my shoulder, thus preventing me from walking straight into the rhino, which stood behind a bush, facing us. I leaped back and ran. Luckily Elsa, who had not seen the rhino, thought I was playing a game and followed me. This was fortunate, for rhinos are unpredictable creatures who are apt to charge anything, including lorries and trains. The next day, however, Elsa had her fun; she chased the animal for two miles across the valley, Nuru loyally panting behind her. After this experience the rhino took itself off to quieter quarters.

By now we had established a routine for Elsa. As soon as it got light Nuru released Elsa and both walked a short distance into the bush. The cub, full of unspent energy, chased everything she could find, including her own tail. Then, when the sun got warm, she and Nuru settled under a shady tree and Elsa dozed while he read his Koran and sipped tea. Nuru always carried a rifle to protect them both against wild animals but was very good about following our instructions "to shout before shooting". He was genuinely fond of Elsa and handled her very well.

About teatime the two of them returned and we took over. First, Elsa had some milk, then we wandered into the hills or walked in the plain; she climbed trees, followed exciting scents, or stalked Grant's gazelle which sometimes played hide-and-seek with her. Much to our surprise, she was fascinated by tortoises, which she rolled over and over; she loved playing, and never missed an opportunity of starting a game with us—we were her "pride" and she shared everything with us.

When darkness fell we returned home and took her to her enclosure, where her evening meal awaited her. It consisted of large quantities of raw meat, mostly sheep and goat; as I held her bones for her I would watch the muscles on her forehead moving powerfully. I always had to scratch the marrow out for her; she licked it greedily from my fingers, resting her heavy body against my arms. While this went on, Pati sat on the windowsill watching us: soon her turn would come and she would spend the night cuddled round my neck.

Till then I sat with Elsa, playing with her, sketching her or reading. These evenings were our most intimate time and I believe that her love for us was mostly fostered in these hours when, fed and happy, she would doze off with my thumb still in her mouth. It was only on moonlit nights that she became restless, listening intently, her nostrils quivering to catch the faintest scent from the mysterious night outside. When she was nervous her paws became damp and I could often judge her state of mind by holding them in my hands.

Elsa Goes to the Indian Ocean

Elsa was now a year old, and she had changed her teeth. To gnaw off her meat she used her molars, not her incisors, but she employed her very rough tongue, covered with minute quills, for rasping it from the bone.

Pati was now getting very old and I kept her as quiet as I could.

Our local leave was due and we planned to spend it by the sea, on a remote part of the coast close to a small Barjun fishing village and not far from the Somali border; the nearest town, called Lamu, was about ninety miles away. It would be a perfect place for Elsa, for we could camp on the beach away from people, with miles of clean sand around us, and a bushy hinterland behind to provide shade.

We took two friends with us, one a young district officer, Don, and the other, Herbert, an Austrian writer who was our guest.

It was a long journey over bad tracks and it took us three days. I usually went ahead with Elsa in my truck, George and the others following in two Land-Rovers with Pati. The country through which we passed was dry, sandy and hot.

One day when it was getting dark I lost my way and ran out of petrol. Hoping that George would follow my tracks, I waited for him. When he arrived after several hours, he said that our camp was already pitched some miles away and told me we must hurry as he had left Pati very ill.

He had given her some brandy to strengthen her but had little hope. The miles back to the camp seemed endless to me. I found Pati in a coma. Her heart was beating so rapidly that it was improbable that it would stand the strain much longer. Gradually she became semiconscious, recognized me and made a weak attempt to grind her teeth, which had always been her way of showing affection. Then her heart slowed down till it had almost ceased to beat, and suddenly her little body quivered in a last convulsion, stretched stiffly and collapsed.

Pati was dead. I held her close, and thought of the many moments of happiness she had given me in the seven and a half years during which we had shared our lives. On many safaris she had been my companion, sometimes for months on end she had been my only friend. How tolerant she had been of the bushbabies, squirrels and mongooses which came and went in our household, and how she loved the lions. At meals she had sat by my plate and taken the titbits gently from my hand.

She had become part of me.

Now I wrapped her in a cloth, carried her some distance away from the camp, and dug her grave. The night was hot and the moonlight softened the shadows in the wide plain around us. All was still and very peaceful.

The next morning we drove on and I was glad that the bad road held my attention.

It was late afternoon when we reached the coast, and the fishermen who came out to greet us told us that a lion was causing a great deal of trouble. Almost nightly it raided their goats and they very much hoped that George would kill it.

There was no time to make a proper camp, so we put our beds out in the open. I was the only woman amongst four Europeans and six Africans and I placed mine at a little distance away. Elsa was secured in my truck next to me. Soon everyone went to sleep except myself. Suddenly I heard a noise and flashed my torch; there, a few yards from my bed, was a lion with the skin of the antelope we had shot that afternoon in its mouth.

For a second I wondered if it might be Elsa, but then I saw her in the back of my car. I looked again, the lion was still staring at me and now he was growling.

I shone my torch into his face and walked backwards towards the camp beds where the men were snoring. Only George woke up. When I told him that a lion was following me he said, "Nonsense." All the same, he picked up his heavy rifle and went in the direction I indicated and there, sure enough, he saw two eyes and heard the growl of a lion. He had little doubt that this was the troublesome lion we had been told about; so he tied a large piece of meat to a tree some thirty yards in front of the car and decided to sit up and wait for him.

After a short time we heard a clatter coming from behind the cars where our evening meal had been cooked. George crept round, levelled his rifle and flashed his torch there; he saw the lion sitting amongst the pots and pans finishing off the remains of our dinner. He pressed the trigger but only a click sounded, and he pressed it again with the same result. He had forgotten to load the rifle! The lion got up and sauntered off. Sheepishly George loaded the rifle and went back to his post.

Much later he heard something tugging at the meat and switched on the car lights; then he saw the lion brilliantly illuminated and shot him through the heart.

He was a young maneless lion, typical of the coast region. When light broke we investigated his pugmarks and discovered that he had first seized the skin of the antelope, then dragged it to within twenty yards of my bed where he had eaten his meal. When replete he had made a leisurely round of the camp. Of all these goings-on Elsa must have been an interested spectator, but she had never uttered a sound.

As soon as the sun was up the whole camp trooped down to the water's edge to introduce Elsa to the Indian Ocean. The tide was receding; at first she was nervous of the unaccustomed roar and rush of the waves. Then she sniffed cautiously at the water and bit at the foam; but her first mouthful of saltwater made her wrinkle her nose in disgust. However, when she saw the rest of the party enjoying a bathe, she decided to trust us and join in the fun. Very soon she became quite water-crazy. Rain pools and shallow rivers had always excited her, but this great ocean was a real heaven. She swam effortlessly, far out of her depth; ducked us and splashed the water with her tail.

The reef in this place was the best of all those along the Kenya coast for coral fish. Armed with harpoon and goggles, George and I dived into a fascinating world. Some of the corals were pagoda-shaped, others looked like the brains of giants, while some fanned out like mushrooms, patterned with purple rosettes or furrowed by emerald creases. Curtains of brilliant coloured seaweed, in the folds of which schools of minute fish were hiding, fingered the current. We swam through deep valleys, which often led into caverns, and we peeped into dimly lit tunnels, out of whose depths coral fish emerged, inquisitive and puzzled by our monstrous bulk; they had good reason for their surprise, since under water everything looks twice its natural size.

On these occasions, Elsa, with someone to keep her company, rested in the shade of a mangrove tree close to the camp. When passing fishermen got to know of this they made a big detour, hitched up their loincloths and waded into the sea. They would have felt less reassured had they known what an amphibious creature she was.

She also loved walking along the beach, where she chased the coconuts bobbing in the surf, getting swamped by the waves in the process. Sometimes we tied a string to a coconut and swung it in a circle above our heads while she jumped high up after it as it flew past. She soon discovered that digging in the sand was a most rewarding game, since the deeper the hole the wetter and cooler it became and therefore the nicer to roll in. But crabs provided her with the best fun of all: she would rush from one to the other, invariably getting nipped on the nose, but undeterred she would pounce again, only to be nipped once more. To the crabs' credit it should be recorded that of all Elsa's opponents, not excluding elephants, buffaloes and rhinos, they were the only ones which stood their ground. Sideways-on they waited, one pink claw erect, and however cunningly Elsa tried to outwit them, they were always quicker than she was and her soft nose would get punctured again.

Feeding Elsa became quite a problem, for the local fishermen were quick to recognize the source of income which she represented and the price of goats soared. In fact, for some time she kept the villagers in luxuries hitherto unknown to them. However, in the end she had her revenge. The herdmen never guarded their animals, which straggled along all day in the bush, an easy prey to leopard and lion. One evening, we were out on the beach, long after bedtime for goats, when Elsa suddenly darted into a bush; there followed a loud bleat and then silence. She must have scented a lone straggler, and pounced on it. But, never having killed before, she did not know what to do next. When we arrived,

George quickly shot the beast while Elsa held it down. As no complaint was made by the owner for its loss, which was no doubt credited to the usual kill of some wild lion, we kept quiet about the incident. We overcame our qualms of conscience with the thought that George had rid the district of its chief goat eater, and also with the recollection of the exorbitant prices we had paid for the most miserable little beasts.

Towards the end of our holiday George became ill with malaria. But he was so keen on fishing that he took much stronger doses of mepacrine than the normal one and also got up before he should.

Returning home one evening from a walk along the beach with Elsa, as I neared the camp I heard an alarming howling and screaming. After securing Elsa in my truck I rushed to the tent, where I found George limp and collapsed in a chair. He was emitting frightful groans and yelling for his revolver, cursing Elsa and shouting that he wanted to shoot himself. Even in his semiconscious condition he recognized me, seized me with an iron grip and said that now that I was there he could relax and die. I was most alarmed for I knew the cause of his condition; he had been poisoned by an overdose of mepacrine, and the reaction was due to the fact that he had gone fishing without giving this dangerous drug time to work.

The boys stayed a few yards away looking very frightened. Our friend Don stood clutching a stick with which he proposed to club George if he should become violent. In whispers they told me that, quite suddenly, George had started to gesticulate wildly, shrieking for me and shouting for his revolver to kill himself. Luckily I had returned soon after.

Although my heart was heavy with fear, I began talking to him in a quiet voice, telling him about our walk along the beach, about the fish we were going to eat for dinner. Like a child, he responded to my efforts to soothe him and calmed down. But his temples grew grey, his nostrils fell in and his eyes closed. He whispered that an icy current was creeping up his legs towards his heart, that his arms were lifeless and cold, and that when both icewaves met at his heart, he would die. Suddenly he was seized by panic, clutched me with a desperate strength, as though hanging on to life. I poured brandy between his dry lips and stroked him gently. Before he fell into an exhausted sleep, the night had passed; during that time he had had several relapses, during which his brain worked with frightening rapidity while he uttered senseless words. The next morning, as soon as he was well enough, we returned to Isiolo.

Like all holidays, ours had passed much too quickly, but by the time we went home we had acquired a deep tan and Elsa, owing to her sea bathing, had developed a beautiful silky coat.

The Man-Eating Lions

One day, soon after our return to Isiolo, George had to deal with two man-eating lions which had killed or mauled about twenty-eight people of the Boran tribe during the last three years. Many and gruesome were the tales told of their marauding. As a rule the Boran are very brave indeed, but in this case the man-eaters completely overawed them. This was partly due to the cunning and boldness of the lions, and partly to the fact that superstition had added its weight to the fear with which they were regarded: it was said that these lions were the spirits of two holy men who had been murdered long ago by the Boran, and who had now come back in this shape to seek their revenge. To add to the legend of the lions, George and other hunters had tried on previous occasions to kill them and had failed owing to lack of time. This confirmed the Boran's opinion that the lions were supernatural beings and that it was useless to hunt them.

So now, in spite of the coming rains, we were determined to break the spell. We set off, Elsa and myself in the truck; George followed with John, a young officer on leave from the King's African Rifles, and a few game scouts, in the Land-Rover and trailer. We were fortunate to find a good camping site set well in the open, an important point when dealing with man-eaters, for they are less likely to raid a camp placed in the open than one surrounded by bush.

After pitching camp, George sent at once for the local headman and elders of the Boran and ordered them to inform their people living along the river that as soon as the lions killed again news was to be brought to him.

These lions covered an area of fifty miles along the Uaso Nyiro River. From the beginning it seemed as if they were aware of our intentions. They had the terrain in their favour and made good use of the almost impenetrable river undergrowth. They were most energetic walkers and thought nothing of covering thirty miles during a night.

To begin with, George had to cover forty miles before he was able to shoot a zebra; he then towed its carcass to within about a mile of our camp and secured it on the ground under an acacia tree, in which, about twelve feet from the ground, we built a platform. For the next three nights George and John kept watch. We heard the lions roaring upriver but nothing happened. I sat in camp listening to their magnificent chorus, with Elsa snoring contentedly by my side, inside the truck. Did she not know that her own kin were nearby?

On the fourth night, weary from sitting up, he and John slept in camp; it was that night that the lions came to the kill. Now another carcass had to be obtained and once more they sat over it for three nights without result. Then once again, exhausted by days spent trying to follow the lions' spoor and sleepless nights, they returned to camp. Once more the lions took the occasion and came to the kill. By that time we were all half inclined to agree with the Boran that perhaps the lions were the spirits of holy men or, more likely, of devils.

Now we changed our tactics and did most of our hunting by day, following the spoor into dense bush. Twice we got close to the lions, only to hear them break away ahead without giving us the chance of a shot. Hunting on foot was most exhausting, nor did the presence of rhino and elephant make our task easier. The rains had started up-country, and the river already showed signs of rising. As the lions kept to the other side of it, we would have to move camp without delay if we were to get across the ford below Merti.

We packed up camp and arrived early in the morning at the ford to find that the water had risen considerably during the night and was still going up; we decided that it was just fordable by cars. First the Land-Rover crept into the river and crossed successfully. Next my truck entered with Elsa, as usual, sitting in the back. The water rushed past at alarming speed, carrying debris. The truck got bravely into the middle, then the engine spluttered and died. Nothing would make it start again. We released Elsa at once; she plunged into the water, splashed about and tried to retrieve the driftwood, as though we had arranged all this for her amusement. Eventually, all hands pushing and pulling, and applauded by the ever-present baboons, we managed to get the truck across.

Camp had to be pitched on the spot, as it took all the rest of the day to dry out our kit. Then, next morning, the river overflowed its banks and we had to move to high ground. During the next night it rained solidly, and we feared this might mean the end of the lion hunt. Nevertheless George shot a zebra and put its carcass beneath a bush for the lions; then, soon after dark, he and John took up watch.

After about an hour George heard the unmistakable sound of a lion tearing at the carcass, but it was a dark night and he could not see anything. They waited for the lion to settle down to his meal, then John switched on his torch and the animal became visible; he had his tail towards them and, with his head buried in the carcass, offered a poor shot till, disturbed by the light, he turned and looked towards it.

George then aimed at his neck and fired. There was a deep grunt, the lion leaped into the air and made off. Evidently he had been hard hit and George was confident of finding him dead at dawn. As soon as it was light enough two game scouts came from the camp and with George and John followed the blood spoor, which led into the dense bush by the river.

If the lion were still alive it would be a very dangerous proposition to follow him in. They advanced cautiously step by step, pausing every few minutes, with ears strained to catch the slightest sound. Suddenly there was a growl and George caught a fleeting glimpse of two lions making off. By now the blood trail had almost disappeared. They had stopped and were carefully examining the ground when a game scout tapped George on the shoulder and pointed back. There, fifteen yards away, he saw a lion looking at them over a low bush. He shot him between the eyes: a big lion, nine feet five inches from nose to tail. George was sure that it must be the animal he had wounded, as there appeared to be two bullet holes in the back of his head, besides the one between the eyes. He assumed that the other lion had escaped across the river.

When I arrived on the battlefield, I gave George full marks for his success. It must have been very frightening to follow a wounded man-eating lion into that thicket. Although we had just spent three weeks hunting these man-eaters, this was the first time that I had actually seen one of them. He was in the prime of life, about eight years old. Of course we were relieved that at last one of the man-eaters was dead but, illogically, we did not enjoy our victory over this splendid animal.

That night, George began to question whether the lion he had killed was in fact the one which he had previously wounded; it was not impossible that the expanding bullet from his heavy rifle had split inside the beast's skull so that perhaps the two holes at the back of the head were made by fragments of the same bullet. In that case, there was still a wounded lion on the same side of the river as our camp was pitched.

George then found a party of six young Boran and suggested that they return next day with their best hunting dogs. News of the first man-eater's death had caused much excitement, and now at last the Boran were convinced that the lions were less than immortal and were keen to help find the other one. In the morning we met them, as arranged, and found them accompanied by the most unlikely-looking hunting dogs, which they however assured us were not afraid of lion.

Once more we entered the bush; after a short time George noticed that the dogs were not displaying much eagerness to go forward. Then the pack leader turned with his tail between his legs and headed for home with the rest following him. We all expected to hear the roar of a charging lion, but nothing happened. Instead we heard the excited barking of baboons, a sure sign that they had seen something alarming; after pausing with ears and eyes strained, we moved on. Then, as George stooped to pass under a bush, something light-coloured caught his eye; in a fortress of thornbush crouched a lion, apparently ready to charge. George was about to fire when the loud buzzing of flies told him that the animal was dead. We found that the bullet fired from the platform had torn its throat, probably damaging the jugular vein. It was a really magnificent lion, not as large as the other, but a much handsomer animal.

Both lions were in perfect condition, about middle-aged, as lions go. Certainly they had no disabilities to justify their man-eating.

Most lions take to man-eating because they have some infirmity: either they have been wounded, or their teeth are in bad condition, or they have porcupine quills in their paws, or they are very old and in this state turn to less agile forms of food than is natural to them. But clearly there are exceptions, cases where one can only guess at the whim of nature that has induced them to change their way of hunting.

Now our task was accomplished, and the Boran would no more be troubled by the spirits of the holy men. We reflected, however, that there was good reason to suppose that the two lions had sired lusty cubs and we could only hope that they had not been trained to their fathers' tastes.

Safari to Lake Rudolf

One afternoon after we had returned to Isiolo, we took Elsa up a hill behind the house, and from the top we saw a herd of about eighty elephant, with many small calves, feeding below. Elsa saw them too and before we could shout "No" she went off downhill and, a few moments later, was advancing cautiously towards the herd.

Nearest to her was a cow with a small calf. Elsa stalked it with great cunning, but the mother elephant was well aware of her intention. We watched, expecting a charge, but to our surprise the mother elephant moved quietly between Elsa and the calf, pushing it slowly towards some big bulls, keeping our lioness on the far side. Disappointed, Elsa tried to provoke other small groups of elephants, advancing to within a few yards of them. But again she was ignored. The sun was getting low; we shouted to her but she obstinately disregarded our calls. Finally we had no alternative but to return home without her.

I waited for her inside the enclosure, reading, but my thoughts were not on the book. I became more and more worried. What would we do? Chaining Elsa up during the elephant season would only frustrate and infuriate her; indeed, it might end by making her dangerous. We had to let her learn by experience the danger of playing with these big animals.

By the time she was three hours overdue I was really afraid, and then suddenly in she came, very thirsty indeed—yet before she went to her waterbowl she licked my face and sucked my thumbs as if to tell me how glad she was to be with me again. She smelled strongly of elephant, and I could well imagine how close she had been to them. By the way she flung herself to the ground with a crash, I could also judge how tired she was. Here was my friend just returned from a world that was utterly denied to me, yet she was as affectionate as ever—did she have any realization of the extraordinary link she was between the two worlds?

Of all animals, giraffe were undoubtedly her favourites. She would stalk them, using every stratagem of her kind, but invariably they would spot her before she got too close; this was mainly because Elsa seemed unable to control her tail. Her body would freeze without so much as the twitch of an ear, but the conspicuous black tassel on her tail would never keep still. Once the giraffe had spotted her she would sit down waiting for them to return and sure enough, after a time they would approach again, advancing slowly step by step, facing Elsa, looking at her with their large sad eyes, while their slender necks arched in an inquisitive way. Then, browsing at their favourite acacia seeds as they went by, they would walk peacefully away.

Our next safari was to take us to Lake Rudolf, a stretch of water some one hundred and eighty miles long, reaching to the Ethiopian frontier. We were to be away for seven weeks and most of the time we would travel on foot with pack donkeys and mules. It would be Elsa's first experience of a foot safari in the company of donkeys, and we could only hope that both sides would accept each other. The pack animals were sent off three weeks ahead to meet us on the shores of the lake, while we travelled the distance of about three hundred miles by motor transport.

It was a big convoy: two Land-Rovers, my one-and-a-half-ton truck with Elsa in the back of it, and two three-ton lorries. The latter were necessary to enable us to carry, as well as the men, sufficient food and petrol for the weeks we should be away, also eighty gallons of water. Our first one hundred and eighty miles led us through the sandy, hot and dusty plains of the Kaisut desert. Then we ascended the volcanic slopes of the Marsabit mountain, an isolated volcanic mass rising to 4,500 feet out of the surrounding desert. Clothed in thick, cool, lichen-covered forest, and often enveloped in mist, it presented a welcome contrast to the hot arid country below.

Here was the last administrative post. From now on we made our way through practically uninhabited country and were cut off from any contact with the outside world. Nothing broke the monotony of the sand gullies and lava ridges. The only incident was a crash which nearly broke my car in half. One back wheel left us and we came to an abrupt stop. Poor Elsa; it took hours to repair the damage and she had to spend the whole time inside the car, since it provided the only shade from the fierce sun. When we were mobile again, we climbed up the most shocking track into the Huri hills on the Ethiopian border. These are desolate and, though higher than Marsabit, attract less moisture. An enervating gale blows across their slopes and Elsa was quite bewildered by it.

George's purpose in visiting these hills was to examine the game situation and to see whether there were any signs of poaching by the Gabbra tribesmen. After a few days spent in patrolling the country we turned westwards, crossing the most depressing, desolate lava country, where sharp rocks jerked the car mercilessly, and Elsa had a tough time as we pushed the vehicles through deep sandy riverbeds or ground our way carefully between boulders, jostling against the large stones.

At last, after two hundred and thirty miles of hustling and bumping, we skirted the Chalbi desert and reached Loyongalane, an oasis of freshwater springs in a grove of doum palms near the south of Lake Rudolf. Here we found our donkeys waiting for us. We took Elsa at once to the lake, which was two miles distant. She rushed into the water, right among the plentiful crocodiles. Luckily they were not aggressive, but all during our safari their floating, horny shapes, silhouetted along the shore, were to make bathing, at least for us, a dubious pleasure.

At Loyongalane we established our base camp and spent the next three days in repairing saddlery and packing donkey loads. Each load weighed approximately fifty pounds, two to each donkey. At last all was ready. There were eighteen donkeys loaded with food and camping gear, four with water containers, six sheep to feed Elsa on the way, one riding mule for anyone who went weak or lame, and five spare donkeys. Elsa watched all our packing with restrained interest, then when we started loading she had to be chained up, for the sight of so much lovely meat braying and kicking and rolling in the sand made her tense with excitement. The main cavalcade started off in the late morning and we followed with Elsa when it was cooler. Our march was northwards along the shoreline. Elsa was very excited and rushed like a puppy from one to the other of us, then she dashed in among the flocks of flamingoes, retrieved a duck we had shot, and finally went swimming in the lake. Later, when we passed a herd of camels, I was obliged to put her on the chain; this made her furious, but I had no wish to see a panic-stricken herd of camels falling over each other, legs intertwined, and Elsa in their midst.

When night fell, we saw the fires of the camp ahead. Again I put Elsa on the chain for fear that she might have enough energy left to chase our donkeys. When we arrived we found camp already pitched and everything laid out for dinner. While we had a belated sundowner we decided that at dawn each morning the lion party—George and I, Nuru, a game scout as guide, and Elsa—would start off, while camp was being struck and the animals saddled and loaded. This would spare any need to keep Elsa on the chain. Then at about nine thirty we would look for a shady place where we could rest during the heat of the day.

We kept to this routine during the whole safari and it worked out very well. We found that Elsa marched strongly until about nine in the morning; then she began to feel the heat and kept stopping wherever a rock or bush gave shade. In the afternoon, she was reluctant to move before five; after that, once her pads had hardened, she could have gone on all night. On average she trotted from seven to eight hours daily, and kept in wonderful condition. Usually we reached camp between eight and nine in the evening; often the donkey party would fire Very lights to guide us.

The second day out we left the last human habitation behind us; it was a small fishing village of the primitive El Molo tribe. This tribe numbers about eighty souls who live almost entirely on fish, varied occasionally by crocodile and hippo meat. As a result of this badly balanced diet and of interbreeding, many of them are deformed and show signs of rickets. Perhaps also owing to malnutrition or, more likely, to the fact that the lake water contains a high proportion of natron and other minerals, they also suffer from bad teeth and gums. They are a friendly and generous people and a stranger is always welcomed with a gift of fresh fish. Their fishing is mostly carried on by means of nets, which they make out of doum-palm fibre, the only fibre that does not rot in the alkaline water; while the giant Nile perch, which runs up to two hundred pounds and over, and crocodile and hippo, are harpooned from rafts made from three palm logs lashed roughly together. These unwieldy craft are poled along in the shallows and never venture far out for fear of the violent winds which often sweep the lake and sometimes reach a velocity of over ninety miles an hour.

The first ten days took us along the lake's shore. The country around was grim: lava, and more lava. In certain places there was deep sand, and as we waded along each step was an effort; at other times we had to make our way across coarse grit or pebbles, and always the hot wind blew, sapping our energy and making us feel dizzy. There was little vegetation, only a few thorny meagre plants which pricked, and razor-edged grass which cut the skin.

To keep Elsa's paws in good condition I had often to grease them, an act which she seemed to like. During the midday rest, I usually lay on my camp bed so as to be able to relax in comfort. Elsa saw the point of this, adopted my idea, and joined me. Soon I considered myself fortunate if she left me a small corner, and every noon saw us curled up together on the bed, I hoping that it would not break beneath our combined weight.

One evening we lost our way and reached the camp late at night. Elsa seemed exhausted, so I left her unchained to recover; but although she looked sleepy, she suddenly rushed at full speed to the thorn enclosure in which the donkeys spent the night, and crashed through the fence. Braying and pandemonium ensued, and before we could intervene all the donkeys had bolted into the darkness. Luckily, we soon caught Elsa and I gave her a good hiding. She seemed to understand that she deserved it and, as far as she could, showed that she was sorry. I felt guilty at having underestimated her natural instinct and the tremendous temptation that a nice-smelling donkey herd must be to her, especially at an hour when the hunting spirit is most alive in wild animals.

Luckily only one poor donkey had received scratches and these were not serious. I dressed them and they soon healed, but this episode was a warning to me never to leave her unguarded.

The route we were taking crossed the western foot of the Longondoti hills. In several places the hills fall straight into the lake, so the donkeys with their bulky loads had to make a detour inland, while the lion party struggled across the rocks and kept to the shore.

Nine days out of Loyongalane, we camped at the northern end of the hills. As usual, we had sent a party of game scouts ahead to spy out the country and keep a lookout for poachers. Early in the afternoon they returned and reported seeing a large body of men in canoes. The only tribe on the lake which possessed proper dugout canoes was the Galubba, a turbulent people who constantly carried out raids from across the Ethiopian border into our territory, looting and murdering. The band which the scouts had seen might be either a raiding party, or a poaching and fishing expedition. In any case, they had no right to be there. Elsa and I remained in camp, with four game scouts to protect us, while the rest of the party went off to reconnoitre.

When they had reached the top of a ridge which overlooked the bay, they saw three canoes with twelve men on board, paddling close inshore in the direction of our camp. However, our party was spotted at once, so that by the time George and the other men had reached the water's edge the canoes were a good two hundred yards out, making for a small island and paddling madly. Looking through glasses, George saw a body of at least forty men on the island and several canoes drawn up on its shore. He watched the canoes reach the beach and an obviously excited group gather round them. Then—since without a boat there was nothing much that they could do—the party returned to camp. That night, extra sentries were posted and every man slept with his rifle loaded beside him. When dawn broke, we saw that the island was deserted. Evidently the Galubba had not liked the look of us and had decided to get away during the hours of darkness. Soon after sun-up we saw a multitude of vultures descending upon the island; this led us to suppose that the Galubba had been on a poaching expedition and had no doubt killed several hippo, on the remains of which the vultures had come to feast.

By now our supplies were running low and it was time to turn back. Instead of retracing our steps, we decided to take an inland route. Our guide did not seem very sure of the way and, what was worse, was not certain whether we should find water when needed. George, however, calculated that we should never be more than a long day's march from the lake so, if pressed for water, could make for it. We missed the cooling breeze off the lake, and there were times when I felt nearly dehydrated by the heat. The country here was even more desolate than on our outward march so, understandably, there was little game. Luckily, although Elsa's living larder was rapidly dwindling away, it was just sufficient to solve her feeding problem. But all of us lost most of our surplus weight.

When we got back to Loyongalane we found that the scouts we had left behind to protect our base had not been idle. They produced four Turkana poachers, who had been caught trapping game. The oldest greeted George with great affection and reminded him that, some ten years ago, George had caught him committing the same offence and had sent him to jail at Marsabit. He said that he had quite enjoyed his enforced stay there but did not wish to repeat it. Owing to his age, George relented and, unofficially, sentenced him to be donkey driver for the rest of the safari.

We spent three days at Loyongalane, mending saddlery and refitting in

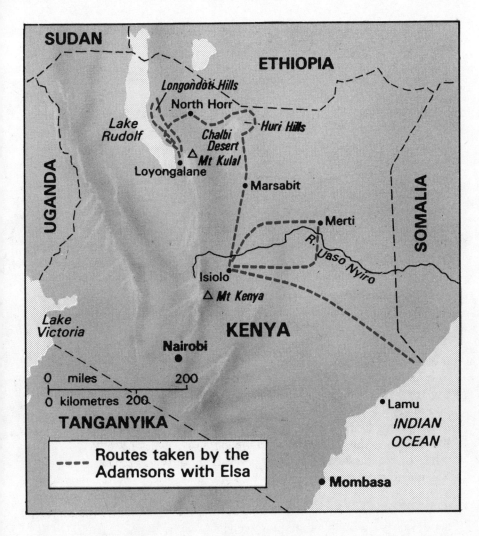

preparation for the second part of our safari, the ascent of Mount Kulal. This mountain, which lies twenty miles east of the lake, rises out of the surrounding desert to about 7,500 feet; it catches all the moisture from the monsoon on its upper levels and has developed rich forest on its summit. It is a narrow extinct volcano, twenty-eight miles long, with a crater in the centre about four miles wide. This crater is split in half and divides the mountain into two sections, with smooth walls and deep crevasses which fall 3,000 feet from the crater's lip. At the bottom, invisible from the top, is a gorge called Il Sigata which leads to the heart of the mountain.

The object of the safari was to find out whether the game on the mountain was holding its own, or decreasing as a result of poaching, by comparing the present situation with that found by George when, twelve years previously, he had last visited the area. In particular, we wanted to investigate the state of the greater kudu.

The first day's march, over thickly strewn lava boulders, was extremely arduous for laden animals. On the second night we were two thirds of the way up the mountain and camped in a precipitous valley near a little spring. This was one of the few waterholes on Kulal and so it was naturally a vital centre for the Samburu tribesmen who bring their livestock up to Kulal in the dry season.

It must have been difficult for Elsa to meet such large herds of camels, cattle, goats and sheep around this and other waterholes; but she was intelligent and good-natured and put up with the tantalizing smell of animals which often passed within a few feet of her. On these occasions we put her on the chain but she made no attempt to attack.

Next day we reached the top of Kulal; it was a relief to be walking on more-or-less even ground. Camp was pitched in a beautiful little glade, close to a rather muddy spring.

In the dense forest belt near the top on most mornings there was heavy mist, so we made a blazing cedar-log fire to keep us warm. At night it was so cold that I kept Elsa in my small tent, made her a nest of lichen and covered her with my warmest blanket. She never made any attempt to tear the tent and get out; on the contrary she remained in it long after her usual waking hour, snuggling in her nest, where she was warm and cosy. But as soon as the sun had cleared the fog away, she came to life.

Because of the shade and altitude, walking during the heat of the day was no effort in this region, and Elsa was able to explore the mountain with us. She watched the eagles circling high in the air and was annoyed by the crows who followed her and dived low to tease her, and on one occasion woke a buffalo out of his sleep and chased him.

One day we stood on the lip of the crater which divided the mountain and looked across to the northern part. Nonchalantly Elsa balanced herself on the edge of the two-thousand-foot precipice, a sight which nearly sent me into hysterics. But animals seem to have no fear of heights. The following day we descended and the safari reached the mouth of the great Il Sigata gorge; there we made camp.

During the day thousands of camels, goats and sheep, herded by tall, good-looking Rendille tribesmen, passed by on their way to water four miles up the gorge. They were followed by women leading strings of camels tied nose to tail and loaded with water containers. These held about six gallons each and were made of closely woven fibre. We walked up the cleft, literally *into* the mountain. The floor of the gorge is a dry watercourse which, for about five miles, rises gently between towering walls which attain some fifteen hundred feet in height and are sheer precipice. In places the gorge is so narrow that two laden camels cannot pass abreast and the cliffs overhang, shutting out the sky. We went far beyond the watering place of the stock, where the trickle of water becomes a sizable brook, with many rockbound pools of clear water. Finally we were halted by a sheer fall of thirty feet.

Il Sigata used to be a favourite place for poachers since it was easy to lie in wait for animals going to water. In fact, once an animal had entered the trap it was doomed, since there was no way out except that which led past the waiting hunters.

From Il Sigata it was a day and a half's march to the top of the northern massif. We saw little game. Buffalo, of which there used to be a lot, had not, we were told, visited the northern end of the mountain for the last six years. There were also no greater kudu to be seen, though we observed the spoor of a few. George considered that this absence of game was probably due to the tribesmen's domestic stock, which were eating up the grazing and rapidly denuding the mountain.

Owing to sharp broken lava, the descent to Loyongalane was a most exhausting struggle and not even the superb view of Lake Rudolf far below, reflecting the setting sun in its lead-coloured surface against deep indigo hills and an orange-yellow sky, could compensate us for our tumbles, which grew more and more frequent.

Towards nightfall we lost our way in the dark. Elsa lay down every few yards, making it very plain that she had had enough. At last some tracer bullets, fired by the advance party, guided us to the camp. When we staggered in Elsa refused food and only wanted to be near me. She, of course, could not know why we were doing such a senseless thing as to struggle across sharp lava at night, and it was only her affection for us and her trust that kept her going. Although she was nearly full-grown she still liked to suck my thumb when she felt nervous, and there was a lot of thumb-sucking that night.

To feel that we were responsible for such a proud, intelligent animal, who had no other living creature to satisfy her need for affection and her gregarious instincts, attached us all the more deeply to her. Sometimes, it is true, she was a nuisance; for instance, because we could not leave her in charge of anyone else, we became to some extent her prisoners, but she gave us so much in return for these small sacrifices. It was very touching to watch her trying to control the strong forces within her and to adapt herself to our way of life in order to please us. Her good nature was certaintly due in part to her character, but part too may have come from the fact that neither force nor frustration was ever used to adapt her to our way of life. For we tried by kindness alone to help her to overcome the differences that lay between our two worlds.

Elsa and Wild Lions

Elsa has charming manners; no matter for how short a time we have been separated, she will greet us ceremoniously, walking from one to the other and rubbing her head against us while miaowing.

Soon after our return from Lake Rudolf, however, when we took her out for her evening walks she began to refuse to return with us. Usually we succeeded in getting her back by going to fetch her in the Land-Rover. In fact, she soon decided that it was a waste of energy to walk home when a car had been specially brought to fetch her, so she would jump onto the canvas roof and loll at her ease as we drove along. This was a very satisfactory arrangement from her point of view but, unfortunately, the manufacturers had not designed the roof as a couch for a lioness. As a result it began to give way under the strain and George had to rig up extra supports and reinforce the canvas.

When she was not with us, Nuru was still always in charge of Elsa; one day we wanted to film him with her and told him that he should wear something rather smarter than his usual tattered shirt and trousers. In a few minutes he reappeared in a startling, close-fitting cream-coloured jacket, with braid and frogging down the front, which he had bought for his wedding. We thought that he looked just like a professional lion tamer in it. Elsa took one look at him and made at once for the bush; from there she peeped out from behind a shrub until she had established his identity.

Elsa was now twenty-three months old and her voice broke to a deep growl. A month later she seemed to be in season. Normally she followed us on our walks wherever we went, but now she seemed determined to cross the valley. On one particular afternoon, she led us in *her* direction, and we soon found the fresh pugmarks of a lion. At dark, she refused to return. We went back to get the Land-Rover, and George set off in it while I stayed at home in case she took a short cut back. Some time after he had gone I heard a shot. Until he came back I was very anxious, and then most upset by what he had to tell me.

He had driven out and called for a good half hour, but Elsa had not shown up. Then he had stopped the car in an opening in the bush, wondering where to look next. Suddenly there had been a great uproar of lions quarrelling. Then, the next moment, Elsa flashed by with another lioness in hot pursuit. As they shot past, George seized his rifle and put a bullet under the second animal, assuming, probably rightly, that she was a jealous lioness bent on Elsa's destruction. Then he jumped into the car and gave chase, flashing a spotlight from side to side, until he was brought up short by a lion and two lionesses, who only very reluctantly moved out of his way, giving loud roars.

Now he had come to fetch me; we drove back to the scene, but though we called desperately for Elsa no familiar sound came in answer. So, with heavy hearts, we turned for home. Had Elsa been killed? In her present condition, she might well have mated with the lion and it was a question whether his lioness would tolerate a rival. However, to our great relief, we had not gone more than a mile along the track when we came upon Elsa. But she utterly ignored us, gazing wistfully into the bush in the direction in which the lions had last been heard. Presently they started calling again, and approached. Thirty yards behind us was a dry riverbed, and here the pride stopped, growling vigorously.

It was now well after midnight. Elsa sat in the moonlight between us and the lions, undecided what to do. For an hour the situation did not alter, then George fired two shots over the lions; this had the effect of sending them off in silence. Then, as Elsa had still not made up her mind, we drove slowly back, hoping that she might follow us; and so she did. Very reluctantly, she walked parallel with the car, looking back many times, till finally she hopped onto the roof and we brought her back to safety. When we arrived home she was very thirsty and exhausted.

What had happened during the five hours which Elsa had spent with the lions? Would a wild pride accept her in spite of the human smell she carried? Why had she returned with us instead of joining her own kind? These were some of the questions we asked ourselves.

After this adventure the call of the wild evidently grew stronger. Often she did not return with us at dark and we spent many evenings looking for her. In the dry season water was our main hold on her, for this she could only get at the house.

Soon after her adventure with the lions Nuru reported that, that morning, Elsa had growled at him repeatedly when he tried to follow her.

Obviously she wished him to remain behind, so she had trotted off quickly into the hills until he lost her tracks in the rocks. In the afternoon we followed her spoor, but soon lost it and could only call her from the foot of the cliffs. A reply came, a strange growl unlike Elsa's voice but undoubtedly that of a lion. Soon afterwards we saw her struggling downhill over the boulders, calling in her familiar way. When she reached us she flung herself exhausted onto the ground, panting and very excited. We had brought water with us and she could not have enough of it. Now we noticed several claw marks on her hind legs, shoulders and neck.

When she had assured herself of our admiration, she threw herself on the ground again and fell fast asleep for two hours. She had obviously just been with a lion when we had interfered by calling to her.

Two days later she spent a whole day and night away, and when we followed her spoor we found her in the company of a lioness, both having laid up several times together.

From this time onwards, Elsa spent more and more nights away. Sometimes she was away, without food or water, for two or three days. Water was still some hold over her, but soon the rains were due and we realized that when they came we should lose all control of her. This raised a problem which we had to solve; it was one which was made more urgent by the fact that our long overseas leave was due in May. Elsa was now twenty-seven months old, almost full grown. We had always known that we could not keep her free indefinitely at Isiolo. Our original idea had been to send her to join her sisters at the Rotterdam zoo, but because we had been so fortunate in bringing her up in her natural environment and because she seemed to be accepted by wild animals, we felt that she might well prove to be the exception to the rule that a pet will be killed by its own kind because of its human smell and ignorance of bush life. To release Elsa back to the wild would be an experiment well worth trying.

We intended to spend two or three more weeks with her, then, if all went well, we would take our long leave; this one is supposed to spend outside Kenya, in order to have a change of climate.

Next we had to consider *where* to release Elsa? Unfortunately Isiolo was far too populated for us to let her go wild there. But we knew of a game reserve which for most of the year was devoid of inhabitants and livestock but had an abundance of game, especially lion.

We received permission to take Elsa to this place and made the necessary arrangements. We would have to travel three hundred and forty miles, crossing the highlands on our way and also the great rift valley. The rains were expected any day, so we had no time to lose.

The First Release

It was after midnight when we had at last secured Elsa in her travelling crate and started off. In the hope of making the trip easier for her I gave her a tranquillizer; we had been told by the vet that the drug was harmless and that the effect would last about eight hours. To give Elsa all the moral support I could, I travelled with her in the open lorry. During the night we passed through country that is 8,000 feet above sea level, and the cold was icy. Owing to the effect of the tranquillizer, Elsa was only semiconscious, yet even in this state every few minutes she stretched her paws out through the bars of the crate, to assure herself that I was still there.

It took us seventeen hours to reach our destination, and the effect of the tranquillizer did not wear off until an hour after we had arrived. During these hours Elsa became very cold, her breathing was slow, and for a time I feared that she was going to die. This experience showed us that one should be very careful with drugs where lions are concerned, for they are far more sensitive to them than other animals.

It was late in the afternoon by the time we reached our destination; there we were met by a friend who was the game warden of this reserve. We pitched camp on a superb site at the base of a thousand-foot escarpment overlooking a vast plain of open bush country. As we were at an altitude of 5,000 feet, the air was fresh and brisk. Immediately in front of our camp lay open grassland sloping towards the plain, on which herds of Thomson's gazelle, topi, wildebeeste, Burchell's zebra, roan antelope, kongoni, and a few buffalo were grazing. It was a game paradise.

Our plan was this; we would spend the first week taking Elsa, perched on the roof of the Land-Rover, round the new country, thus getting her used to it. During the second week we intended to leave her overnight, and to visit and feed her in the mornings. Afterwards we would reduce her meals, in the hope that this would encourage her to kill on her own.

On the morning after our arrival we started our programme. First, we took off the collar she always wore, as a symbol of liberation. Elsa hopped onto the roof of the Land-Rover and we went off. After only a few hundred yards we saw a lioness walking parallel to us, downhill; we drove closer. Elsa displayed much excitement, jumped off her seat and, making low noises, cautiously followed this new friend. But as soon as the lioness stopped and turned round, her courage failed her and she raced back as fast as she could to the safety of the car.

We drove on and surprised a hyena chewing a bone. Elsa jumped off and chased the startled animal, who made good her escape but lost her bone in the process.

Later we passed through herd after herd of antelope, whose curiosity seemed to be aroused by the sight of a Land-Rover with a lion on it and who allowed us to approach within a few yards of them. All the time Elsa watched carefully, but did not attempt to leave the car unless she spotted an animal off guard, grazing with its back towards her, or fighting; then she would get down quietly and creep forward with her belly close to the ground, taking advantage of every bit of cover. But however cunning she was, she never got close enough to kill.

On another day, from the car, we watched a buffalo cantering across the plain. Quickly Elsa jumped to the ground and, using the cover of a bush, set out to stalk him. The buffalo had the same idea and also used this cover but starting from the opposite direction. We watched until we saw them nearly collide. Then it was the buffalo who bolted, with Elsa following him.

On another occasion, from her seat on the Land-Rover, she saw two buffaloes asleep in a bush. Off she went; bellows, crashing, and a wild commotion followed, then the buffaloes broke through the thicket and galloped away in different directions.

She loved climbing trees, and sometimes when we had looked in vain for her in the high grass we found her swaying in the crown of a tree. More than once she had difficulty in getting down again. Once, after trying various possibilities, and making the branch she was on bend alarmingly under her weight, we saw her tail dangling through the foliage, followed by her struggling hind legs, till finally she fell onto the grass well over twenty feet below. She was most embarrassed at having lost her dignity and walked quickly away from us, so we gave her time to regain her self-respect.

One morning we followed circling vultures and soon found a lion on a zebra kill. He was tearing at the meat and paid no attention to us. Elsa stepped cautiously from the car, miaowing at him and then, though she did not get any encouragement, advanced carefully towards him. At last the lion looked up and straight at Elsa. Evidently poor Elsa did not like this, for she returned as fast as she could to the safety of the car. The lion continued feeding and we watched him for a long time, hoping that Elsa might regain her courage; but nothing would induce her to leave her safe position.

Next morning we had better luck. We discovered a young lion resting in the high grass, sunning himself. He was a magnificent young male with a beautiful blond mane: just the right husband for Elsa, we thought. We drove to within thirty yards of him. The lion looked mildly surprised when he saw his prospective bride sitting on the top of a car, but responded in a friendly manner. Elsa, apparently overcome by coyness, made low moans but would not come off the roof. So we drove a little distance away and persuaded her to get down, then, suddenly, we left her and drove round to the other side of the lion: this meant that she would have to pass him in order to reach us. After much painful hesitation, she plucked up enough courage to walk towards the lion. When she was about ten paces away from him, she lay down with her ears back and her tail swishing. The lion got up and went towards her, with, I am sure, the friendliest intentions, but at the last moment Elsa panicked and rushed past to the car.

We drove away with her and, strangely enough, right into a pride of two lions and one lioness on a kill.

This was luck indeed. They must have killed very recently for they were so intent upon their meal that however much Elsa talked to them they paid not the slightest attention to her. Finally they left the kill, their bulging stomachs swinging from side to side. Elsa lost no time in inspecting the remains of the carcass, her first contact with a real kill. Nothing could have served our purpose better than this meal, provided by lions and full of their fresh scent. After Elsa had had her fair share, we dragged the kill back to the handsome young lion who had seemed so friendly. We hoped that if Elsa provided him with a meal he would have a favourable opinion of her. We found him still in the same place, so we left her and the kill near to him and drove away.

Early next morning, anxious to know the outcome of the experiment, we set off to visit her, hoping to find a happy pair. What we found was poor Elsa, waiting at the spot at which we had left her, but minus the lion and minus the kill. She was overjoyed to see us but when she had calmed down and even felt safe enough in our company to fall asleep, we decided, rather sadly, that we must break faith with her again and we sneaked away.

Till now we had always given her her meat already cut up, so that she should not associate her food with living animals. Now we needed to reverse our system, so during her midday sleep we drove sixty miles to shoot a small buck for her. We had to go this distance because no one was allowed to shoot game near the camp. We brought her a complete buck, wondering if she would know how to open it, since she had had no mother to teach her the proper way of doing it. We soon saw that by instinct she knew exactly what to do: she started at the inner part of the hind legs, where the skin is softest, then tore out the guts, and after enjoying these delicacies, buried the stomach contents and covered up the blood spoor, as all proper lions do. Then she gnawed the meat off the bones with her molars and rasped it away with her rough tongue.

It was time for us to let her do her own killing. The plain was covered with isolated bush clusters, ideal hideouts for any animal. All the lions had to do, when they wanted a meal, was to wait under cover until an antelope approached downwind, rush out and get their dinner.

We now left Elsa alone for two or three days at a time, hoping that hunger would make her kill. But when we came back we always found her waiting for us and hungry. It was heartbreaking having to stick to our programme, when obviously all she wanted was to be with us and sure of our affection. This she showed very clearly by sucking my thumbs and holding onto us with her paws. All the same we knew that for her own good we would have to persevere.

By now we realized that it was going to take us much longer to release her to nature than we had expected; we therefore asked the government if we could use our long leave in the country for the purpose of carrying out this experiment and, very kindly, they consented.

We now increased the number of days on which Elsa was left on her own. One evening, while sitting in our tent, we suddenly heard Elsa's miaow and before we could stop her, she crept in and settled down with us. She had walked eight miles back.

The next time we took her a longer distance away from camp.

As we drove we met two young lions sitting on the grass in the open. They looked to us ideal companions for Elsa, but by now she was very suspicious of our tricks and would not leave the car, although she talked very agitatedly to them; as we had no means of dropping her off we had to miss this opportunity and went on until we met two Thomson's gazelles fighting; this sight caused Elsa to jump off and we drove quickly away, leaving her to learn more about wildlife.

It was nearly a week before we returned. We found her waiting, and very hungry. We dropped some meat which we had brought with us and she immediately started to eat it. Suddenly we heard unmistakable growls and soon saw two lions trotting fast towards us. They were obviously on the hunt and probably they had scented the meat; they approached very quickly. Poor Elsa took in the situation, bolted hurriedly leaving her precious meal, and watched from a distance. In the circumstances it seemed hard that the two lions took no interest in anything but their food and completely ignored her. To compensate her for her disappointment we took her away.

While we were in camp we had some human visitors. Late one morning a Swiss couple, having heard that we had a lion cub, came to see it. I think they had visions of something small which could be picked up and cuddled, but seeing the three-hundred-odd-pound Elsa on the roof of the Land-Rover made them pause, and it was a little time before we could persuade them to get out of their car and join us at lunch. Elsa was courtesy itself, welcomed the strangers, and only once swept the table clear with her tail. After this, they could not have enough of her and had themselves photographed with her at every angle.

We had been in camp for four weeks and although Elsa had spent most of the last fortnight in the bush, she had not yet started killing for herself. By now, the rains had begun and every afternoon there were heavy showers. The conditions in this region were very different to those at Isiolo; for one thing it was much colder, for another while the ground at Isiolo is sandy and dries within a few hours, here there was black cotton-soil which turns into a morass after rain; moreover, it is covered with waist-high grass which prevents it drying for weeks on end. At home Elsa had enjoyed the rains, but here she was very miserable.

One night at least five inches came down before daybreak and the country was flooded. In the morning we waded out often knee-deep in mud, and we met Elsa already halfway back to the camp. She looked so unhappy and wanted so desperately to stay with us that we took her home. That evening we suddenly heard a terrified galloping come past our camp, followed by a stillness. What drama was happening outside? Next arose the hysterical chuckles of hyena mingled with the yells of jackal, but these were soon silenced by the growls of at least three lion. We realized that they must have killed just outside the camp. What a chance for Elsa. But while we listened, fascinated, to the deep guttural rumblings, she rubbed her head against us and showed how glad she was to be inside the thorn fence in our company.

After a few days the rain decreased and we renewed our efforts to turn Elsa into a wild lioness. But she had become so suspicious of being deserted that we decided to wait till she came into season again, then perhaps she would choose her own mate by mutual attraction.

Meanwhile we would concentrate our efforts on training her to kill her food and thus to become independent of us. The plains were still under water and most of the game had concentrated on the few bits of slightly higher ground, which were drier. Elsa loved one little hillock which was studded with rocks, and we therefore chose this place as her experimental headquarters.

We left Elsa on her hillock. Late that afternoon a deluge descended with such torrential force that soon our camp was in the middle of a running stream. For hours the flood continued. I imagined poor Elsa alone in this icy night; thunder and lightning added to my nightmare. Next morning we waded to the ridge where we had left her. As usual, she was waiting for us, overjoyed to see us and we decided that, though it would interrupt her education, we could not leave her out in such weather. Unlike the local lions, used to this climate, she came from semi-desert country and could not quickly adapt herself to very different conditions.

Next day she was ill. When she moved she was in great pain, her glands were swollen and she had a temperature. We made her a bed of grass in the annexe to George's tent and there she lay, panting, listless and pathetic. I treated her with M and B, the only drug which I thought might help. She wanted me near her all the time, which, of course, I was.

We believed that she had become infected by some local tick-borne virus. If this proved true it would suggest that an animal, immune to diseases in its own environment, when transferred to another does not carry the same immunity to local strains.

Elsa became so ill that for a time we did not think that she would recover. Her coat was dull, like cotton wool, and she developed many white hairs on her back. Her face became ash grey. She had difficulty in dragging herself from the tent into the sparse sunshine; the only hopeful sign was her appetite. We gave her as much meat and milk as she wanted although both had to be fetched from a long distance. We also succeeded, in spite of the transport difficulties arising from the weather, in corresponding regularly with the veterinary laboratory in Nairobi, but as no sign of a parasite was found in the samples we provided we had to treat her more or less by guesswork.

During her illness, because she lived so intimately with us, Elsa became more dependent on us and tamer than ever. It was now five weeks since her illness had started, and her condition had improved only slightly. It was plain that the climate in this region was against her. In every way she belonged to the semi-desert and not to the highlands. Also, being in a game reserve meant that George had to go twenty miles by car to shoot meat for her outside the reserve; nor could he take Elsa hunting with him and thereby give her the opportunity of being in at the kill and getting the feel of pulling down a live animal—an experience which, in her wild state,

The cubs at seven weeks old (below) with Pati, their self-appointed nanny. Pati had a weakness for spirits and whenever possible would make straight for the whisky bottle (right).

Elsa and her sisters at six months old (above). One of their favourite games was playing with a hessian bag filled with inner tubes (left). Elsa loved water, and her trip to the Indian ocean was a great success (right). At Lake Rudolf (below right) she strode into the water, ignoring the crocodiles.

Game Scouts offer a catfish to Elsa by Lake Rudolf (left). Elsa (above) sharing an affectionate moment with Joy and (right) interrupting George.

KGR 608

Elsa on the Land-Rover (far left) and standing on her favourite rock (inset). She enjoyed going fishing with George (above) and would carry home the catch; at night she slept by his camp bed, often putting out a paw to make sure he was still there.

A morning walk (above) was part of Elsa's routine. It was a great achievement for Elsa when she overpowered a bull buffalo and dragged him into the river (above right). During her releases into the wild she was always pleased to see the Adamsons, and made herself at home in the camp.

The first sight of Elsa's cubs was when she brought them across the river (far left) to see Joy.

Elsa and the cubs were often seen near the river (above) and came to the camp for food (below).

Jespah, Gopa and Little Elsa. The inset shows two of the cubs alerted by nearby game.

Elsa and her family relax by the river.

The three cubs take an evening drink (above). Joy lights the candles for Christmas (left) with Jespah looking on.

she would have gained from her mother. It was evident therefore that after having camped here for three months we would have to try to choose a better home for her.

It was not easy to find an area which had a suitable climate, permanent water, enough game to supply her with food, and no tribesmen or hunting parties; moreover, it needed to be accessible by car. Eventually we discovered such a paradise and received the government's permission to release a lion there. As soon as the rains ceased we decided to go there. Although, up to now, there was no record of a hand-reared lion being successfully liberated, we still hoped that Elsa would be able to adapt herself to wild life, a life to which she had always been so close.

The Second Release

Elsa's new home was truly remote. To reach an ideal campsite, George and the boys cut a new track through thick bush; it took them four days. Our final camp was on a beautiful river lined by walls of doum palms, acacias and fig trees. The water rushed foaming and bubbling through rapids, passed between islands covered with reeds, and in the further reaches calmed into many rockbound pools of cool, clear water, deep enough to hold many fish. It was a fisherman's paradise and George could not wait to set out his rod.

The country was quite different from the region we had left. It was much hotter; there were no great herds of game grazing peacefully on grassy plains. When we left the lush tropical greenery, which was confined to the river banks, there was only thornbush, with visibility reduced to a few yards—a hunter's nightmare. But it was only thirty-five miles from Elsa's birthplace and was the type of country that was natural to her.

The great attraction of the place was a huge ridge of reddish rock with cliffs and caves, in whose shadows we saw hyrax dashing about. It was an ideal lion's home, with a splendid lookout. From its top, we watched giraffe, waterbuck, lesser kudu, gerenuk and bushbuck moving towards the river which was their life artery in this otherwise waterless semi-desert country. We called the crest the Big Rock and it soon became Elsa's favourite retreat.

Either as a result of our treatment or owing to the change in climate, Elsa's condition improved daily, so we were able to re-start her education. Every morning as soon as it got light we took Elsa for a walk, and again in the afternoon. These walks, which took us along the numerous game paths and sandy watercourses, were full of interest. Elsa loved them; she sniffed and followed the spoor of animals which had been there during the previous night.

Here too, unlike the first place to which we had taken her, Elsa was able to go out hunting with George. We both hate killing animals, but now we had to make some sacrifices to Elsa's education, and knowing that in her natural state she would have been killing them on her own account appeased our qualms. The sooner she learned to do it properly, the better for all concerned. For the present she would have to stalk her quarry, then, if she were not able to kill, George would bring the animal down with a bullet and leave her to give the coup de grace. After this she would be left to protect her kill against vultures, hyenas and lions, and in this way would meet these animals in natural circumstances.

We heard several lion close to the camp and often saw their pugmarks.

One morning a waterbuck offered an excellent opportunity for initiating Elsa into killing. George shot it, but before it fell Elsa jumped at its throat and hung on like a bulldog until in a few minutes the animal died. It was her first experience of killing a large animal. Now she seized the buck by the neck, and straddling it between her forepaws, dragged it into a shady thicket some fifty yards away. One frequently hears stories of lion carrying their victims away by swinging them across their backs, but neither George nor I have ever seen a lion act in this way; they always drag anything large in the way which Elsa did on this occasion.

We left her there to guard her kill from vultures and hyena. When it became dark she did not return, but about three am we were awakened by a heavy cloudburst and soon after this she appeared and spent the rest of the night in camp.

Early in the morning we all went out to see what had happened to her kill. Of course it had disappeared, and the ground was patterned with lion and hyena spoor. Nearby, we heard some lion grunts; these made us wonder whether it was the rain or the lions which had made Elsa leave her kill during the night.

Although Elsa's health had greatly improved, she was still far from her usual self and preferred to spend most of her day in camp. In order to break this habit and to make her lie up in the cool shade of the river, George took her out fishing with him. She would watch intently for the slightest ripple in the water and as soon as he hooked a fish she plunged in to retrieve the wriggling creature. This new game was great fun, but we needed to find another device to attract her away from the camp.

Close to the river stood a magnificent tree, its branches nearly sweeping the water. Under its green canopy, protected by its cool shade and subdued light from the glaring sun, I felt as though I were under a dome. Here, concealed by the low branches, I watched many wild creatures come to the river to drink: kudu and bushbuck, storks and baboons. Sitting there with Elsa close to me, I felt as though I were on the doorstep of paradise; man and beast in trusting harmony, the slow-flowing river adding to the idyll. I thought that this place would make a stimulating "studio" for me to paint or write in, so we improvised a table and bench, and soon I began to work there.

Standing on her hind legs, Elsa inspected my paintbox and typewriter suspiciously; then she settled down at my feet and I began, full of inspiration; but I had not reckoned with our audience. As soon as I tried to concentrate I heard the inquiring bark of a baboon peeping through the foliage; then the bush on the opposite bank became alive with inquisitive watching faces. Soon they came more into the open, swinging from tree to tree, screaming and barking, hopping and swaying in the treetops until one little chap fell with a splash into the river. At once an old baboon came to its rescue, and clutching the wet, struggling creature, raced off with it to safety. At this, the screeching was deafening. Elsa, who could tolerate the noise no longer, plunged into the river and swam across. As soon as she had reached firm ground she jumped at the nearest of the little tormentors. He swung tantalizingly low but nimbly avoided her. The others joined in the game, and the more infuriated Elsa became, the more they enjoyed teasing her.

After this the baboons looked every day for Elsa, and both sides got to know each other very well. As she took to ignoring their provocations they grew bolder and bolder. Often they squatted for their daily drink at the edge of the rapids, separated from her by only a few yards of water. One would keep sentry duty while the others slowly drank their fill.

Our idyll would have been perfect if Elsa had not been a carnivore who had to be trained to kill. Every day a buffalo approached our camp, until one morning he became a victim: George shot him. Although he was dead long before Elsa arrived, she went wild with excitement—indeed, she got far more worked up over this carcass than we had ever seen her before at a kill. She pounced madly on the dead buffalo, attacking from every side and turning somersaults across the body. Finally she tapped the buffalo on the nose with her paw to make sure that he was dead.

George's main purpose in shooting such a big beast had been to attract wild lion. We hoped that if they came, Elsa could join in the feast and make friends with them. In order to control whatever might happen, we decided to secure the carcass with a chain to a tree close to the camp and then leave Elsa in charge of it. She guarded it jealously during the whole of the following day and night. Judging by the never-ending chorus of high-pitched chuckles from hyena, she was kept very busy after dark but next morning when we returned she was still protecting the carcass. Only then did she leave it, making it very plain that it was now *our* turn to be on guard while she trotted away to the river.

After a short time she spotted a hyena making its way slowly towards the kill. Immediately she froze, then, with the utmost caution, lowered herself into the straw-coloured grass till she was almost invisible, and watched the hyena hobbling peacefully along. When it came to within a few yards, Elsa rushed forward and gave it a well-aimed smack. With a yell the animal rolled over and lay on its back emitting howls and long-drawn moans. Elsa looked at us, then started licking her paws and appeared utterly bored by the miserable creature in front of her. Gradually the hyena pulled itself together and eventually, still whining protests, sneaked away.

Although Elsa had no mother to teach her, she knew by instinct how far she could go with wild animals. Many times on our walks through the bush we watched her sniffing the air and then stalking determinedly in one direction until we heard the crashing of big bodies breaking through the woods. On several occasions she detected rhino and chased them away from us; in fact she was an excellent watchdog.

One morning George shot a waterbuck which was standing in the river. Badly hit, it dashed across to the opposite side, followed by Elsa, who splashed unbelievably fast through the deep water. When we arrived at the other bank we found her amongst the river bush, panting, on top of the dead buck. She was very excited and did not allow us to touch her kill. So we decided to return home and leave her to guard it. As soon as we started wading back through the water she began to follow us, but seemed torn between conflicting impulses: she did not want to be left on the wrong side of the river with her kill, on the other hand she did not want to lose it. Eventually she returned to it, and now we saw her dragging the buck into the water. What was she up to? Surely she could not bring this heavy animal across alone? But Elsa was not going to be defeated. She held the carcass in her mouth and swam with it through the deep water, her head often submerged to get a better grip. She hauled and tugged, pushed and pulled, and often disappeared from view. After half an hour of strenuous effort, she trailed her quarry proudly through the shallow water into a little sheltered bay where the current could not carry it away.

We left her with her kill and went back to camp to have our overdue breakfast. Although we had left the kill fairly near the camp, we soon heard her dragging it along with the intention, no doubt, of bringing it inside. We quickly closed the thorn fence, locking her out with her smelly buck. Poor Elsa; the best thing she could do now was to place it against the outside of the thorn fence and this she did.

One day we were very tired and I was walking along absentmindedly behind Elsa. Suddenly she reared up on her hind legs and leaped back. We were passing a tree which forked about five feet above the ground and now coiled up in it I saw a red cobra, erecting its hood. Thanks to Elsa, nothing happened, but to pass a cobra at such close range might have been serious. It was the first time I had seen one in a tree. Even Elsa was impressed, and during the next few days she made a careful detour whenever we came near to that tree.

At this time it was very hot and Elsa spent much of her time in the river. Often she stood half submerged in the cool water; although we often saw crocodiles, they never seemed to worry her. Whenever George shot a guinea fowl near the river, Elsa retrieved it from the water and used its rescue as an excuse for prolonged splashings with the bird in her mouth; she enjoyed the game just as much as we loved watching her.

She had now completely recovered and was perfectly fit. She was very conservative in her habits and except for slight variations our routine was the same every day: an early-morning walk, followed by her midday slumber close to me by our tree on the river bank. This lasted until teatime, then came our afternoon stroll. On our return she found her meal waiting for her; she usually carried it onto the roof of the Land-Rover, where she remained until the lights were put out and everybody went to bed. Then she joined George in his tent, sleeping next to his bed on the ground, a paw always in touch with him.

One afternoon Elsa refused to come for a walk. When we returned after dark she had disappeared and did not return until early next morning. Later we found large pugmarks close to camp, and when she came back I again noticed the peculiar smell which was typical of her being in season.

We knew now by experience that this period lasted about four days. The right moment seemed to have come, so we decided to withdraw tactfully and leave her alone—we hoped in the company of a mate. We had to act quickly. In order to avoid her seeing our departure we arranged that, while I looked after her, George would break camp, drive the loaded cars a distance of about one mile, and send a message to me to join him when everything was ready.

I took Elsa away from the camp to our tree. Would this be the last time we should see it together? She knew something was wrong; and, though I tried to keep to our normal routine and had taken the typewriter along, she was not reassured, nor could I type properly for I was too upset. Although we had prepared ourselves for this release and hoped it might give Elsa a happier future than she would have living in captivity, it was a different matter when it came to making the break. Elsa must have felt my emotion for she rubbed her silky head against me.

The river flowed slowly in front of us, as it had flowed yesterday and it would flow tomorrow. A hornbill called, some dry leaves fell off the tree and were carried away by the water. Elsa was part of this life. She belonged to nature. I had just given her a kiss to give her a feeling of security, but was it a kiss of betrayal? How could she know that it needed all the strength of my love for her to leave her now and give her back to nature?

Nuru came and called me away. He had brought some meat along and Elsa followed him trustfully into the reeds and started to eat—then we stole away.

The Final Test

We drove ten miles to another river where we intended to spend a week. Late in the afternoon George and I strolled along the bank; we walked quietly, our thoughts with Elsa. I felt desperately lonely. I realized acutely how much I had become dependent on her; how for nearly three years I had shared her feelings, interests and reactions. We had lived so intimately together that being alone seemed unbearable.

Suddenly George stopped, pointing ahead, and we sank to the ground. A kudu advanced towards us, nibbling gracefully at the young buds of the undergrowth. Then it stopped grazing, lifted its head and looked cautiously around. Its perfect proportions, its exquisite body-markings and white stripes and the magnificently shaped horns make this antelope one of nature's masterpieces. We watched the kudu with intense pleasure while it browsed slowly from bush to bush till it eventually disappeared.

The sun was sinking now, and its warm light was reflected on the shiny fronds of the doum palms, tinting their tops with a golden glow.

Again I thought of Elsa—what a beautiful world she had been born into. Whatever losing her might mean to me, we had to try our utmost to give her back to this life.

At last, the week of anxiety ended and we went back to see how Elsa had stood up to the test.

When we arrived at our former camp, we looked at once for her pugmarks; there was no sign of them. I began to call. Soon afterwards we heard her familiar "hnk-hnk" and saw her coming from the river, trotting as fast as she could. Her welcome showed us that she had missed us as much as we had missed her. We had brought her a buck, but she hardly glanced at it and continued her greetings. I looked at her stomach: it was full. This took a great load off my mind for it meant that she was now safe. She had proved that she could fend for herself and be independent of us, at least so far as food was concerned.

While our tents were being pitched I took her to the river and there we rested together. I was happy now and could relax, feeling that Elsa's future was assured. She must have felt the same, for she laid her big soft paw on me and dozed off.

Now that our minds were at ease regarding Elsa's future, we decided to wait till an opportunity occurred of making the final break in some way which would not be too painful. We took up our life where we had left it off. Although Elsa seldom let us out of her sight, we thought it a good omen that she continued to follow her hunting instinct.

To make her more independent of our camp life we regularly took her out for the whole day. After an early-morning walk of two or three hours we would settle down in a shady place along the river. We picnicked and I took out my sketchbook. Elsa soon dozed off and I often used her as a pillow when I read or slept. George spent more of the time fishing and usually produced our lunch straight out of the river. Nuru and the gun bearer proved to be excellent chefs and roasted our meal as soon as it had been caught.

These excursions brought all of us much closer together and even Nuru and the gun bearer felt so much at ease in Elsa's presence that they did not bother to get up when she strolled over to them for a nose-rubbing or sat on them, in her playful way. Nor did they mind sharing the back of the Land-Rover with her and when she dumped her three hundred pounds between their bony legs, they only laughed and petted her, while she licked their knees with her rough tongue.

By now, Elsa's fame had spread far and wide and a party of American sportsmen paid us a visit specially to film her. She entertained them royally and did everything she could to please them. She climbed a tree, played in the river, hugged me, joined us for tea and behaved in such a docile manner that none of our guests could believe that she was a full-grown lioness, who shortly before they arrived had been equally at ease in the company of wild lions.

Early one morning when we were out on our pre-breakfast walk, Elsa took the lead and with great determination headed in a set direction, leaving us behind. A few moments later, in the far distance, we heard the faint call of a lion. She stayed away all that day. Late in the evening we heard her call a long way off mingled with that of another lion. During the night, hyena were much in evidence and kept us awake with their inane laughter. She did not return until early on the fifth morning, when she was very hungry and ate until her belly was near to bursting. After that, she retired to my camp bed and made it clear that she was not to be disturbed. In the afternoon, she did not want to go for a walk and sat on the roof of the Land-Rover until dark, then she disappeared into the night. Some two hours later we heard a lion's roar in the distance and Elsa's immediate reply.

She was away for two days. During this time she returned for one brief visit to George's tent, when she was most affectionate and nearly broke his camp bed by sitting on top of him as he lay asleep. After a short meal, she went off again, and kept away for three more days, returning each evening for a few minutes just to show us her affection, but going off again without touching the meat which was ready for her. When she returned after such escapades she always seemed more affectionate than ever, as though she wished to make up for having neglected us.

The rains had started and after the first downpour the dry, grey thornbush changed within a few days into a Garden of Eden. Every grain of sand seemed to give way to a seed bursting up from beneath. We walked along tracks of luxuriant sap-green growth; each bush a giant bouquet of white, pink or yellow blossom. There were rain pools everywhere and near each was a concentration of freshly marked game tracks. Elsa would often leave us to go hunting.

One morning we were walking quietly along the river, intending to spend the day out; Elsa was with us, full of energy and, judging by the twitching of her tail, was having a wonderful time. After walking for two hours I saw her stop abruptly, her ears cocked and her body tense. The next moment she was off, jumping noiselessly down the rocks which flank the river at this point; then she disappeared into the thick undergrowth below. Then came—as I thought—the unmistakable sound of elephant trumpeting. George disagreed, saying that the noise was made by a buffalo. He leaped down the rocks, saying that Elsa was in trouble. I followed, as fast as I could, but was brought to a halt by a fresh outburst of violent bellowings just ahead. When I finally broke through the bush to the river bank, what I saw was Elsa, dripping wet, sitting on top of a bull buffalo in the middle of the rapids. His head was half submerged, while Elsa tore away at his thick skin and attacked from every angle. Elsa must have disturbed the buffalo, an old bull past his prime, and chased him towards the river. Then in his attempt to cross, he must have fallen on the slippery rock of the rapids; and Elsa had taken advantage of his predicament, jumped on him and held his head under water until he was half drowned and too exhausted to get up.

Even for a wild lion, it would have been a remarkable achievement to kill a buffalo bull single-handed, let alone for Elsa, who had only recently learned the art of hunting from her very inferior foster-parents, and I felt very proud of her.

Not long afterwards we were again walking together along the shady river bank when Elsa sniffed with great interest at a bush and wrinkled up her nose, a thing she often did when scenting a lion. Now we saw fresh pugmarks nearby and Elsa, who was purring distinctly, followed the spoor and disappeared. She kept away all night and the following day. When, in the afternoon, we looked for her, we detected her through field glasses outlined on her favourite rock. It was a splendid place where she found the breeze cool, where no tsetse fly molested her and from which she could watch the animals below. She must have spotted us, but she made no attempt to move from her position. Thinking she might be near wild lions, we did not want to interfere, and returned home.

While we were having our dinner next evening, she walked into the tent, rubbed her head affectionately against me and then went out and spent the night away. In the morning we tracked her spoor over a long distance; it led far away. That evening she failed to come back and during the night we were awakened by the most alarming lion growls mixed with the laughing of hyenas. We listened, expecting Elsa to come in at any moment, but morning dawned and she did not return. As soon as it became light we went in the direction from which the growls had come, but stopped after a few hundred yards, startled by an unmistakable lion grunt coming from the river below us. Creeping cautiously through thick undergrowth down to the river, we found the fresh pugmarks of at least three lions in the sand; they led across the river. Wading through, we were following the still wet spoor up to the opposite bank, when through the dense bush I noticed the shape of a lion not fifty yards away. It was Elsa. George called to her. She walked away from us. When George repeated his call she only trotted faster along the game path until we saw the black tuft on the end of her tail switch for the last time through the bush.

We looked at each other. Had she found her destiny? She must have heard us; by following the lions she had decided her future. Did this mean that our hopes for her to return to her natural life had been fulfilled?

We returned to camp alone.

Elsa's Cubs

To us it seemed impossible, after more than three years of such close companionship, that we should lose all touch with Elsa, so long as she was willing to keep in touch with us.

As George, in the course of his duties, was constantly travelling, we endeavoured to pay a visit to the area where Elsa lived at intervals of about three weeks. On arrival in camp we always fired a shot or two or let off a thunderflash, and on nearly every occasion she came running into camp within a few hours, giving us a great welcome and showing more affection than ever.

The months went by. Towards the end of August, when she would again be in season, George was obliged to go on his own to Elsa's area for game control and arrived at six pm at her camp to spend the night there. He fired off two thunderflashes to attract her attention. At about eight pm he heard a lion downriver and let off another thunderflash. The lion continued to call throughout the night, but there was no sign of Elsa. Next morning George found the pugmarks of a young lion or lioness close to camp. He had to leave immediately afterwards but returned at four pm. An hour later Elsa came across the river, looking very fit and full of affection. Although she was not hungry, she ate a little of the buck which George had brought her and then dragged the carcass into the tent. Soon after dark a lion began to call. Much to George's surprise she completely ignored the invitation which continued throughout most of the night.

Early next morning she had a hearty meal and then, without any show of hurry, disappeared in the direction from which the lion had called. Guessing the direction she had taken, George followed and found her tracks heading for the river. Presently he saw her sitting on a rock almost hidden by bush. She seemed very restless. First she miaowed, then with a startled "whuff-whuff" dashed down the rock, and next moment a young lion appeared, evidently in hot pursuit. George withdrew and moved camp.

When on his return to Isiolo he told me what he had seen, I could hardly bear not to start off for the camp alone, for I was afraid that Elsa might now follow her mate into a world beyond our reach.

But when we arrived she was there waiting for us by her favourite rock. She was very affectionate and also very hungry.

That night she slept in front of my tent, but just before dawn her lion started calling and she went off in his direction.

Their calls were easy to distinguish; Elsa had a very deep guttural voice, but after her initial roar only gave two or three whuffing grunts, whereas her lion's voice was less deep and after his roar he always gave at least ten or twelve grunts.

During Elsa's absence we broke camp and left for Isiolo hoping that she was in the company of her mate.

Three weeks later we were able to return: an hour after our arrival we saw her swimming across the river to greet us, but instead of the exuberant welcome she usually gave us, she walked slowly up to me. She did not seem to be hungry and was exceptionally gentle and quiet.

Patting her, I noticed that her skin had become extremely soft and her coat unusually glossy. I saw, too, that her nipples were very large. She was pregnant. There was no doubt about it. She had conceived a month ago.

It is widely believed that a pregnant lioness who is handicapped in hunting by her condition is helped by one or two other lionesses who act as "aunts". They are also supposed to assist in looking after the newborn cubs, for the male is not of much practical use on such occasions, and indeed is often not allowed near the young lions for some weeks.

Since poor Elsa had no "aunts", it would be our job to replace them. George and I talked over plans to help to feed her and avoid any risk of her injuring herself during her pregnancy. I was to spend as much time in camp as I could spare from Isiolo and, at the nearest game-scout post, some twenty-five miles away, we would establish a herd of goats from which I could collect a few in my truck at regular intervals. Nuru would remain with me to help with Elsa, and George would visit us as often as his work allowed.

During the following days Elsa shared her time between her mate and me. On our last night in camp Elsa made a terrific meal of goat and then, very heavy in the belly, went to join her lion who had been calling for her for many hours. Her absence gave us an opportunity to leave for Isiolo.

In the second week of November we were on our way back to Elsa. She seemed very fit and was not hungry. She left at dawn, but returned at teatime when we were setting out for our walk. We climbed up Elsa's big rock and sat watching the sun sink like a fireball behind the indigo hills.

At first Elsa blended into the warm reddish colour of the rock as if she were part of it, then she was silhouetted against the fading sky in which a full moon was rising. Instinctively I stretched my hand towards her; she belonged to this world and only through her were we allowed to glance into a paradise which we had lost. I imagined Elsa in the future playing with her cubs on this rock. Carefully I laid my hand below her ribs to feel whether any life were moving within her, but she pushed it away making me feel as though I had committed an indiscretion.

Soon we had to return to camp, to the lamps and rifles with which we armed ourselves against those dark hours in which Elsa's real life began. This was the moment we parted, each to return to our own world.

We wanted to help Elsa through her pregnancy by providing her with regular food, but we did not wish to interfere with her relations with her mate by our continued presence in the camp. He had a good right to resent this, but did he in fact object to us? On the whole, we thought that he did not, and I think we were justified in our opinion for, during the next six months, though we did not see him, we often heard his characteristic whuffing grunts and recognized his spoor, which proved that he remained Elsa's constant companion. In view of his attitude we stilled our qualms of conscience and stayed on.

It was now nearly mid-December and we believed that the cubs might arrive at any moment.

Elsa was so heavy that every movement seemed to require an effort; if she had been living a normal life she would certainly have taken exercise, so I did my best to make her go for walks with me, but she kept close to the tents. We wondered what place she would choose for her delivery and even thought that since she had always considered our tent as her safest "den" the cubs might be born in it.

The river was now in flood and George and I decided to walk three miles downstream to look at some cataracts which are very impressive when the water is high. Elsa watched our departure from the top of the Land-Rover. She made no attempt to join us and looked sleepy.

The cataracts were a magnificent sight, the foaming water cascading through the gorges, thundering across the rocks and then flooding out into deep whirlpools.

On our way back, we soon saw Elsa trotting along the path as quickly as she could to join us. I was very touched that she had made the effort, the more so since though her lion had roared desperately for her during the whole of the previous night and had gone on doing so until nine in the morning, she had made no attempt to join him.

This was very gratifying but it also reminded us of our fear that her lion might get tired of sharing her with us. It had taken us a very long time to find a mate for her; it would be unforgivable if our interference now caused him to leave her. We wanted her cubs to grow up as wild lions, and to do this they needed their father.

We decided to go away for three days. It was of course a risk, for the cubs might be born during this time and Elsa might need us, but we thought the danger that her lion might desert her the greater of the two evils—so we left.

We returned on the 16th of December and found a very hungry Elsa waiting for us. For two days she remained in camp; she did, however, to our surprise, take a few short walks, always to the Big Rock, but returned quickly. She ate ravenously and we felt that she was stocking up a reserve for the days that lay ahead.

The next day when George and I went for a walk Elsa followed us, but she had to sit down at intervals panting and was plainly in great discomfort. When we saw this we turned back and walked very slowly. Suddenly to our astonishment she turned off into the bush in the direction of the Big Rock.

She did not return during that night, but in the morning we spotted her through our field glasses. She was standing on the Big Rock and from her silhouette we saw that she was still pregnant.

We climbed up and found her lying close to a large boulder which stood at the top of a wide cleft in the rock; near to it there was some grass and a small tree providing shade. This place had always been one of Elsa's favourite lookouts and we felt that it would make an ideal nursery, since inside the cleft was a rainproof and well-protected cave.

We left her to take the initiative and presently she came slowly towards us, walking very carefully and obviously in pain. She greeted us very affectionately, but when I came near her she got up and moved to the edge of the rock, and remained there with her head turned away from us, making it plain that she wished to be left alone.

We went a short distance away and for half an hour watched her through our field glasses. She rolled from side to side, and moaned repeatedly. Suddenly she rose, went very carefully down the steep rock face and disappeared into the thick bush at its base.

Since there was nothing we could do to help her, we went back to camp. After dark we heard her lion calling; there was no reply.

I lay awake most of the night thinking about her. When, towards morning, it started to rain my anxiety increased and I could hardly bear to wait till it was light to go out and try to discover what had happened.

Very early, George and I set out; first we followed the spoor of Elsa's lion. He had been close to the camp, then he had walked to the rock near to the place where we had seen Elsa disappear.

We wondered what we should do next. We did not want our curiosity to bring any risk to the cubs and we were aware that captive lionesses who have been disturbed soon after giving birth to cubs have been known to kill their young. We also thought that her lion might be very near, so we decided to stop our search; instead George went off and shot a large waterbuck to provide Elsa and her mate with plenty of food.

I, in the meantime, climbed the Big Rock and waited for an hour, listening for any sound which might give us a clue to Elsa's whereabouts. I strained my ears but all was still; finally I could bear the suspense no longer and called. There was no answer. Was Elsa dead?

Hoping that the lion's spoor might lead us to her we took up his tracks where we had left them and traced them till they reached a dry watercourse near the rock. There we left him some meat, thinking that if he came for it this might help us to find Elsa.

During the night we heard him roaring in the distance and were therefore surprised next morning to find his pugmarks close to the camp. He had not taken any of the meat. We felt it would be unwise to continue our search so went back to camp and left three new lots of meat in different places before night fell.

As soon as it was light we went to inspect the deposits; all of them had been taken by hyenas.

By the river we found the spoor of Elsa's mate, but there was no sign of her pugmarks. Again we put out meat close to the rock and near to the camp. In the morning we found that Elsa's lion had eaten some of it, while the rest had been disposed of by hyenas.

It was now four days since we had seen Elsa and six since she had eaten anything. We believed that she had given birth to the cubs on the night of the 20th of December and we did not think that it could be a coincidence that her lion, who had not been about for days, had reappeared on that night and remained close to the rock ever since.

On Christmas Eve George went to get a goat while I continued the fruitless search and called to Elsa without getting any answer.

It was with a heavy heart that I prepared our little Christmas tree, complete with glittering tinsel branches, sparkling decorations and candles. I placed it on a table outside the tents which I had covered with flowers and greenery. Then I collected the presents which I had brought for our African servants and the sealed envelopes containing money for them on which I had painted a Christmas-tree branch.

I changed quickly into a frock and by then it was dark enough to light the candles. I called the men, who came dressed up for the occasion, grinning but a little shy, for never before had they seen a Christmas tree of this kind. I must admit that I myself was deeply moved when I saw the little silver tree sparkling in the vast darkness of the surrounding bush, bringing the message of the birth of Christ.

Early on Christmas morning we went in search of Elsa. We followed the lion's spoor across the river, and again screened the bush all round the spot to which he had dragged the waterbuck. After hours of fruitless tracking we came back for breakfast.

Later we set out once more for the rocky range; something seemed to tell us that if Elsa were still alive that was where she would be. When we were all tired out we sat down to rest in the shade of an overhanging rock and discussed every possible fate which might have overtaken Elsa. We were very depressed and even Nuru spoke in a subdued voice.

At midday we returned to camp and began a very gloomy and silent Christmas meal.

Suddenly there was a swift movement and, before I could take in what was happening, Elsa was between us sweeping everything off the table, knocking us to the ground, sitting on us and overwhelming us with joy and affection.

Her figure was normal again, she looked superbly fit but her teats were very small. Had the cubs died? And if so, why had she waited for five days before coming to us for food?

After she had had a good meal and drunk some water she rubbed her head affectionately against us, walked about thirty yards down the river, lay down and had a doze. We left her alone, so that she should feel at ease. When I looked for her at teatime she had gone.

We followed her spoor for a short way; it led towards the rock range, but we soon lost it and returned none the wiser about her cubs. However, now that we were reassured about Elsa our morale was restored.

Next day we began to worry about the cubs. If they *were* alive, was their mother able to suckle them? We felt we simply had to know about the cubs and rescue them if necessary. So the next morning we searched for five hours, but we did not find so much as a dropping or a crushed leaf to show where Elsa's nursery was.

We carried on equally unsuccessfully in the afternoon. Back at the camp, however, we found that Elsa had arrived.

She was most affectionate to us and although we were alarmed to observe that her teats were still small and dry, one of the boys assured us that when she had arrived they and her milk glands had been enormous, hanging low and swinging from side to side. She had, he said, "tucked them up", and told us that if a lioness could not do this she would be greatly handicapped by her heavy undercarriage, and besides this her teats might be injured by the thorny bush.

Meanwhile Elsa, having eaten enormously and methodically cleaned up every scrap, much to our relief disappeared into the dark. We were now convinced that she was looking after her cubs.

On our next visit we hooted several times before we reached camp to let Elsa know we were arriving. We found her waiting for us on top of a large boulder at the point where the track passes the Big Rock. She hopped in among the boys at the back of the Land-Rover, then she went to the trailer in which there was a dead goat. I had rarely seen her so hungry.

After she had spent seven hours in camp, however, we thought this a bad sign and began to be afraid that she no longer had any cubs to look after. She only left us at two in the morning.

Very early we set out and followed her spoor which led towards the Big Rock. As we called loudly, she suddenly appeared out of a cluster of bush only twenty yards away. She kept silent and very still as though hoping we would not come nearer. Then, after a few moments, she walked up to us and was very affectionate. But soon she went slowly back to the bush and stood, for about five minutes, with her back turned towards us. Then she sat down, still with her back turned to us. It was as though she wanted to say to us: "Here my private world begins and you must not trespass."

It was a dignified demonstration and no words could have conveyed her wishes more clearly.

We sneaked away as quietly as we could, and decided that we must respect Elsa's wishes and not try to see the cubs until she brought them to us, which we felt sure she would do one day. I determined to stay on in camp in order to provide her with food, so that she would have no need to leave her family unguarded for long periods while she went out hunting for them. We also decided to take her meals to her, so as to reduce the time during which she had to desert the cubs.

We put our plan into immediate operation and that afternoon went by car close to her lie-up. We knew that Elsa would associate the vibrations of the engine with us and with food.

Soon she came, was as affectionate as usual and ate a lot. While she had her head in a basin, which we had sunk in the ground to keep it steady, and was busy drinking, we went off. She looked round when she heard the engine start but made no move to follow us.

During the following days I went on taking food to the spot near to where we believed the cubs were. Whenever I met Elsa on these occasions, she took great pains to conceal the whereabouts of her lie-up, often doubling back on her tracks, no doubt to puzzle me.

One afternoon in early February while I was writing in the studio, the servants came running to tell me that Elsa was calling in a very strange voice from the other side of the river. I went upstream, following the sound, till I broke through the undergrowth at a place where in the dry season there is a fairly wide sandbank on our side and on the other a dry watercourse which drops abruptly into the river.

Suddenly I stopped, unable to believe my eyes.

There was Elsa standing on the sandbank within a few yards of me, one cub close to her, a second cub emerging from the water shaking itself dry and the third one still on the far bank, pacing to and fro and calling piteously. Elsa looked fixedly at me, her expression a mixture of pride and embarrassment.

I remained absolutely still while she walked up to the landing cub, licked it affectionately, then turned back to me and began rolling on her back and showing her affection; it seemed that she wanted to prove to her cubs that I was part of the pride and could be trusted.

Reassured, the two cubs crept cautiously closer and closer, till they were within three feet of me. I found it difficult to restrain an impulse to lean forward and touch them, but I remembered the warning a zoologist had given me: never touch cubs unless they take the initiative, and this three-foot limit seemed to be an invisible boundary which they felt that they must not cross.

While all this was happening the third cub kept up a pathetic miaowing from the far bank, appealing for help.

Elsa watched it for a time, then she walked to the water's edge, at the point at which the river was narrowest. With the two brave cubs beside her she called to the timid one to join them. But its only response was to pace nervously up and down; it was too frightened to try to cross.

When Elsa saw it so distressed she went to its rescue accompanied by the two bold ones who seemed to enjoy swimming.

Soon they · were all on the opposite side again where they had a wonderful time climbing up the steep bank, rolling down it, landing on each other's backs and balancing on the trunk of a fallen doum palm.

I watched them for about an hour and then called Elsa who replied in her usual voice, which was quite different from the one she used when talking to the cubs. She came down to the water's edge, waited till all her family were at her feet and started to swim across. This time all three cubs came with her.

As soon as they had landed she licked each one in turn and then walked up slowly, rubbed herself gently against me, rolled in the sand, licked my face and finally hugged me. I was very much moved by her obvious wish to show her cubs that we were friends. They watched us from a distance, interested, but puzzled and determined to stay out of reach.

The evidence suggested that they were six weeks and two days old. I could not tell their sex, but they were in excellent condition and though they still had a bluish film over their eyes they could certainly see perfectly. Their coats had fewer spots than Elsa's or her sisters' and were also much less thick than theirs had been at the same age, but far finer and more shiny. Elsa was very gentle and patient with her family and allowed them to crawl all over her and chew her ears and tail.

Gradually she moved closer to me and seemed to be inviting me to join in their game. But when I wriggled my fingers in the sand the cubs, though they cocked their heads, kept their distance.

When it got dark we all sat together on the grass, Elsa leaning against me while she suckled her family. Suddenly two of the cubs started quarrelling over a teat. Elsa reacted by rolling into a position which gave them better access. In doing so she came to rest against me and hugged me with one paw, including me in her family.

The evening was very peaceful, the moon rose slowly and the doum palms were silhouetted against the light; there was not a sound except for the suckling of the cubs.

So many people had warned me that after Elsa's cubs had been born she would probably turn into a fierce and dangerous mother defending her young, yet here she was as trusting and as affectionate as ever, and wanting me to share her happiness. I felt very humble.

Two weeks passed before she brought the cubs to camp to introduce them to George. This was not entirely her fault, for during this time we had been obliged to go to Isiolo for a couple of days and while we were away she and the cubs had arrived at the camp one morning looking for us, but had only found the boys.

At teatime on the day of our arrival we saw Elsa and the cubs on the opposite side of the river, but when she spotted us she moved her family a short distance downstream. Later, they all got thirsty and came to the water's edge to drink, their round foxy faces stretched forward between the pointed elbows of their front legs, which were bent. At first they just lapped noisily, then they plunged into the shallow water and began to play. A big boulder surrounded by water made a perfect setting for playing "king of the castle", and I thought of the days when Elsa and her sisters had to be content with a potato bag on our veranda at Isiolo for their "castle". How lucky these little cubs were to be living in such a lovely and exciting place!

They were now about nine weeks old and for the first time we knew that the family consisted of two lions and a lioness. It was now that we gave them their names. The boys had already called the boldest cub, a male, by a name which was, they said, very popular with the Meru tribe. It sounded like Jespah. I asked where the name came from. They said it was out of the Bible, but as each boy pronounced it slightly differently it was difficult for me to trace it. The nearest phonetic association I could find was Japhtah, which means "God sets free". If that were the origin of the little cub's name it could not be more appropriate. We called Jespah's brother, who was very timid, Gopa, for in Swahili this means timid, and his sister we named Little Elsa.

When they were ten weeks old Elsa began to wean them. Whenever she thought they had had enough milk she either sat on her teats or jumped onto the roof of the Land-Rover. The little ones resented this very much; they stood on their hind legs against the car, miaowing up at their mother, but she sat and licked her paws, as though she were quite unaware of the whimpering cubs below. So if the cubs did not want to starve they had to eat meat.

The next two evenings Elsa came to camp without her family. She was exuberantly affectionate to us and swept the table clear of our sundowners. On the third evening she brought the cubs with her and behaved in the same way. They now seemed quite at home in our presence, but we were rather surprised to observe that they were not in the least startled when our supper landed on the ground with a clatter.

During all that night it poured without stopping. On such occasions Elsa had always taken refuge in George's tent, and now in she came, calling to the cubs to follow her. But the youngsters' inbred fear of man was so great that they preferred to soak outside. This trait was the most obvious sign of their wild blood and it was something we were determined to encourage, even in defiance of Elsa's wish to make them into friends of ours. Often she called to them, but whatever she did they never overstepped their self-imposed frontier.

It seemed that our rearing of their mother in domesticity had in no way impaired the instincts which all wild animals possess. Moreover, Elsa herself had shown by concealing her cubs from us for five or six weeks, that her own instinct for protecting her young was still alive.

Unfortunately, if the way in which the cubs were developing into true wild lions exceeded our hopes, their father was a great disappointment to us. No doubt we were partly to blame, for we had interfered with his relationship with his family—but certainly he was of no help as a provider of food for them; on the contrary, he often stole the meat we provided. Moreover, he caused us a lot of trouble. One evening he made a determined attempt to get at a goat which was inside my truck, and another time when Elsa and the cubs were eating outside our tent she suddenly scented him, became very nervous, cut her meal short and hurriedly removed the cubs.

George went out with a torch to find out what the trouble was; he had not gone three yards when he was startled by a fierce growl and saw the cubs' father hiding in a bush just in front of him. He retreated rapidly and luckily so did the lion.

Meanwhile, however, I was immensely interested in observing the cubs' development. Already they stretched their tendons; they stood on their hind legs and dug their claws into the rough bark of certain trees— preferably acacias—and in so doing they exposed the pink bases of their claws. When they had finished this exercise, the bark showed deep gashes.

The cubs were very easily distinguishable. Jespah was much the lightest in colour, his body was perfectly proportioned and he had a very pointed nose and eyes so acutely slanted that they gave a slightly Mongolian cast to his sensitive face. His character was not only the most nonchalant, daring and inquisitive, but also the most affectionate. When he was not cuddling up against his mother and clasping her with his paws he demonstrated his affection to his brother and sister.

His timid brother Gopa had very dark markings on his forehead but his eyes, instead of being bright and open like Jespah's, were rather clouded and squinted a little. He was bigger and more heavily built than his brother and though he was by no means stupid, he took a long time to make up his mind and, unlike Jespah, was not venturesome; indeed, he always stayed behind till he was satisfied that all was safe.

Little Elsa fitted her name, for she was a replica of her mother at the same age. She had the same expression, the same markings, the same slender build. Her behaviour too, was so strikingly like Elsa's that we could only hope that she would develop the same lovable character. She knew of course that for the moment she was at a disadvantage compared with her two stronger brothers, but she used cunning to restore the balance.

Though all the cubs were well disciplined and obeyed Elsa instantly on all important occasions, when playing they showed no fear of her and were only occasionally intimidated by the cuffs she gave them when they became too cheeky.

I was always touched by the way in which she discriminated when she played with me or with them. With the cubs she was often rather rough, pulling their skin, biting them affectionately or holding their heads down so that they should not interfere with her meal; it would have been most painful if she had treated me in the same way, but she was always gentle when we played together.

By the time the cubs were eighteen weeks old Elsa seemed to have become resigned to the fact that their relationship with us would never be the same as ours with her. Indeed, they were growing more shy every day and preferred to eat outside the area lit by our lamp, except for Jespah, who, as he followed his mother everywhere, often came with her into the "danger zone". Elsa now often placed herself between us and the cubs in a defensive position.

As they were in excellent condition we thought that we should risk leaving them to hunt with Elsa, for a few days at least. Their father had been about lately and as the family had only come into camp for short feeding visits, we assumed that they were spending most of their time with him.

On our visit in June to celebrate the cubs' six months' birthday, George shot a guinea fowl. Little Elsa, of course, took possession of it and disappeared into the bush. Her indignant brothers went after her but returned defeated, and tumbling down a sandy bank landed on their mother. She was lying on her back with her four paws straight up in the air. After a splendid game together, Elsa got up and walked up to me and embraced me gently as though to show that I was not to be left out in the cold. Jespah looked bewildered. What could he make of this? Here was his mother making such a fuss of me, so I couldn't be bad, but all the same I was so different from them.

Elsa dozed off with her head on my lap. This was too much for Jespah. He crept up and began to scratch my shins with his sharp claws. I could not move my legs because of the weight of Elsa's head resting on them, so in an effort to stop him I stretched my hand slowly towards him. In a flash he bit it and made a wound at the base of my forefinger. It was lucky that I always carry sulphanilamide powder with me, so I was able to disinfect it at once. All this happened within a few inches of Elsa's face but she diplomatically ignored the incident and closed her eyes sleepily.

I stayed on watching the last glow of the sinking sun gild the tips of the doum palms, then all colour vanished and darkness fell.

After this we all returned to camp and Jespah seemed so friendly that I began to wonder whether when he bit me it was only in play. Certainly, between himself and his mother, biting was a proof of affection.

But now we were beginning to worry about his relationship with us. We had done our best to respect the cubs' natural instincts and not to do anything to prevent them from being wild lions, but inevitably this had resulted in our having no control over them. Little Elsa and her timid brother were as shy as ever and never provoked a situation which required chastisement, but Jespah had a very different character, and I could not push his sharp, scratching claws back by saying, "No, no," as I used to do when Elsa was a cub. Our only hope seemed to lie in establishing a friendly relationship with Jespah, but for the moment his variable reactions made a truce more realistic than friendship.

Indeed, by the beginning of August he had become increasingly obstreperous. For instance he now took much too much interest in our flock of goats. One evening when Nuru was herding them towards my truck, he made a beeline for them, rushed through the kitchen, dodged between the water containers and round the open fire and arrived at the truck just as the goats were about to enter it.

There was no doubt as to his intentions, so I ran and grabbed a stick, and holding it in front of him shouted, "No, no," in my most commanding voice. Jespah looked puzzled, sniffed the stick and began spanking it playfully, which gave Nuru time to lift the goats into the truck. Then Jespah walked back with me towards Elsa who had been watching the game. Often she helped me to control him, either by adding a cuffing to my "nos'" or by placing herself between the two of us. But I wondered how long it would be before, even with her support, my commands and my sticks failed to have any effect. Jespah was so full of life and curiosity and fun; he was a grand little wild lion, and a very fast-growing one too, and it was high time that we left him and his brother and sister to live a natural life.

One evening the tsetse flies were particularly active and Elsa and her two sons were rolling on their backs inside my tent trying to squash their tormentors. In doing so they knocked down two camp beds which were propped up against the wall. Elsa lay down on one of them and Jespah on the other, while Gopa had to be content with the groundsheet. The sight of two lions lolling in bed, while far from our ideal picture of Elsa's family returned to a wild life, was comic enough. Only Little Elsa stayed outside: she was as wild as ever and nothing would induce her to enter the tent, so she at least appeased my conscience.

We were both very interested in observing the different relationships which Elsa's cubs were developing towards us. Jespah, prompted by an insatiable curiosity, had overcome his earlier inhibitions, mixed with us and was most friendly, but allowed no familiarities.

Little Elsa was truly wild, snarled if we came close and then sneaked away. Gopa, on the other hand, quite often made use of the tent when the tsetse flies were most active. One evening I was sitting at the entrance of the tent while he was in the annexe at the far end. When Gopa started chewing at the tent canvas, I said as firmly as I could, "No, no"; to my surprise, he snarled at me, but stopped chewing. A little later he took up the canvas again and, though my "no" was answered with another snarl, he again stopped.

So far, all the cubs responded when we said no, although we had never enforced our prohibition with a stick or anything else which could frighten them. But we did not want to push our luck. George had things to attend to back at Isiolo, and it seemed to be a good time for us to leave the camp. They were now powerful young lions, and it was time that they should hunt with their mother and live their natural life.

We decided to space our absences. On the first occasion we had intended to leave for only six days, but in fact, because of very heavy rains, it was nine before I could return. Elsa did not turn up in answer to the shots we fired, nor were there any signs of spoor around the camp, but these might well have been washed away by the flooding of the river. After a while, I walked towards the Big Rock and came upon Elsa trotting along with the cubs; they were panting and had probably come a long way in answer to my signal. They were delighted to see me and all were in excellent condition. Elsa had a few bites on her chin and neck but nothing serious. Gopa had grown a much longer and darker mane than Jespah, whose colouring was very light in comparison to his brother's. In a year's time I thought, what a handsome pride they would make, with two slender graceful lionesses accompanied by one blond and one dark lion.

Reassured, I went back to Isiolo and left the cubs to a longer spell of wild life.

As a treat on the cubs' first birthday, in December, I had brought a guinea fowl, which I cut up into four portions so that each should have a share. After gobbling these titbits Elsa hopped onto the Land-Rover while the cubs tore at some meat we had prepared for them. As all the lions were happily occupied I went for a walk. As soon as I set out Elsa jumped off the car and followed; then Jespah, seeing his mother disappear, stopped his meal and ran after us, and we had not gone far before I saw Gopa and Little Elsa, parallel to us, chasing each other through the bush.

When we came to the place where the track comes nearest to the Big Rock, the lions sat down and rolled in the sand. I waited for a little while and watched the setting sun; then since Elsa looked settled, I walked back, expecting the family to spend the evening on the Rock. I was surprised when she followed me. She kept close and Jespah trotted next to us like a well-trained child. Gopa and Little Elsa took their time; they scampered about a long way behind us and we often had to stop to wait for them.

Elsa seemed to have come along just to join me in my walk; this was the first time she had done so since the cubs were born. I thought it a charming way of celebrating their birthday.

Next morning we found the spoor of a lioness upstream, but no trace of Elsa. She did not turn up that day or during the following night. On the second night we heard two lions roaring and understood why she had not come to camp. She brought her cubs in for dinner that night but when a lion started roaring she left at once, crossing the river.

Elsa and the cubs returned in the early morning and when, after breakfast, I strolled along the road to read in the sand the report on last night's visitors, she and the cubs followed me.

We went on until we came to a rain pool where the lions had a drink. By now the sun was getting hot and it would not have surprised me had Elsa decided to spend the day in this place, but good-naturedly she turned back when I did and trotted slowly home with me.

George arrived at about teatime with the Christmas mail. We gave the family their supper which kept them occupied while I arranged the table for our Christmas dinner. I decorated it with flowers and tinsel ornaments and put the little silver Christmas tree I had kept from last year in the middle and a still smaller one which had just arrived from London in front of it. Then I brought out the presents for George and the boys.

Jespah watched my preparations very carefully and the moment I turned my back to get the candles he rushed up and seized a parcel which contained a shirt for George, and bounced off with it into a thicket. Gopa joined him immediately and the two of them had a wonderful time with the shirt. When at last we rescued it it was in no state to give to George.

By now it was nearly dark and I started to light the candles. That was all Jespah needed to make him decide to come and help me. I only just managed to prevent him from pulling the tablecloth, with the decorations and burning candles, on top of himself. It needed a lot of coaxing to make him keep away so that I could light the rest of the candles.

When all was ready he came up, tilted his head, looked at the glittering Christmas trees and then sat down and watched the candles burn lower and lower. A few yards away Elsa and her cubs rested peacefully in the grass, hardly visible in the fading light. I could not help feeling as though we were all one family.

Editorial Postscript

In January 1961, a month after the events described above, Elsa died in the bush after an illness lasting several days. A postmortem established that she died from babesia, a parasite which destroys the red blood corpuscles.

The cubs immediately became very wild and, for a few weeks, only came to the camp after dark to be fed. Then they disappeared.

Shortly afterwards the Adamsons learned that they had been attacking goats belonging to local tribesmen and it became essential to catch them and move them to an uninhabited area. This highly difficult operation, which involved trapping the cubs and transporting them seven hundred miles to the Serengeti National Game Park, Tanganyika, was achieved in May, 1961.

Joy Adamson

Joy Adamson was born in 1910 in Vienna, and educated there. In 1937 she visited Kenya for the first time and became fascinated by the country; a talented artist, she began to paint its landscapes and people. Then, when she married game warden George Adamson in 1944, animals became her second great passion, which dominated the rest of her life. After writing the phenomenally popular Elsa books, Mrs. Adamson made a study of cheetahs and then set up a leopard research camp near Mount Kenya. Tragically, she was murdered there in 1980, but George Adamson still carries on their work, rehabilitating captive lions to be returned to the wild.

The Year of the
Greylag Goose

A PICTURE FEATURE TAKEN FROM THE BOOK BY
Konrad Lorenz
WITH PHOTOGRAPHS BY
Sybille and Klaus Kalas

Konrad Lorenz, the great animal scientist, has always been fascinated by greylag geese. In order to study the family life of this beautiful species, Lorenz established a colony of geese on an idyllic, secluded lake high in the Austrian mountains; the geese were free-living but tame, and many had actually been reared by human foster-parents. Here, living in perfect harmony with the greylags, the author was able to observe the remarkably "human" characteristics displayed in their domestic lives. His text, accompanied by spectacular photographs, provides a fascinating record of the complete annual cycle of one of nature's most captivating creatures.

I AM STANDING at a place in the Alm Valley of Austria, near my ancestral home in Altenberg, where I sometimes have a rendezvous with the greylag geese. It is early morning. The mountain peaks are partly lit by the sun, while the valley still bears the greyness of dawn. Just above the spot where I am standing is a layer of cloud. Suddenly I hear, high in the air over my head, the calls of geese in their morning flight. I call out an answer, which evokes further calling in response, and then I see them through a small blue hole in the cloud layer, highlighted by the sun and shining like stars. The geese fly further down the valley until they reach the end of the clouds, drop downwards, and wheel back towards me underneath the cloud layer. Their wing beats die away and they glide lower and lower, before turning in a sharp dive to land at my feet.

Greylag geese have fascinated me for years. I am often asked why I have made them the subject of such intensive studies, and I reply that there are many reasons. There is one outstanding feature that makes the social behaviour of the greylag goose suitable for ethological study: greylag geese reared from the egg under human care transfer all their natural loyalty and attachment to their human foster parents. It may sound sentimental, but it is a fact that our geese, because of their lasting friendship with us, remain in the area where we want to study them. They will even lead their offspring back to the site of their infancy and bring them up before our eyes.

But far and away the most important reason for my enduring interest in greylag geese is that their family and social life exhibits striking parallels with human behaviour. The wild goose species can know happiness and deep sadness in much the same way as we do; they are capable of love and attachment; of courage and jealousy, and of lasting bonds of genuine friendship. In addition, geese have a veritable human capacity for grief. Quite literally, a grief-stricken goose will hang its head, lose its appetite, and be indifferent to its surroundings. Just as grief-stricken humans will become vulnerable to accidents because of their reduced alertness, so geese will fly into high-tension cables or fall prey to predators. And their sudden defencelessness will be exploited with astonishing speed by former subordinates.

In lectures, I frequently tell my listeners: "Animals are much less intelligent than you are inclined to think, but in emotions they are far less different from us than you assume."

A strong bond between the members of a greylag pair is forged by their joint love for their offspring, which on their part are equally loyal to their parents. If, during a breeding season, a pair of greylag geese lose their clutch or their goslings, their young from the previous year will usually return to them, and a goose that has lost its partner will return in the same way to rejoin either its parents or its still unpaired siblings. In short, the social behaviour of greylag geese contains a great deal that is of interest to us.

When I retired as director of the Max Planck Institute for Behavioural Physiology, my investigations into the social behaviour of the greylag goose were in full swing. To enable me to continue the project, a research station affiliated to the Austrian Academy of Sciences was generously set up for me near my home in Altenberg, in the Alm Valley. Lake Alm, where our valley begins, is the source of the narrow and rapid-flowing River Alm. About five miles downstream the river broadens and here, in harmony with the fairy-tale surroundings of pine trees and mountain peaks, we have constructed ponds and islands, and set up a settlement for geese and humans which we call Obergansbach (literally, Upper Goose Stream). Further downstream, our actual research institute is housed in the converted old mill of Auingerhof.

What we were trying to do at Auingerhof was to establish a tame but free-living colony of geese so that their social behaviour could be studied in a natural habitat. We began by transferring four flocks of hand-reared geese from the Max Planck Institute, relying on their attachment to their human "parents"; fortunately we had three willing foster-parents, three girls and a young man, and the move was made successfully. Soon our colony was settled.

That first winter the geese would pass the night on the great expanse of Lake Alm, where they were safe from foxes, and every morning after sunrise they would come flying down the valley from the lake. The many upcurrents that prevail in this mountainous area give them the opportunity to climb to considerable heights without exerting themselves, and the geese would fly high and joyously over the icy river before landing beside us on the gravel banks near the station building.

Even after having seen it many times, I still find it utterly enthralling to witness free-flying birds moving towards me from a long distance away. After all, most poor souls never see wild animals except *from behind*—for in all the lands of the earth where man has come in contact with wild animals, he is recognized as the most dangerous and merciless predator of all. There is hardly an animal, no matter how big or strong or how effective its weapons, that will not flee when it sees a human being. Only in places where man is unknown will the local animals approach him with complete trust.

Man regards himself as lord of the earth, but he has in reality been exiled from the paradise of peaceful coexistance with his fellow creatures. That is why, when free-living animals approach me from a long distance away, not because they have failed to notice me but for the very reason that they *have* seen and heard me, it is as if this exile from paradise had been lifted.

I WOULD NOT WANT to live in a country where the four seasons are not sharply distinct from each other, and in the Alm Valley spring appears with striking suddenness. Nowhere is spring as beautiful as it is in the Alps. The carpet of snow is replaced almost overnight by an array of flowers. As soon as the snow-free patches appear on the ground, one can find Christmas roses, the tender blossoms of the purple crocus, golden saxifrage and the large spring snowflake.

The geese also show signs of the awakening spring—the time of love. Pair formation ("marriage") among greylag geese follows almost exactly the same course as with ourselves. The young male exhibits a sudden infatuation with a particular female, followed by intensive courtship of her—sometimes with considerable interference from an angry father. His courtship is in many details almost laughably similar to that of the young human male. The young gander shows off his strength and courage; he will drive off other ganders, even those he is normally afraid of—though only if the object of his love is watching. In her presence, he will accelerate his takeoff; and he will brake spectacularly when landing alongside his girlfriend, behaving just like a young man on a motorcycle or in a sports car. If the female responds to his courtship, the two greylags celebrate their partnership with the so-called triumph-call—a distinctive, gabbling call uttered with necks outstretched. The "engagement" can now be regarded as concluded and, provided that no dramatic circumstances intervene, a greylag goose pair formed in this manner will remain faithful for life.

However, just as with humans, dramatic circumstances can intervene, and a gander or a goose may "fall in love" with a different partner despite a pre-existing "engagement". Such infidelity usually only occurs when something has been amiss in the original pair formation; for example, when a goose or gander has lost its first great love and acquired the present partner as a substitute. And it is extremely rare for a pair to split up that has bred and successfully reared young.

If a paired female is unfaithful, her bridegroom sticks close to her wherever she goes and bars her passage if she moves towards his rival. If he is extremely provoked, he will even bite her—something he would never do under normal circumstances. A gander forced to guard his female in this manner cannot attack his rival, because the unfaithful female will break away the moment he leaves her side; he cannot feed properly, and if the drama lasts many weeks he loses weight visibly. From dawn to dusk, these unhappy goose "trios" scurry to and fro, the rival in front, followed by the goose, with the gander jealously maintaining his guard between them.

When the goose is undecided about the object of her affection, duels between rival ganders can be fierce and fatal. Geese are well equipped for aerial combat: one will climb above the other in the sky, dive downwards rapidly like a bird of prey, and swoop past to strike his opponent with a wing shoulder (the anatomical equivalent of our wrist). On the ground, a greylag goose possesses two weapons: its beak, which can inflict a painful bite, and its wing shoulder, which is armed with a small, thornlike projection called the carpal spur. Fighting ganders grasp each other with their beaks by the neck or breast, draw close, and then strike blows with the wing shoulders. One wing is spread in counterbalance, the other flails at the opponent. Hearing the battle, other ganders rush up excitedly to watch. When one contestant flees, the victor stands proudly with wings outspread, brandishing his shoulder spurs like brass knuckles. The unfortunate loser is subsequently bullied by even the weakest of the colony; he has lost his social standing along with his wife.

Soon after this period of pair formation and its resulting jealousies, individual pairs split away from the flock, mate, and seek out nesting sites. When a clutch of eggs is laid, the goose pulls the down feathers from her own belly and tucks them between and beneath the eggs; when she leaves the nest to drink and graze she hides the eggs, with down feathers, from the sharp eyes of her great enemies, marauding crows and ravens.

The goslings hatch after about a month of incubation. Hatching begins when the gosling uses its beak to break the membrane separating it from the air cavity at the blunt end of the egg. Now the gosling breathes with

On cold winter days mist forms over the relatively warm waters of Lake Alm.
The geese stand in the water to keep their feet warm.

The geese begin their courtship in early spring, the ganders (centre left) circling round their chosen mates with necks held at a characteristic angle. Sometimes a pair is threatened by a rival male and the gander (above) must jealously guard his goose, sometimes having to block her physically (below left) from joining his rival. Often a fight will occur (right), the ganders grasping each other with their beaks and striking with their wing shoulders.

After mating, the female's eggs begin to mature and her swollen belly (inset) shows that she is ready to lay. During the brooding period she will pluck quantities of down from her breast to make a warm lining for the nest.

This egg (left) was moved to an incubator so that hatching could be observed. As the gosling emerges from the egg it lies exhausted. To crack open the shell, it has used its yellow egg tooth, which can be seen (right) on the tip of the beak. It will drop off in a few days. When the goslings first leave the nest (above) their father keeps a watchful look out.

When the goslings are cold they burrow beneath their mother's feathers (right), sometimes emerging higher up. As they grow older their plumage changes. Here (above), their father keeps watch while they preen themselves.

Hand-reared geese must be made familiar with their environment and walks (right) are an important part of their upbringing. The geese enjoy taking a break on these excursions, eating favourite plants (below); and while a midday rest in the rain is not so pleasant for their foster-parents, the geese fall asleep quite happily (above).

The young geese return from their practice flights, sometimes veering from side to side as they learn to keep their balance while gliding down to land.

Shortly before touching down the geese thrust their feet forward and brake with powerful wing beats. On stormy days (inset) the migratory instinct is aroused and the geese often fly high over the mountains in a "V" formation.

*As winter returns the flock huddles
closely together, all rivalries forgotten.*

its lungs for the first time, and it also starts to utter calls. When the egg becomes too cool the gosling produces a plaintive "lost piping", and it responds with a two-part "greeting call" when a comforting reply is given by the mother. Such "conversations" with an unbroken egg never fail to intrigue me.

The first round of communication between mother and offspring constitutes the vital process of *imprinting*, which can never be repeated or reversed. When the dialogue takes place between a gosling and a human being, the gosling accepts the human as its mother. I was to find out how rigid the bond is with my very first gosling. I took it out from under the domestic goose that had hatched it for just a few minutes and elicited the greeting response. From then on, the gosling obstinately refused to accept the domestic goose as its parent: I was its mother.

Wild goslings leave the nest after a few days to follow their mother in tight-packed formation. In their first few days of life they must be frequently warmed, roughly every fifteen or twenty minutes; while this is happening, they will often thrust their heads out through the mother's feathers and look up at her face with a greeting cackle, indicating the family bond. If the mother gets up, the goslings follow closely, watching to see what she eats and then pecking at the same objects.

Foster-parents, in order to play their maternal role with complete success, must now devote themselves exclusively, and of course under natural conditions, to their charges. The foster-children cannot be left for a moment or they will immediately "cry" in confusion, an emergency signal to which their natural parents would respond at once. The human foster-parent must do exactly the same or the goslings will become seriously neurotic.

Day after day, around the clock, the foster-parent shares in all the little joys and sorrows of the goslings. One must smile in sympathy with them when they tread on a patch of nettles and pipe in distress, share their pleasure when they utter calls of contentment while feeding. And human foster-parents must also teach their goslings to find appropriate food by stabbing at it with a finger.

In good weather, with the sun shining warmly down, being a substitute mother for water fowl hardly seems like work. On the other hand, when it is pouring with rain it is a major undertaking to spend day after day with young geese. Geese are very well protected by nature against the weather and are not at all bothered by rainstorms—but their plumage is a great deal more waterproof than the foster-parent's raincoat!

At a very early age the siblings begin to develop a social hierarchy, and sometimes, tiny goslings quite abruptly start fighting vigorously, in a sort of general free-for-all. The response of the parents, who are obviously disturbed by the situation, is to stare tensely and excitedly at the fighting goslings, often spreading their wings and hissing. However, the parents never intervene to stop the fighting, except that the mother will offer protection to any defeated goslings that flee from the fight and attempt to bury themselves beneath her.

In their fights the goslings display exactly the same behaviour as adult geese: they bite, pull at an opponent's feathers, and will bend their wings at the wrist joint and attempt to strike, although the wing is so short that the gosling succeeds only in striking its own flank.

Goslings grow swiftly, and the touchingly pretty appearance of the very young changes in the course of four or five days. Their behaviour changes just as rapidly as their appearance. They are now highly mobile. In their very first days, it is usually the parents' decision when to move off, and in what direction. As the goslings grow, they become increasingly independent, and never more so than when they are too hot. When the young geese are only a few weeks old, their downy feathers are replaced by their definitive plumage. They are, in a sense, carrying double plumage, and they easily become overheated, even though the temperature may be perfectly acceptable to the parents. Then they will energetically head for shade, obliging their parents to follow them by uttering persistent plaintive calls.

Just before fledging, orientation lessons begin with our fostered goslings: young geese have to be made familiar with the surrounding countryside, and with us they must learn from ground level what their own parents would shortly teach them from the air. Wandering through the Alm Valley at the footpace of a flock of geese, which never exceeds 1.25 miles an hour, is remarkably tiring for their human companions but, happily, the regular schedule of a goose's day includes a bath taken around noon, followed by preening, and then a nap. The human parents sleep even more soundly than their charges, and when the weather is warm, nothing is cosier than such a siesta shared by man and beast; the trilling call of young geese as they fall asleep is the sweetest lullaby imaginable. That makes it all the more infuriating when, as is typical in the Alm Valley, a rain cloud abruptly pours a cold shower on our resting bodies. Birds and humans react quite differently. Only the latter wake up cursing and reach for their raincoats; the geese sleep on undisturbed.

During the period when the young geese are fledging, their parents shed all their primary feathers. Barely a week after their loss, the new primaries have grown considerably; and in three or four weeks more the parents can fly again, by which time their offspring, too, are ready to take wing—a beautiful example of natural adaptation. When the youngsters fly off, the parents take off after them, assume the lead at once, and thus determine the landing site. Since the parents' wings are still relatively short, they fly carefully, avoiding sharp turns and flashy braking manoeuvres. Without the offsprings' being aware of it, the parents are giving them valuable guidance. And as the young gain experience, the parents take them on more ambitious excursions over the surrounding countryside.

In a strict sense, our young fostered geese do not have to learn to fly, since the coordination patterns required for takeoff, level flight, braking and landing are completely innate. But the youngsters must be taught that they can land only against the wind, for if they land with it, they may turn the most awful somersaults. To teach them this, foster-parents must choose a moment when their charges are flying low against the wind. Then, if the foster-parent stoops rapidly, or falls flat on the ground, the young geese will respond as they would to guiding parents—they will land at any cost.

It is heartening when the time for learning to fly passes without loss. Again and again one is amazed to see how in four short weeks the fluid content of an egg can bring forth a downy gosling that will cry and make greetings, grieve and be happy, and is capable of attaching itself to one certain individual—either greylag goose or human being. And every year it is a renewed source of wonderment how in eight more weeks the pretty little balls of fluff have changed into full-grown wild geese that fly way up into the sky in orderly formation, and brave the storm.

On clear September days the Alm Valley still has the appearance of high summer. Then suddenly one morning the mountains are covered with snow, the leaves turn an autumn yellow, and the spiders' webs are coated with pearls of dew at daybreak. Then our geese become very restless indeed, as their motivation to fly off increases. Hand-reared geese, since their foster-parents are unable to show them the path of autumn migration, stay at the place they were reared. We are well aware how dangerous such a migration can be. Nevertheless, we would be glad to have our geese resemble their wild counterparts, and when they fly high above us uttering their migratory chorus, we stand by, way down on the earth, with mixed feelings.

At this time of year I am always reminded of something that remains fixed in my mind, even though it happened almost seventy years ago. I am sure I had not started going to school and could not yet read. While out walking in the watermeadows of the Danube, I had disobediently run ahead, against the wishes of my anxious mother, and was standing in a small clearing near the river when I heard above me some peculiar metallic calls and then saw, far up in the sky, a flock of wild geese heading downstream. Human emotions develop early and remain unchanged for life. I can still relive today exactly what I felt at that moment. I did not know where the birds were flying, but I wanted to migrate with them. I was filled with a romantic, heart-bursting longing to travel. For me, that childhood romance is inextricably linked with the time when the geese migrate. It is reawakened whenever our wild geese fly overhead, and a childhood dream comes true when I call them and they magically fly down towards me.

Autumn gives way to winter's reign earlier than we would like in the Alm Valley. As soon as the snow lies thick on the ground, the geese, who until then have grazed in the meadows around the research station, restrict their activities to the riverbanks, where they can find food. They have become more settled; the period of migratory restlessness has passed, and there is not much of interest to observe in their behaviour, although we still spend as much time with them as we can, in order to maintain the trusting relationship they have with us. Even in our thickest clothing, we feel the cold far more than the geese and can only marvel at the efficiency of their insulating plumage. When there is heavy frost, the geese do not walk around much, but stand in the relatively warm shallows of the river. Lake Alm is fed by artesian springs originating deep in the rock, and even in winter the waters of the lake, and the river flowing from it, are so warm that they never freeze over.

How beautiful the cold, clear winter days are in the Alm Valley, with the sun lighting the mountain crests, shadows in the valley, and a fine mist hanging over the water. What a magnificent sight it is to see the oblique rays of the morning sun slanting through the cloud and spotlighting a flock of geese flying above. And how dramatic it is when the geese break through the mist to land on a sandbank, sending up swirls of frosty snow in the draught from their wings.

The idea of producing a book took shape at Auingerhof, where on winter evenings (which can seem very long in the Alm Valley) we would analyse the photographic records which form the basic documentation for comparative behavioural research. All my students are more accomplished photographers than I am, but not all have achieved the mastery of Sybille and Klaus Kalas. They have taken innumerable photographs for scientific purposes, directing their attention not to the beauty of the subject but to an exact recording of animal behaviour. Nevertheless, their pictures of the annual cycle of greylag geese are outstandingly beautiful, and as we relived the splendid hours we had passed in taking them, we felt certain that the pictures would appeal to a wider audience. That is how the idea came about.

Far too much of civilized mankind today is alienated from nature. Most people seldom encounter any but man-made things in their daily lives, and have lost the capacity to understand living things or to interact with them. But people respond to beauty, and we hope that perhaps the beauty of these pictures may inspire them with a sense of what is good and of their duty to protect and preserve all nature's living things.

This is not a scientific study. I have merely written a background to the pictures. They tell the real story.

THERE IS STILL HEAVY frost about, but the days are a little longer, the sun shines more strongly, and the geese are becoming more active. One evening, the south wind will come blustering over the mountains into the valley, the snow will melt, and it will be spring. For the geese, that marks the onset once again of a period of excitation, of love and jealousy. For the human observer too, it is the beginning of another spell of excitement and exertion. Now we must get up especially early and be continually on duty. Experience has taught us that most of the events of greatest importance to our research take place in early spring. It is a time when we look forward to new discoveries and, no less, to many new goose families. It is a time of hope.

Konrad Lorenz

Konrad Lorenz was born in Vienna in 1903. After studying medicine and biology he became one of the founders of a new science, ethology— the study of animal behaviour. Between 1961 and 1973 he was head of the Max Planck Institute for Behavioural Physiology in Bavaria, and when he retired he set up his own research station at Grünau in Austria. He was awarded the Nobel Prize for Medicine in 1973.

Sybille Kalas was born in Germany in 1949, and since 1971 has worked as Professor Lorenz's assistant. In 1976 she married fellow biologist Klaus Kalas; the couple both work at Grünau.

The
WHISPERING
LAND

A condensation of the book by

Gerald Durrell

Illustrated by Ralph Thompson

No one but Gerald Durrell could wake up under a
Land-Rover in the cold Argentinian dawn and
watch a family of foxes performing a ballet with a
roll of lavatory paper, and no one else could
describe it so vividly. It's just one of many
amusing incidents from the famous naturalist's
account of his expedition to South America
to collect animals for his Jersey zoo. On his travels,
from windswept Patagonia to the tropical
paradise of Jujuy, Durrell encounters eccentric
locals and elusive wildlife: penguins, pumas and
peccaries, and a particularly foul-mouthed
parrot. And everything seems to do its best to
make life unpredictable!

Readers familiar with Gerald Durrell's many
books and television films need no introduction
to this popular author. Those who come anew
to his adventures will find a colourful and very
special world, described with perception
and a great deal of humour.

Part One
The Customs of the Country

BUENOS AIRES, decked out for spring, was looking her best. The tall and elegant buildings seemed to gleam like icebergs in the sun and the broad avenues were lined with jacaranda trees covered with a mist of mauvy-blue flowers. The spring-like atmosphere seemed to have infected the pedestrians, who fled across the road through the traffic with even less caution than usual, while the drivers vied with each other in the time-honoured Buenos Aires game of seeing how close they could get to each other at the maximum speed without actually crashing.

Not having a suicidal streak in me, I had refused to drive in the city, and so we swept on our death-defying way in the Land-Rover with Josefina at the wheel. Short, with curly auburn hair and big brown eyes, Josefina had a smile like a searchlight that could paralyse even the most unsusceptible male at twenty paces. By my side sat Mercedes, tall, slim, blonde and blue-eyed. These two girls were part of my private army of feminine pulchritude which I used in dealing with Argentine officialdom. At that precise moment we were heading towards the massive building in whose interior lurked the most formidable enemy of sanity in Argentina: the aduana, or customs. When I, my wife Jacquie, and Sophie, my secretary, had arrived some three weeks earlier with the express purpose of filming animals, and also of collecting them for my zoo on the island of Jersey, the customs had let in the Land-Rover and my highly dutiable cameras and so on, without a murmur; but for some unknown reason they had confiscated my nets, traps, cage fronts and other worthless but necessary items of collecting equipment. So, for the past three weeks Mercedes, Josefina and I had spent a good part of every day in the bowels of the customs house, being passed from office to office with a frustrating regularity which made you begin to wonder if your brain would last out the course.

Mercedes regarded me anxiously as Josefina wove in and out of fleeing pedestrians in a way that made my stomach turn over.

"How are you feeling today, Gerry?" she asked.

"Wonderful, simply wonderful," I said bitterly; "there's nothing I like better than to feel that I have the whole sunlit day ahead in which to get on more intimate terms with the customs."

"But today we are going to see Señor Garcia," said Mercedes, with the air of one promising a sweet to a child.

I snorted. "To the best of my knowledge we have seen at least fourteen Señor Garcias in that building. The Garcia tribe treat the customs as though it's an old family firm."

"Oh dear, promise that you won't lose your temper again," said Mercedes, turning her kingfisher-blue eyes on me pleadingly.

"De hand ... de hand ..." Josefina said suddenly and loudly. I stuck my arm out of the window, and the speeding line of traffic behind us screeched to a shuddering halt as Josefina swung the Land-Rover into a side turning. The shouts of rage mingled with cries of "*Animál!*" faded behind us.

"Josefina, I do wish you would give us all a little more warning when you're going to turn," I said. Josefina turned her glittering smile on me.

"Why?" she inquired simply.

"Well, it helps you know. It gives us a chance to prepare to meet our Maker."

"I 'ave never crash you yet, no?"

We swept majestically across an intersection at forty miles an hour, and a taxi coming from the opposite direction had to apply all its brakes to avoid hitting us amidships.

"Blurry bas-tard," said Josefina tranquilly.

"Josefina! You must not use phrases like that," I remonstrated.

"Why not?" asked Josefina innocently. "You do."

"That is not the point," I said severely.

"But it is nice to say, no?" she said with satisfaction. "And I 'ave learn more; I know blurry bastard ..."

"All right, all right," I said hastily. "I believe you. But for Heaven's sake don't use them in front of your mother, otherwise she'll stop you driving for me."

"De hand ... de hand," cried Josefina again, and again we swept across the road, leaving a tangle of infuriated traffic behind us, and drew up outside the massive and gloomy facade of the aduana.

THREE HOURS LATER we emerged, our brains numb, our feet aching. That was, however, almost the last of our bedevilments, for a day or two later the customs suddenly released my equipment.

So, with our problem solved, Jacquie, Sophie and I got out the maps and planned our route to the south, to Deseado and the Patagonian coastline where the penguins and the seals which I wished to photograph, gambolled in the icy waters. At first sight everything seemed to be quite straightforward. Marie, another of the army of friends we had already made, had obtained leave from her job and was to come with us to act as interpreter. Our equipment was checked and carefully packed and we began to feel that at last we were on our way. Then, at our last council of war (in the little cafe on the corner), Marie produced an argument that she and Jacquie had obviously been brooding upon for some considerable time. "I think it would be a good idea if we take someone who knows the roads, Gerry," she said. "Patagonian roads are quite different from anywhere else in the world, you know."

"How different?" I inquired.

"Worse," said Marie, who did not believe in wasting words.

"We've heard the most awful reports of those roads," said Jacquie. "If we could get someone who knows them to drive us down, then you would know what to expect on the way back."

"But there *is* no one," I said irritably.

"There is Dicky," said Marie.

I stared at her. "Who is Dicky?"

"A friend of mine," she said carelessly. "He is a very good driver, he knows Patagonia, and he is a very nice person. He is quite used to going on hunting trips, so he does not mind suffering."

"When can he come and see us, Marie?" said Jacquie.

"Well, I told him to meet us here," said Marie. "I thought Gerry would want to see him."

I gazed at them speechlessly.

"I am sure you will like Dicky ..." began Marie, and at that moment Dicky arrived.

At first glance I decided that I did not like Dicky at all. He did not look the sort of person who had ever suffered or, indeed, was capable of suffering. He was exquisitely dressed. He had a round, plump face, with boot-button eyes, a rather frail-looking moustache like a brown moth, and dark hair so plastered down that it looked as if it had been painted on to his scalp.

"This is Dicky de Sola," said Marie, in some trepidation.

Dicky smiled at me, a smile that transformed his whole face.

"Marie have told you?" he said, dusting his chair fastidiously with his handkerchief before sitting down at the table. "I am delight to come with you if you are happy. I am delight to go to Patagonia, whom I love."

I began to warm to him.

"If I am no useful, I will not come, but I can advise if you will allow. You have a map? Ah, good, now let me explanation to you."

Within half an hour Dicky had won me over completely. Not only did he have an intimate knowledge of the country, but his own brand of English, his charm and infectious humour had decided me.

"Well," I said, as we folded the maps away, "if you can really spare the time, we'd like you to come very much."

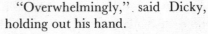

"Overwhelmingly," said Dicky, holding out his hand.

And on this rather cryptic utterance the bargain was sealed.

WE SET OFF for the south in the pearly grey dawn light of what promised to be a perfect day. The air was chilly, and Dicky had dressed for the occasion. He was wearing a long tweed overcoat, white gloves, and a ridiculous deerstalker hat which he wore, he explained to me, in order to "keep the ears heated". Sophie and Marie crouched in the back of the Land-Rover, on top of our mountainous pile of equipment, and Jacquie and I sat next to Dicky in the front seat, a map spread out across our laps.

Soon we had left the edge of the city and were out in the open countryside. Some of the places we came to had delightful names: at one point we passed through two villages, within a few miles of each other, one called "The Dead Christian" and the other "The Rich Indian". Marie's explanation was that the Indian was rich because he had killed the Christian and stolen all his money, but, attractive though this story was, I felt it could not be the right one.

For two days we sped through the prosperous, almost monotonous, landscape of the Pampa, flat golden grassland in which the cattle grazed knee-deep; occasional clumps of eucalyptus trees; small, neat *estancias*, gleaming white in the shade of huge *ombú* trees, that stood grimly on their enormous squat trunks. The neat fences that lined the road were hung with electric-blue flowers the size of saucers, and upon every third or fourth fence post there was balanced the football-like nest of an ovenbird.

On the third day, our destination was Carmen de Patagones, a town on the north bank of the Rio Negro that Charles Darwin had stayed in for some time. I was interested in seeing it, but we lost our way and when we eventually arrived at two o'clock in the morning every house was blank-faced and tightly shuttered. We stopped in the main square of the town and were arguing irritably over the problem of finding a place to stay when suddenly, under one of the pale, trembling street lights, appeared an angel of mercy in the shape of a tall policeman. He saluted smartly, bowed to the female members of the party, and with old-world courtesy directed us up some side roads to an hotel.

We came to a great gloomy house, with a massive front door that would have done justice to a cathedral. We beat a sharp tattoo and the door swung mysteriously open, displaying a long, dimly lit passageway, and a marble staircase leading to the upper floors. Dead tired and extremely hungry, we marched into the echoing hall like an invading army. We stood there and shouted *"Hola!"* but there was no response.

"I think, Gerry, that sometimes they are all deceased," said Dicky gravely.

"Well, if they are I suggest we spread out and find ourselves beds."

So we climbed the staircase and, by the simple expedient of opening every door in sight, found ourselves three bedrooms, with beds made up. Then Dicky and I went downstairs to see if the hotel boasted of any sanitary arrangements. The first door we threw open led us into a dim bedroom in which was an enormous double-bed hung with an old-fashioned canopy. Before we could back out a figure surged from under the bedclothes like a surfacing whale, and waddled towards us. It turned out to be a colossal woman, clad in a flowing flannel nightie, who must have weighed some fifteen stone. She came out, blinking, into the hallway, pulling on a flowing kimono of bright green covered with huge pink roses, so the effect was rather as if one of the more exotic floral displays of the Chelsea Flower Show had suddenly taken on a life of its own. Over her ample bosom spread two long streamers of grey hair which she flicked deftly over her shoulder as she did up her kimono, smiling at us with sleepy goodwill.

"Buenas noches," she said politely.

"Buenas noches, señora," we replied, not to be outdone in good manners at that hour of the morning.

"Hablo con la patrona?" inquired Dicky.

"Si, si, señor," she said, smiling broadly, *"que quieres?"*

Dicky apologized for our late arrival, but *la patrona* waved away our apologies. Was it possible, Dicky asked, for us to have some sandwiches and coffee? Why not? inquired *la patrona*. Further, said Dicky, we were in urgent need of a lavatory. With great good humour she led us to a small tiled room, showed us how to pull the plug, then puffed her way to the kitchen and cut us a huge pile of sandwiches and made a steaming jug of coffee. Having assured herself that there was nothing further she could do for our comfort, she waddled off to bed.

The next morning we did a rapid tour of the town. As far as I could see, apart from the introduction of electricity, it had changed very little since Darwin's day, and so we left and sped across the iron bridge that spanned the rusty-red waters of the Rio Negro. By that simple action of crossing a river we entered a different world.

Gone were the lush green plains of the Pampa, and in their place was an arid waste stretching away as far as the eye could see, a uniform pelt of grey-green scrub composed of plants about three feet high, each armed with a formidable array of thorns and spikes. Nothing appeared to live in this dry scrub, for when we stopped on the rutted, potholed road there was no bird or insect song, only the whispering of the wind.

We drove into Deseado at ten o'clock one windswept morning. It was the most extraordinarily dead-looking town I had ever been in. It resembled the set for a rather bad Hollywood cowboy film, and gave the impression that its inhabitants had suddenly packed up and left it alone to face the biting winds and scorching sun. As we drove slowly into the centre of the town we saw only a dog, trotting briskly about his affairs, and a child, crouched in the middle of a road, absorbed in some mysterious game of childhood.

In the bar of an unprepossessing hotel we found the proprietor, who led us through dim passages to three small grubby rooms. Dicky, his deerstalker on the back of his head, stood in the centre of his room, pulling off his white gloves, surveying the sagging bed and its grey linen with cat-like fastidiousness.

"You know what, Gerry?" he said with conviction. "This is the stinkiest hotel I ever dream."

"I hope you never dream of a stinkier one," I assured him.

Presently we went out to call on one Señor Huichi to whom I had an introduction. Huichi's house was on the outskirts of Deseado, and Huichi himself was a man I took an instant liking to. Short, squat, with a weather-browned face, he had kind, humorous dark eyes with crow's feet at the corners, and an air of quiet, unruffled confidence that was very reassuring. Señor Huichi agreed to let us stay at an *estancia* he owned near the main penguin colony of Puerto Deseado, and said he would accompany us there himself to show us the best places to photograph penguins.

The next day Dicky had to return to Buenos Aires. We knew we were going to miss him, and he was equally depressed at having to leave us just when the trip was starting to be interesting. After we had seen him off on the plane, Marie, Sophie, Jacquie and I picked up Señor Huichi, who took over the wheel of the Land-Rover. I was heartily glad of this when we branched off the road on to something so vague that it could hardly be termed a track. Occasionally this would disappear altogether, and Huichi would aim the Land-Rover at what appeared to be an impenetrable thicket of thorn bushes, we would tear through it, the thorns screaming along the sides of the vehicle like so many banshees, and there, on the further side, the faint wisp of track would start again.

Gradually, as we got nearer to the sea, the flat landscape changed. It became gently undulating, and here and there the wind had rasped away the topsoil and exposed large areas of yellow and rust-red gravel. These seemed to be favoured by the Patagonian hare, for it was always on these brilliant expanses of gravel that we found them, sometimes in pairs, sometimes in groups of three or four. They were strange creatures that looked as though they had been put together rather carelessly. They had blunt, though rather hare-like faces, small, neat, rabbit-shaped ears, slender forelegs and large, muscular hindquarters. The most attractive part of their anatomy was their eyes, which were large, dark and lustrous, with a thick fringe of eyelashes. They would lie down on the gravel, sunning themselves, gazing aristocratically down their blunt noses, looking like miniature Trafalgar Square lions. They would let us approach fairly close, and then suddenly their long lashes would droop over their eyes seductively, and with amazing speed they would launch themselves at the heat-shimmered horizon in a series of gigantic bounding leaps, as if they were on springs, the black and white pattern on their behinds showing up like a retreating target.

Presently, towards evening, we switchbacked over a series of low hills and saw, in the lee of further hills, a cluster of green trees, the first we had seen since leaving Deseado. As we drew nearer we could see that this little oasis of trees was surrounded by a white fence, and in the centre stood a neat wooden house, gaily painted in bright blue and white.

Huichi's two peons came to meet us, wild-looking characters with long black hair and dark, flashing eyes, and dressed in *bombachas*—the plus-four-like native trousers—and tattered shirts. They helped us unload our gear and then, while we unpacked and washed, they went with Huichi to kill a sheep and prepare an *asado* in our honour.

It was dark by the time we made our way down to the *asado* ground at the bottom of the slope on which the house was built. An *asado* needs a fierce fire, and in windswept Patagonia you have to be careful not to set fire to the tinder-dry scrub for miles around. So Huichi had planted a great square of cypress trees so close together that their branches formed an almost impenetrable hedge. He had carved a narrow passageway into the centre of this box of cypress, and had there chopped out a room, some twenty feet by twelve. Here one of the peons had kindled an immense fire.

Near it a great stake had been stuck in the ground; on this a sheep, split open like an oyster, had been spitted.

I have been to many *asados* in the Argentine, but that first one will always remain in my mind as the most perfect. The wonderful smell of burning brushwood mingling with the smell of roasting meat, the pink and orange tongues of flame lighting up the green cypress walls of the shelter, and the sound of the wind battering ferociously against these walls and then dying to a soft sigh in the mesh of branches, and above us the night sky, trembling with stars, lit by a fragile moon. To gulp a mouthful of soft, warm red wine and then to lean forward and slice a fragrant chip of meat from the brown, bubbling carcass in front of you, dunk it in the fierce sauce of vinegar, garlic and red pepper, and stuff it, nut-sweet and juicy, into your mouth, seemed one of the most satisfying actions of my life.

Presently, when our attacks on the carcass had become more desultory, Huichi took a gulp of wine, wiped his mouth with his hand, and beamed at me across the embers of the fire, lying like a great sunset on the ground. "*Mañana*," he said, smiling, "we go to the *pinguinos?*"

"*Si, si,*" I responded sleepily, "*mañana* the *pinguinos.*"

A Sea of Head Waiters

Early the next morning we set off to find the penguins. Knots of blank-faced sheep scuttled across the nose of the Land-Rover as we drove along, their fleeces wobbling as they ran, and at one point we passed a long, shallow dewpond, caught in a cleft between the hills, where six flamingoes were feeding, pink as cyclamen buds. Then Huichi swung the Land-Rover off the main track and headed across country, up a gentle slope of land. As we came to the top of the rise, he turned and grinned at me.

"*Ahora*," he said, "*ahora los pinguinos*."

Ahead of us was a great desert of sun-cracked sand, separated from the sea beyond by a crescent-shaped ridge of white sand dunes, very steep and some two hundred feet high. It was in this protected desert area that the penguins had created their city. As far as the eye could see on every side the ground was pockmarked with nesting burrows, some a mere half-hearted scrape in the sand, some several feet deep, making the place look like a small section of the moon's surface seen through a powerful telescope. In among these craters waddled the biggest collection of penguins I had ever seen, like a sea of pygmy head waiters, solemnly shuffling to and fro as if suffering from fallen arches due to a lifetime of carrying overloaded trays.

Slowly we drove to the edge of the colony and then we stopped and got out of the Land-Rover. We stood and watched the penguins, and they stood and watched us with immense respect and interest. As long as we stayed near the vehicle they showed no fear. The greater proportion of birds were, of course, adult; but each nesting burrow contained one or two youngsters, still wearing their baby coats of down, who regarded us with big, melting dark eyes, looking rather like plump and shy debutantes clad in outsize silver-fox furs. The adults, sleek and neat in their black and white suits, had red wattles round the base of their beaks, and bright, predatory street-peddler eyes. As you approached them they would back towards their burrows, twisting their heads from side to side in a warning display, until sometimes they would be looking at you completely upside down. If you approached too close they would walk backwards into their burrows and gradually disappear, still

twisting their heads vigorously. The babies, on the other hand, would turn and dive into the burrows, so that their great fluffy behinds and frantically flapping feet were all that could be seen of them.

At first the noise and movement of the vast colony was confusing. As a background to the continuous whispering of the wind were the peeting of the youngsters, and the loud, prolonged, donkey-like bray of the adults, standing up stiff and straight, flippers spread wide, beaks pointing to the blue sky as they brayed joyfully and exultingly. The movement was constant, and most of it was due to the vast numbers of adult birds that passed to and fro, some making their way towards the sea, others coming from it. This trek to the sea occupied a large portion of the penguins' day, and it was such a tremendous feat that it deserves to be described in detail. By carefully watching the colony, day by day, we discovered that this is what happened:

Early in the morning one of the parent birds (either male or female) would set out, leaving its mate standing by the burrow in charge of the nestlings. In order to get to the sea the birds had to cover about a mile and a half of the most difficult terrain imaginable. First they had to pick their way through the vast patchwork of burrows that made up the colony, and when they reached the edge of this they were faced by an area where the sand was caked and split by the sun into something resembling a gigantic jigsaw puzzle. Quite early in the day, it would get so hot that it was painful to touch, and yet the penguins would plod dutifully across it, pausing frequently for a rest, as though in a trance. This used to take them about half an hour. But, when they reached the other side of the desert, they were faced with the sand dunes. These towered over the diminutive figures of the birds like a snow-white chain of Himalayan mountains, their steep sides composed of fine, shifting sand. We found it difficult enough to negotiate these dunes, so it must have been far worse for such an ill-equipped bird as a penguin.

When they reached the base of the dunes they generally paused for about ten minutes to have a rest. Some just sat there, brooding, while others fell forward onto their tummies and lay panting. Then they would climb sturdily to their feet and, gathering themselves, would rush at the slope, obviously hoping to get the worst of the climb over as quickly as possible. But about a quarter of the way up their progress would slow down, and they would often pause to rest. As the gradient grew steeper and steeper they would eventually be forced to flop down on their bellies, and use their flippers to assist them in the climb. Then, with one final, furious burst of speed, they would triumphantly reach the top, where they would stand up straight, flap their flippers in delight, and then flop down onto their tummies for a rest. They had reached the halfway mark and, lying there on the top of the dunes, they would see the sea, half a mile away, gleaming coolly and enticingly. But they had still to descend the other side of the dune, cross a quarter of a mile of scrubland and then several hundred yards of shingle beach.

Going down the dune presented no problem to them, and they accomplished this in two ways, both equally amusing to watch. Either they would walk down, starting very sedately and getting quicker and quicker until they were galloping along in the most undignified way, or else they would slide down on their tummies, using their wings and feet to propel their bodies over the surface of the sand exactly as if they were swimming. With either method they reached the bottom in a small avalanche of fine sand, and they would get to their feet, shake themselves, and set off grimly through the scrub. But it was the last few hundred yards that seemed to make them suffer most. There was the sea, blue, glittering, lisping seductively on the shore, and to get to it they had to drag their tired bodies over the stony beach, where the pebbles wobbled under their feet, throwing them off balance. But at last it was over, and they ran the last few feet to the edge of the waves in a curious crouching position, then suddenly straightened up and plunged into the cool water. For ten minutes or so they twirled and ducked in a shimmer of sun ripples, fluttering their hot, sore feet in ecstasy, whirling and bobbing, disappearing beneath the water, and popping up again like corks. Then, thoroughly refreshed, they would set about the stern task of fishing, undaunted by the fact that they would have to face that journey again before the food they caught could be delivered to their young.

Once they had plodded their way—full of fish—back to the colony, they started on the hectic job of feeding their ravenous young, a fascinating feat that resembled an all-in wrestling match. There was one family that lived close to the spot where we parked the Land-Rover each day, and got so used to our presence that they allowed us to sit and film them at a distance of about twenty feet, so we saw every detail of the feeding process very clearly. Once the parent bird reached the colony it had to run the gauntlet of several thousand youngsters before it reached its own nest burrow. All of these were convinced that, by launching themselves at the adult bird in a sort of tackle, they could get it to regurgitate the food it was carrying. So the adult had to dodge to and fro like a skilful centre-forward on a football field, and generally ended up at its burrow, still hotly pursued by two or three strange chicks. Then it would suddenly lose patience with its pursuers, and would proceed to peck at them so viciously that large quantities of the babies' fluff would float like thistledown across the colony.

Having routed the strange babies, it would then turn its attention to its own chicks, who were by now attacking it in the same way as the others had done, uttering shrill wheezing cries of hunger and impatience. It would squat down at the entrance to the burrow and stare at its feet pensively, making motions like someone trying to stifle an acute attack of hiccups. On seeing this the youngsters would work themselves into a frenzy of delighted anticipation, flapping their wings frantically, pressing themselves close to the parent bird's body, and stretching up their beaks and clattering them against the adult's. This would go on for perhaps thirty seconds, when the parent would suddenly—with an expression of relief—regurgitate vigorously, plunging its beak so deeply into the gaping mouths of the youngsters that you felt sure it would never be able to pull its head out again. The babies, satisfied and apparently not stabbed from stem to stern by the delivery of the first course, would squat down on their plump behinds and meditate for a while, and their parent would seize the opportunity to have a quick wash and brush up, carefully preening its breast feathers, picking minute pieces of dirt off its feet, and running its beak along its wings with a clipper-like motion. Then it would yawn, bending forward like someone attempting to touch his toes, wings stretched out straight behind, beak gaping wide. Then it would sink into a trance-like state. All would be quiet for five minutes or so, and then suddenly the parent would start its strange hiccupping motions again and pandemonium would break out immediately. The babies would rouse themselves from their digestive reveries and hurl themselves at the adult, each trying its best to get its beak into position first. Once more each of them in turn would be apparently stabbed to the heart by the parent's beak, and then once more they would sink back into somnolence.

The parents and young who occupied this nest-burrow were known, for convenient reference, as the Joneses. Quite close to the Joneses'

establishment was another burrow that contained a single, small and very undernourished-looking chick whom we called Henrietta Vacant-tum. Henrietta was the product of an unhappy home life. Her parents were, I suspected, either dim-witted or just plain idle, for they took twice as long as any other penguins to produce food, and then only in such minute quantities that Henrietta was always hungry. An indication of her parents' habits was the slovenly nest-burrow, a mere half-hearted scrape, totally unlike the carefully dug villa residence of the Jones family. So it was not surprising that Henrietta had an ill-cared-for look that made us feel very sorry for her. She was always on the lookout for food, and as the Jones parents had to pass her front door on their way to their own neat burrow, she always made valiant attempts to get them to regurgitate before they reached home.

These efforts were generally in vain, and all Henrietta got for her pains was a severe pecking. She would retreat, disgruntled, and with anguished eye watch the two disgustingly fat Jones babies wolfing down their food. But one day Henrietta discovered a way to pinch the Jones family's food without any unpleasant repercussions. She would wait until the parent Jones had started the hiccupping movements and the baby Joneses were frantically gyrating and then, at the crucial moment, she would join the group, carefully approaching the parent bird from behind. Then, wheezing loudly, and opening her beak wide, she would thrust her head under the adult's wing. The parent Jones, its mind fully occupied with the task of regurgitating a pint of shrimps, did not seem to notice the introduction of a third head into the general melee and when the final moment came it would plunge its head into the first gaping beak that was presented, with the slightly desperate air of an aeroplane passenger seizing his little brown paper bag at the onset of the fiftieth air pocket. Only when the last spasm had died away would it realize that it had been feeding a strange offspring, and then Henrietta had to be pretty nifty on her great, flat feet. But even if she did not move quickly enough, and received a beating up for her iniquity, the smug look on her face seemed to argue that it was worth it.

The Golden Swarm

The penguin colony was our southernmost goal, and we stayed there for three weeks. Then we said goodbye to Huichi, who had done so much for us, and drove northwards towards Peninsula Valdés, where, I had been assured, I would find large colonies of fur seal, and the only remaining colony of elephant seals in Argentina.

Peninsula Valdés, a mass of land some eighty miles long by thirty broad, is shaped rather like an axe-head, being connected to the mainland by such a narrow neck of land that you can see the sea on both sides of the road. Entering the peninsula was like coming into a new land. For days we had driven through the monotonous purple scrubland of Patagonia.

Now suddenly we drove into a buttercup-yellow landscape. The bushes were larger, greener, and each decked with a mass of tiny blooms; the countryside, no longer flat but gently undulating, stretched away to the horizon like a yellow sea, shimmering in the sun.

Not only had the landscape changed but it had suddenly become alive. We were driving down the red earth road, liberally sprinkled with backbreaking potholes, when suddenly I caught a flash of movement in the undergrowth and immediately trod on the brakes. To one side of the road, standing knee-deep in the yellow bushes, stood a herd of six guanacos, watching us with an air of intelligent interest. Now guanacos are wild relatives of the rather stocky, dingy brown llama, and I was totally unprepared for the magnificent sight they made.

What I took to be the male of the herd was standing a little in front of the others. He had long, slender racehorse legs, a streamlined body and a graceful neck reminiscent of a giraffe's. His face was much longer and more slender than a llama's but wearing the same supercilious expression. His eyes were dark and enormous. His small neat ears twitched as he put up his chin and examined us as if through a pair of imaginary lorgnettes. Behind him, in a timid bunch, stood his three wives and two babies, each about the size of a terrier, and they had such a look of wide-eyed innocence that it evoked strange gurgles and gasps from the feminine members of the expedition. Instead of the dingy brown I had expected, these animals almost glowed. The neck and legs were the colour of sunshine on sand, while their bodies were covered with a thick fleece of the richest biscuit-brown.

Grabbing the camera I very slowly got out of the Land-Rover. The male guanaco put both ears forward with manifest suspicion. Slowly I started to lift the camera. But this was enough. He uttered a snort, wheeled about, and galloped off, herding his females and babies in front of him. The babies were inclined to think this was rather a lark, and started gambolling in circles, until their father called them to order with a few well-directed kicks. When they got some little distance away they slowed down into a sedate, stiff-legged canter, looking like some strange gingerbread animals, mounted on rockers, tipping and tilting their way through the golden scrub.

By the evening we were nearing Punta del Norte on the east coast of the peninsula, where the biggest concentration of fur seals lived, and we began to look for a campsite. We found one without too much difficulty, a flat grassy space, sheltered on all sides by a gentle rise in the ground. Even so there was a strong wind blowing from the sea, and now that it was evening it became very cold. It was decided that the three female members of the party would sleep inside the Land-Rover, while I slept under it. Then we dug a hole, collected dry brushwood and, taking great care, built a fire to make tea.

The sun set in a nest of pink, scarlet and black clouds, and there was a brief green twilight. Then it darkened, and a huge yellow moon appeared and gazed down at us as we crouched round the fire, huddled in all the clothes we could put on.

Presently the Land-Rover party crept inside the vehicle, with much grunting and argument as to whose feet should go where, and I put earth on the fire and then fashioned myself a bed under the back axle. In spite of the fact that I was wearing three pullovers, two pairs of trousers, a duffel coat and a woolly hat, and had three blankets wrapped round me, I was still cold.

I awoke in the dimly lit silence just before dawn, when even the sound of the sea seemed to have hushed. The hills around were black against the blue-green of the dawn sky, and there was no sound except the hiss of the wind and the faint snore of the surf. I lay there, shivering in my cocoon of clothes and blankets, and debated whether or not I should get up and light the fire and make some tea. Cold though I was under my clothes, it was still a few degrees warmer than wandering about collecting brushwood, and so I decided to stay where I was. I was just trying to insinuate my hand into my duffel-coat pocket for my cigarettes, when I realized that we had a visitor.

A guanaco stood before me, as if conjured out of nothing. He stood some twenty feet away, quite still, and surveyed me with a look of surprise and displeasure, his neat ears twitching back and forth. He wore a faint aristocratic sneer, as if he knew that I had slept in my clothes for the past three nights. He lifted one forefoot daintily and peered down at me, and after a pause for meditation, he belched.

It was not an accidental gurk, the minute breach of good manners that we are all liable to at times. This was a premeditated, rich and prolonged belch, with all the fervour of the Orient in it. He paused for a moment, glaring at me, to make sure that his comment on my worth had made me feel properly humble, and then he turned and disappeared as suddenly as he had come.

Once the sun was up we breakfasted, and then set off on foot to look for the fur seals. As we approached the coast, we became aware of a strange sound, like the frenzied roar of a football crowd heard distantly.

We walked through waist-high golden scrub until we came out on the edge of a small cliff, and there on the shingle beach below us, at the edge of the creaming waves, lay the fur-seal colony.

When we reached this vantage point the noise of the animals smote us roar, bleat, gurgle and cough, like the boiling of an enormous cauldron of porridge.

The colony, consisting of about seven hundred animals, lay so tightly packed that, as they shifted and moved in the sun, they gleamed gold, like a restless swarm of bees. I squatted on the edge of the cliff, staring down at this wonderful collection of animals, completely entranced.

It was the adult bulls that first caught and held my attention, for they were quite the most extraordinary-looking animals I have ever seen. They sat with their shaggy necks bent back so that the fat was scalloped into folds, their snub noses and fat beery faces peering up into the sky with all the pompous arrogance of the Tenniel illustration of Humpty Dumpty.

They had physiques like boxers, the tremendous muscular shoulders tapering down to slender hindquarters and ending, incongruously, in a pair of ridiculous feet which had long slender fingers, carefully webbed. The impression was that the seal was wearing a pair of very elegant frogmen's flippers.

Sometimes you would see an old bull stretched out asleep in the sand, blubbering and snoring to himself, while at the end of his body he would be waving his flippers to and fro, pointing the slender fingers with all the grace of a Balinese dancer.

When these bulls walked, their huge frog-like feet stuck out on either side, and as the motion of the animal's body was rather like a rumba, the effect was extremely funny.

In colouring, the bulls ranged from chocolate to a rich biscuit-brown, fading to russet on the shaggy fur round their shoulders and necks. This made a nice contrast to the wives, who were very much smaller and decked out in silver or golden coats. And whereas their husbands were enormous blundering tanks of animals, the wives were slim, sinuous and sexy, with neat pointed faces and big melting eyes. They were the personification of feminity, graceful to a degree, beautiful, coquettish and at the same time loving.

They were heavenly creatures, and I decided that should I ever have the chance of being an animal I would choose to be a fur seal so that I might enjoy having such a wonderful wife.

Although they had some six miles of beach to use, the colony chose to lie in an area only a quarter of a mile in length. Packed tightly like this, each bull was in a constant state of nerves over his little group of wives, and throughout the colony there were fights breaking out all the time.

A lot of blame for these, I am afraid, was due to the females who—as soon as they thought their husband was not watching—would undulate gracefully across the sand towards the next group, and sit there watching the bull with languishing eyes. It would take a very staunch Presbyterian fur seal to resist the appeal of those pleading melting eyes.

But before any infidelity could take place the husband would suddenly make a rapid count and discover that he was a wife short. As soon as he spotted her, he would surge after her, his enormous bulk scattering the shingle like spray, and from his mouth, with its great white fangs, would issue a prolonged lion-like belching roar. Reaching her, he would catch her by the scruff of the neck and shake her savagely from side to side. Then, with a jerk of his head, he would send her spinning across the sand towards his harem.

By this time the other bull would feel that the husband was too close to *his* wives for safety, and so he would lunge forward with open mouth and the two would join in battle. Most of these fights were merely mock combats, and after a good deal of mouth-opening, roaring and lunging, honour would be satisfied. But occasionally both bulls would lose their tempers, and then it was frightening to watch how two such ponderous creatures could turn into such swift and deadly fighters. The shingle would be churned up as the two colossal creatures snapped and barged at each other's fat neck, and the blood spurted out over the fascinated audience of wives and babies. One of the favourite gambits during these fights was to undulate across the shingle towards your opponent, waving your head from side to side, like a boxer feinting. Then, when you got near enough, you would lunge forward and, with a sideways and downward bite, try to slash open the thick hide of your antagonist's neck. Most of the old bulls on the beach had fresh wounds or white scars decorating their necks, and one I saw looked as though someone had slashed him with a sabre.

When a bull waddled back to his wives after such a battle they would gather round him in admiration and love, elongating their sinuous necks so that they could reach up and nuzzle and kiss his face, rubbing their bodies against his barrel chest, while he stared up into the sky arrogantly, occasionally condescending to bend his head and bite one of his wives gently on the neck.

A lot of the nervous tension among the bulls with wives was due to the gay, slim young bachelor bulls who had been unable to acquire wives at the beginning of the breeding season when the courtship battles take place. These young bulls spent most of their time just sleeping or swimming. But, every now and then, one of them would be smitten with an impish desire to irritate his elders and betters. He would swagger slowly along the colony, gazing about with a benign air of innocence. Then, as he passed a family group in the centre of which squatted an old bull stargazing, the young bachelor would suddenly swerve and break into an undulating run, getting faster and faster as he approached the group. The females would scatter wildly as he burst through their circle, he would hurl himself at the old bull, give him a quick bite on the neck, and then undulate rapidly away before the old bull really knew what was happening. Then, with a roar of rage the old bull would give chase, but by then the gay bachelor had reached the sea and plunged in, so the old bull, grumbling to himself, would return to round up his scattered wives.

The ones that seemed to lead the most carefree and pleasant lives were the young but fully adult bulls, who had succeeded in getting themselves only one wife. They generally lay a little apart from the main colony, their wife and cub alongside them, and spent a lot of time sleeping. They could afford to do this, as it was obviously easier to control one of these high-spirited female seals than to try to cope with the vagaries of six or seven. I was lucky enough to see one of these newly-wed couples consummate their marriage, as it were, and I have never seen such a delicate and beautiful piece of love-play between two animals.

The young bull had dug himself the fur-seal equivalent of a honeymoon cottage in the shingle near the base of the cliff from which I was filming. This cottage consisted of a large, deep hole scraped out with his fore flippers, so that the cool damp shingle beneath the sun-heated top layer was exposed.

He lay in this hole with his wife in a very typical attitude, his great head resting on her back as she lay asleep, at right angles to him. They had lain like this, almost unmoving, for the whole morning. Now, at mid-day, with the fierce sun directly overhead, the bull started to wave his hind flipper in the air, shift his bulk about uneasily, and scoop up great flippersful of damp shingle and shovel them onto his back, in an effort to keep cool. His wife, disturbed by his movements, woke up, yawned widely, and then gave a deep, contented sigh, gazing round placidly with her great, dark eyes.

After a few minutes' contemplation she shifted her body round so that she was lying parallel to the bull, thus depriving him of his headrest. Then she leaned forward and started to bite at his mouth and chin, very delicately, and in a slow and languorous manner. The bull kept his eyes tightly shut, occasionally snorting as if he were embarrassed. But at last the female's love-play seduced him, and he opened his eyes and started to bite at the back of her glossy neck. With these signs of affection from her lord the female became as excited as a puppy, rolling and wriggling under his great head as he bit her, nibbling at his pigeon-chest and uttering subdued "woofing" noises through her nose, so that her long whiskers stood out like fans of spun glass round her neat muzzle. But now she was straining up her face to his so that their whiskers entwined, biting his muzzle, his nose and his throat, and he in his turn engulfed her neck or her throat in savagely restrained bites. When they had reached a climax they relaxed and lay side by side, gently nibbling one another's mouths and faces with a tenderness that was remarkable.

The whole thing had been beautiful to watch.

I have not as yet mentioned the pups which were such an important and amusing part of the colony. There were hundreds of them, sleeping on the shingle in the most extraordinary abandoned attitudes or moving like animated black ink-blots through the mass of sleeping, love-making, bickering adults.

There appeared to be a crèche system in operation for some of the pups, for in places there would be groups of ten or twenty, looking like heaps of curiously shaped coal. There would be a young bull or a couple of females sleeping nearby who were apparently in charge. If one of the babies wandered, an adult would rouse itself, undulate after it, catch it up in its vast mouth, give it a good shaking and throw it back into the nursery again. I wanted to film the daily behaviour of a pup and in order to do this I picked out the only one I saw that was recognizable. He had obviously been born later than the others, for he was only half their size, but what he lacked in inches he more than made up for in determination and personality.

When I first noticed Oswald (as we christened him) he was busily engaged in stalking a long ribbon of glittering green seaweed that he obviously thought was some sort of monstrous sea-serpent which was threatening the colony.

He shambled towards it, and stopped a yard or so away to sniff. A slight wind twitched the end of the seaweed, and at this obviously threatening display Oswald turned and lolloped off as fast as his flippers would carry him. He stopped a safe distance away and peered over his shoulder, but now the seaweed lay still.

Carefully he approached it again, almost tiptoeing on his great flat flippers, his fat little body taut and trembling. Still the seaweed made no movement. Cheered by this display of cowardice, Oswald decided that it was his duty to save the colony. He shuffled his bottom to and fro ridiculously so that his hind flippers got a good grip in the shingle, and then launched himself at the seaweed. In his enthusiasm he rather overshot the mark, and ended up on his nose in a fountain of shingle. But when he sat up, the seaweed dangled from either side of his

mouth like a green moustache, and he looked very pleased that his first bite had apparently disabled the enemy completely.

He galloped off along the beach trailing the weed on each side of him, occasionally shaking his head vigorously, as if to make sure his victim was really dead.

For a quarter of an hour he played with it, until there was nothing left but a few tattered remnants. Then he flung himself down on the shingle, exhausted, and sank into a deep sleep.

Presently, when he woke up, he remembered that he had been looking for his mother before his attention was distracted by the weed. So he made off down the beach, bleating soulfully. Suddenly, in the middle of his grief, he noticed a seagull squatting on the shingle near him. Forgetting about his mother he decided that the seagull should be taught a lesson, so he humped himself up indignantly and rumbaed towards it ferociously, a look of grim determination on his face. Each time Oswald charged, the gull side-stepped neatly, pattering a few paces on its webbed feet, with the air of a professional matador eluding a very inexperienced bull.

Four times this happened, and the gull grew bored. At the next charge

he opened his wings, gave a couple of lazy flaps, and glided off down the beach to a more restful spot.

Oswald, the object of his wrath having vanished, remembered his mother again and started out to search for her, bleating loudly. He ploughed his way through the most crowded part of the colony, treading with complete impartiality on cows and bulls alike, leaving behind him a wake of infuriated adults who had been woken from a refreshing sleep.

At one point he discovered a cow lying on her back, and he decided that it would be a suitable opportunity to stop for a snack. He had just taken a firm hold of one of her teats, when the cow woke up. For a second, still half asleep, she gazed at him fondly; then she suddenly realized that he was not her son, but some dastardly interloper helping himself to a free drink. With a grunt of wrath she pushed her nose under his fat tummy, and, with a quick flip of her head, sent Oswald somersaulting through the air to land on the head of a sleeping bull. The bull was not amused. He sat up, snorted indignantly, and seized Oswald in his great mouth by the scruff of the neck. Then he decided that a little swimming lesson would do Oswald no harm, and so he flopped his way down to the sea, Oswald dangling from his mouth as limp as a glove.

I had often watched the bulls giving the pups swimming lessons, and I felt sorry for Oswald. The bull paused at the edge of the surf, shook Oswald to and fro, and then hurled him some twenty feet out into the waves. After a prolonged submersion Oswald surfaced, spluttering and coughing, and struck out towards the shore. But the bull lumbered into the water, caught him, and proceeded to hold him under the water for five or ten seconds, at last releasing his hold so that Oswald popped up like a cork, gasping for breath.

After this had happened three or four times Oswald was so frightened that he tried to attack the bull's great bulk with open mouth, uttering spluttering yarring cries. At this, the bull simply picked up Oswald, shook him well, flung him out to sea again, and repeated the whole process.

Eventually, when it was obvious that Oswald was exhausted, the bull took him into the shallows and let him rest for a little while, standing guard over him so that he could not escape.

When he was rested Oswald was picked up and thrown out to sea again. The lesson went on for half an hour and would have gone on longer, but another bull came and picked a quarrel with Oswald's instructor, and while they were fighting it out in the shallows Oswald scrambled back to shore as fast as he could, bedraggled and thoroughly chastened by his experience.

It was not until evening that the colony as a whole went swimming. First the cows of a family group would enter the shallows and tumble and curve with gentle movements in the water, their wet coats gleaming and black.

For some time the bull would watch them in a lordly manner; then he would shoulder his huge bulk into the surf and the tempo of the females' play would quicken. They would close in round the bull, curving over and under him, so that he was like a stocky maypole with the slim, swift ribbon of female seals drifting and fluttering round him, gliding faster and faster, demanding his attention as he peered, supremely smug, into the sky.

Suddenly he would bend his head, and bite playfully at a passing body. This was the signal for the water ballet to begin.

The females' arrow-swift bodies and the bulk of the male would entwine like a gleaming black plait, curving and twisting through the water, sliding free of it without a ripple or bursting out in a white rose of foam, their shining bodies curving like boomerangs before plunging into the water again, then as they rolled and twisted, you could see them

biting at each other with a sort of languorous lovingness, the gentle bites of affection, possession and submission.

By this time the sun would have sunk into a sunset of pink, green and gold, and we would make our way back to camp to crouch shivering over the fire, while in the distance, carried by the night wind, we could hear the noises of the seals, belching and roaring and splashing along the empty coast.

The Bulbous Beasts

After we had spent some ten days filming the fur seals I decided that we really ought to locate the elephant seals before they migrated southwards. So, for the next four days, we drove to and fro about the peninsula searching for an *elefantería*, as their colonies were called, and seeing a variety of wildlife, but no elephant seals.

A creature that we saw very frequently was the Darwin's rhea, the South American counterpart of the African ostrich. These birds were

delicate in build and a pearly-grey in colour. They were generally in small flocks of five or six, and on many occasions we saw them moving through the scrub in conjunction with a flock of guanaco. I think one of the loveliest sights we saw was a herd of six guanaco with three graceful cinnamon-coloured babies, trotting slowly through the golden scrub in company with four Darwin's rheas who were ushering along a swarm of twelve young, each dressed in its striped baby plumage, so that they looked like a line of tiny fat wasps.

Rheas are so prolific that their eggs and, to a large extent, their young, form an important item of diet for the predators of the peninsula, among which the pampas fox is one of the most common. These slim, grey, dainty little animals would suddenly dash across the road in front of us, their bushy tails streaming out behind them like puffs of grey smoke. On reaching the other side of the road they would skid to a halt and, squatting on their haunches, examine us craftily.

At one of the places in which we camped a pair of these little foxes paid us a visit. It was about five in the morning, and from my bed under the rear axle of the Land-Rover I was watching the sky turn green with dawn. Suddenly, from the yellow scrub around us, two foxes appeared as unexpectedly and as silently as ghosts.

Having cautiously circled the camp without mishap, they grew bolder. They approached the ashes of the fire, sniffed at them deeply, and then frightened each other by sneezing violently. Recovering from this shock they continued their investigation and found a large roll of bright pink toilet paper. Having proved that it was not edible, they discovered that if it was patted briskly with a paw it unravelled itself in the most satisfactory manner.

So, for the next ten minutes, they danced and whirled on their incredibly slender legs, hurling the toilet roll to and fro, occasionally taking streamers of it in their mouths and leaping daintily into the air, returning to earth with the paper wrapped intricately round their necks and legs.

The whole campsite was taking on a gay carnival air, when somebody in the Land-Rover yawned. The foxes froze instantly. The yawn was repeated, and they vanished as silently as they had come, leaving—as a souvenir of their visit—some hundred feet of pink paper fluttering in the breeze.

Another creature which we met on the roads was the hairy armadillo. These were most frequently seen towards evening, trotting to and fro over the road surfaces, sniffing vigorously, their little clockwork legs moving so

fast they were a mere blur beneath the hairy shell. Frequently they could be seen right down on the seashore, trotting briskly along the tide line, looking like small, rotund colonels on a Bournemouth seafront imbibing the health-giving ozone, though occasionally they would spoil the illusion by stopping to have a light snack off a dead crab, a thing I have never seen a colonel do.

Watching all this wildlife was, of course, fascinating, but it was not bringing us any nearer to the elephant seals. We had, by now, covered quite a large area of the coast and I began to think that the elephant seals were already drifting southwards towards the Falkland Islands.

Then one day we were walking along a beach that was covered haphazardly with grey and fawn coloured boulders, some as large as a cottage. We struggled through and over them for some distance, and then sat down on one that made a natural seat and unpacked our food and wine. I was convinced by then that there was not an elephant seal for miles, and I was thoroughly depressed.

"Well, we might find some tomorrow," said Jacquie soothingly, handing me a sandwich.

"No," I said, refusing to be comforted, "they've had their babies and left."

Marie, with the air of one who is making the best of a disaster, seized a bottle of wine, and as the cork popped out of the bottle a large, egg-shaped boulder some ten feet away gave a deep and lugubrious sigh, opened a pair of huge, gentle, liquid-looking eyes of the deepest black, and gazed at us placidly.

Once it had thus revealed itself as an elephant seal, a close and excited scrutiny of the surrounding beach showed us that we were, in fact, sitting next to twelve of the gigantic beasts, all closely resembling the rocks amongst which they lay, and all calmly continuing to sleep while we walked among them.

We soon discovered that of the twelve animals three were males, six were females, and three were well-grown young. The babies measured about six feet in length, and the females twelve to fourteen feet. The real bulk was reserved for the males. Two of these were young bulls, each about eighteen feet in length, while the last was a fully adult bull, and measured twenty-one feet.

This bull was a magnificent beast, with a huge barrel-like body, and the great carunculated nose of a confirmed gin-drinker. He lay on the shining shingle like a colossal blob of putty, occasionally sighing deeply so that his nose wobbled like a jelly. When we approached within three or four feet to measure and take photographs, all he did was to open his eyes, survey us dreamily, and sink back into sleep again.

For me this was a tremendously exciting experience. My ambition had always been to see a live elephant seal in his natural environment, and here I was within five feet of one who lay there looking not unlike a baby barrage balloon which has, unaccountably, been filled with dough. With a sandwich in one hand and a stopwatch in the other I checked on his breathing, which is one of the many remarkable things about an elephant seal. They breathe fairly regularly some thirty times during five minutes, and then they stop breathing for a time, which varies from five to eight minutes. Presumably this is of great use to them when they are at sea.

I was so carried away, lying there with this gigantic animal within touching distance, that I began to give the others a lecture on the elephant seal.

"It's quite extraordinary, the soundness of their sleep. Do you know there was one naturalist who actually went and lay on top of an elephant seal without waking it?"

Jacquie surveyed the colossal animal in front of me.

"Rather him than me," she said.

I went on to other things: there are several that strike one immediately about elephant seals. The first is their ridiculous hindquarters. The fur seal (which is really a sea lion) has the hind limbs well developed as legs, so that it can hoist itself up on to all fours and walk as a dog or a cat would. But in the elephant seal, which is a true seal, the hind limbs are minute, with stupid flippers that make the animal look as though it had a couple of empty gloves attached to its rear end. All the propulsion comes from the front flippers, and the humping of the massive back, a slow, ungainly method of movement.

There was quite a colour variation among the herd we had found. The old bull was a rich, deep slate-grey, tastefully speckled here and there with green marine algae. The young bulls and the cows were a much paler grey. The babies, unlike their bald and leathery parents, were wearing a fine fur coat of moon-white hair, close and tight as plush. The adults had folds and wrinkles all over them, but the babies were so rotund and glossy they looked as though they had been blown up with pumps, and would, if they were not careful, take to the air.

From the point of view of filming, the elephant-seal colony was, to say the least, difficult. The only real movement they made was to open and close their huge nostrils as they breathed, and occasionally one would shovel some shingle onto its back. They lacked action, which, after all, is necessary for a moving picture. Now one of the extraordinary things about these seals is the flexibility of the backbone. In spite of their bulk they can bend themselves backwards, like a hoop, until the head touches the uplifted tail. How to get them to demonstrate this was somewhat of a puzzle. At last, however, we were successful with the old bull, by the simple expedient of throwing handfuls of fine gravel onto his tail. It did not, of course, hurt him, but a constant rain of shingle on your rear end when you are trying to sleep can be extremely irritating. He suddenly became very wide awake and reared up so that he was like the letter J with his head high in the air, his mouth opened wide uttering a loud hissing roar, an oddly reptilian sound for such a monstrous mammal to make. Four times he reared up like this, and then, seeing that the display was having no detrimental effect on our morale, he did what all seals do in moments of crisis: he burst into tears. Great black tears oozed out of his eyes and trickled forlornly down his cheeks and he proceeded to hump backwards towards the sea, like a gargantuan caterpillar, the fat along his back rippling into waves as he moved. At last, with a final plaintive roar, he backed into the water. The rest of the herd, alarmed at their lord and master's disappearance, raised their heads and looked at us uneasily. Then one of the babies panicked, and hunched its way down to the sea, tears streaming down its white face. This was the final straw, and within a minute the whole herd was rushing seawards.

Sadly we packed up our equipment and started up the cliff, sadly because we had just completed our last photographic task, and must leave the wonderful peninsula and head back to Buenos Aires and the next stage of the expedition. As we made our way along the twilit cliff path we saw the old bull for the last time. His head appeared out of a wave, his dark eyes surveyed us puzzledly. He snorted, a reverberating noise that echoed along the cliffs. Then, still watching us sadly, he sank slowly beneath the icy waters and disappeared.

Part Two
The Customs of the Country

The plane taxied out across the dark airfield to the lighted runway, revved up its engine, and then suddenly rushed forward. The striplights fled past, and we were airborne, the plane tipping from side to side like a slightly drunken swallow as it climbed. Below me, Buenos Aires lay spread in the warm night like a chessboard of multicoloured stars. I unfastened my safety belt, lit a cigarette and lay back in my seat, feeling very mellow. At last I was on my way to a place I had long wanted to visit, a place with a magical name: Jujuy.

When we returned from the south, Jacquie had had to return to England, Marie had gone back to her job, and this left Sophie and me to finish the trip. So, while I collected animals in various places, Sophie remained in our little villa to look after them as I brought them back. Now I was making tracks for Jujuy, to try to add to the collection.

As the plane droned on through the night I tried to remember the little I knew about Jujuy. It is a northwestern province of Argentina, bordered by the mountains of Bolivia and Chile and by the desiccated province of Salta. It is a curious place in many ways, but chiefly because it is like a tropical tongue, as it were, inserted into Argentina, where I knew that I could find the exciting tropical fauna that I was after. Thinking about these magnificent animals I fell into a deep sleep, only to be awoken by the steward at two in the morning. Apparently we had arrived at some godforsaken place, and all passengers had to disembark while the plane refuelled. As soon as they would allow I got on the plane again, settled down and tried to sleep.

Almost immediately I was roused by what appeared to be a ten-ton weight descending on my arm. I extricated it with difficulty and glared at the person responsible. This was not very effective as the plane was lit by what appeared to be a series of anaemic fireflies. All I could see was that the next seat to me (until now mercifully empty) was being inundated—there is no other word—by a female of colossal proportions, and what she could not cram into her own seat was overflowing into mine.

"*Buenas noches,*" she said pleasantly.

"*Buenas noches,*" I mumbled, and closed my eyes in order to put an end to the conversation. Fortunately my companion, after this exchange, settled herself down for sleep, with much grunting and shifting and deep shuddering sighs that were vaguely reminiscent of the elephant seals.

When I awoke it was light, and I surreptitiously examined my sleeping  companion. She was a fine figure of a woman—all twenty stone of her. She had clad her generous body in a silk dress in yellow and green and she was wearing scarlet shoes, both now some distance from her feet. Her hair was bright glossy black and carefully arranged in tiny curls all over her head, and to crown this she was wearing a straw hat to which half the fruit and vegetable produce of Argentina appeared to have been attached. Her hands were folded demurely in her lap, and though they were work-roughened they were tiny and beautifully formed, like the hands of so many fat people. As I was watching her she suddenly gave a last shuddering sigh and opened large, pansy-dark eyes and gazed about her with the vacant expression of an awakening baby. Then she focused on me and her dumpling face spread into a dimpled smile.

"*Buenos dias, señor,*" she said, inclining her head.

"*Buenos dias, señora,*" I replied, also inclining my head gravely. Wedged as I was there was no escape.

"Where are you travelling to, *señor?*" she asked.

"Jujuy, *señora,*" I replied.

"Ah, Jujuy?" she said, opening wide her kindly eyes and raising her eyebrows, as though Jujuy was the most interesting and desirable place in the world. "You are German?" she asked.

"No, English."

"Ah, English?" again with the delighted surprise.

I felt it was time I took a more active part in the conversation. "I do not speak Spanish at all," I explained, "only a very little."

"But you speak *beautifully*," she said, patting my knee, and then qualified it by adding, "and I will speak slowly so that you may understand."

I sighed and gave myself up to my fate. Evidently she had concluded that I would get a better grasp of her conversation if she shouted, so now the whole plane was party to our confidences. Her name, it appeared, was Rosa Lillipampila and she was on her way to visit her married son, one of six children, whom she had not seen for three years. This was her first flight in a plane and she was taking a childlike delight in it. She kept breaking into shrill cries (which made the more nervous of the other passengers jump) in order to lean over me, enveloping me in scent and bosom, to peer at some landmark below. When the steward came round with morning coffee she fumbled for her bag to pay, and when it was explained that it was free she was so delighted that you would have thought the rather grubby paper cup was a magnum of champagne. Presently the red lights went on to tell us that we were landing yet again to refuel, and I helped her get the safety belt round her enormous girth. This was a strenuous task, and her shrieks of merriment at our efforts echoed up and down the plane.

A moment later, we clambered out onto the tarmac, stiff and crumpled, and I found that my girlfriend moved with the grace and lightness of a cloud. With a courteous, old-world gesture I offered her my arm, and she accepted it with a beaming, coquettish smile. Linked together like a courting couple we made our way towards the airport's inevitable small cafe, and were informed that we would be delayed two hours. There was, however, a company bus which would run all passengers into town, and there, at an hotel, we could have anything we wanted at the air company's expense. My girlfriend was delighted. Such generosity! Such kindness! I helped her into the bus, and we rattled into the town and drew up outside a curiously Victorian-looking hotel.

Inside, there were imitation brown marble pillars, pots and pots of decayed-looking palms, an endless mosaic of tiny tables, and flocks of waiters who looked like ambassadors on holiday. My companion held very tight to my arm as I steered her to a table. All this splendour seemed to bereave her of speech, but soon, under the influence of five large cups of coffee with cream, a plate of hot *medialunas* and butter, followed by six cream cakes and half a pound of grapes, she lost her awe of the place, and even ordered one of the ambassadors to fetch her a plate to put her grape-pips on.

Presently, replete with free food, we went for a walk round the town. My girlfriend was delighted to act as a guide to a real foreigner, and there was nothing she did not show and explain to me. This was a shoeshop ... see, there were shoes in the window. Ah, and here we had a chemist's shop, where you purchased medicines when you were not well. She stood in front of the chemist's window giving such a realistic display of suffering that I expected someone to call for an ambulance. Altogether our tour was a great success, and I was quite sorry when we had to return to the airport and board the plane for the last leg of our journey.

Hitherto the country we had been flying over had been typical flat Pampa; but now hills became more and more frequent, and higher and higher, covered with gigantic cacti like huge green surrealistic candel-abra. And then the airpockets started. The first was quite a big one, and one felt one's stomach had been left at least a hundred feet up as the plane dropped. My companion, who had been in the middle of a story about some remote cousin, uttered a cry of such a piercing quality that the whole of the aircraft was thrown into confusion. Then, to my relief, she burst into peals of happy laughter.

"What was that?" she asked me.

I did my best, in my limited Spanish, to explain the mysteries of airpockets, while she waited expectantly for the next one so that she could enjoy it to the full, for, as she explained, she had not been prepared for the first. She was soon rewarded with a real beauty, and greeted it with a scream of delighted laughter. She was like a child on a switchback in a fair; the whole thing might have been another special treat which the air company had provided. The rest of the passengers, I noticed, were not treating the airpockets in the same light-hearted way, and the man across the gangway had grown progressively greener. My friend noticed this too, and was all commiseration. She leaned across the gangway.

"Are you ill, *señor?*" she inquired. He nodded mutely.

"Ah, you poor thing," she said, and burrowing into her bag produced a huge bag of very sticky and pungent sweets. "These are very good for sickness," she proclaimed. "Take one."

The poor man took one look into the paper bag and shook his head vigorously. My friend gave him a glance of pity and popped three of the sweets into her mouth. As she sucked vigorously and loudly she suddenly noticed something that had escaped her sharp eyes before, the brown paper bag in a little bracket attached to the back of the seat in front of us.

She peered inside, obviously wondering if some other magnificent largesse was concealed inside it. Then she turned a puzzled eye on me.

"What is this for?" she asked in a penetrating voice.

I explained. She held it aloft and examined it minutely.

"Well," she said at last, "if I wanted to get sick I should want something *much* larger than *that*."

The vision conjured up by her words was too much for the man across the gangway. He cast one look at her, then dived precipitately for his own bag and buried his face in it.

When the plane eventually touched down my girlfriend and I were the only ones who didn't look as though we had just been through a hurricane.

At the airport her son was waiting, a pleasant-faced man who was identical in shape to his mother. Uttering shrill cries they undulated towards each other and embraced with a quivering crash. When they surfaced, I was introduced and commended for the care I had taken of my protégée en route. Then, because the driver who was to meet me was nowhere to be seen, the entire Lillipampila family (son, wife, three children and grandmother) hunted round the airport like foxhounds until they found him. They saw me to the car, embraced me, and stood, a solid facade of fat, beaming and waving as I drove off on my way to Calilegua, the place where I was to stay.

Jujuy

Calilegua was primarily a sugar-producing estate, a flat plain cupped in a half-moon of mountains that were covered with thick, tropical forest. It was curious how suddenly you came upon this lushness of vegetation. We left the airport and for the first hour or so drove through a desiccated landscape of semi-eroded hills, dotted here and there with giant cacti or with the great swollen trunks of the *palo borracho* trees, their bark as thickly covered with spines as a hedgehog's back. Then we sped down a hill into the valley of Calilegua, and the vegetation changed so suddenly to the vivid greens of the tropics that it was almost painful to the eye. Shortly afterwards, a small flock of parakeets swooped across the road, wheezing and chittering. Then we passed a group of Indians, dressed in tattered shirts and trousers and gigantic straw hats. They were short and squat, with Mongolian features and the curious sloe-coloured eyes over which there seems to be a bloom like a plum that covers thought and expression.

After the flat scenery of the Pampa, the Indians, the parakeets and the vividness of the country went to my head like wine.

Presently the driver swung off the main road onto a rough track, thickly lined on both sides by gigantic bamboos that bent gracefully over it, intertwining their fluttering green leaves so that it was like driving down the nave of a cathedral. Presently we stopped at a villa half hidden in a riot of flowers and creepers. Joan Lett, who, with her husband Charles, had invited me to Calilegua, came out to greet me, took me inside and gave me a most welcome cup of tea. When Charles returned from his work, we sat on the balcony in the fading indigo evening and discussed my plan of campaign.

It has always been my experience that if you go to an area which is fairly well populated you can obtain most of your common fauna without much difficulty, for the local people either keep the creatures as pets, or rear them to form the basis of a meal. I propounded this philosophy to Charles, as the ice tinkled musically in our gin-and-tonics, and he promised that he would get one of his more intelligent helpers to make inquiries in the village.

The next morning, after breakfast, I was out in the garden watching a flock of gold, blue and silver butterflies feeding on some scarlet blooms, when I heard a man singing in a pleasant tenor voice, as he came down the avenue of bamboo.

As he reached the gate he clapped his hands in the customary manner of anyone in South America when arriving at your house, opened the gate and joined me. He was a tiny man, about five feet in height and as slender as a boy. He had a handsome, faintly skull-like face, huge dark eyes and black hair cropped close to his head. He held out a hand that looked as fragile as the butterflies we were surrounded by.

"Señor Durrell?" he inquired.

"Yes," I replied, shaking his hand gently, for fear it should break.

"I am Luna," he said, as if this should be sufficient explanation.

"Señor Lett sent you?" I asked.

"*Si, si*," he answered, giving me a smile of great charm and sweetness.

There was a pause, and we smiled at each other amiably while I racked my brain for Spanish phrases.

"You speak English?" I inquired hopefully.

"No, very small," said Luna, spreading his hands and smiling gently, as if deploring this terrible gap in his education.

It seemed obvious that his knowledge of English was about as extensive as mine of Spanish. This later proved to be true. Both of us could understand each other's language, but both were incapable of speaking more than a few ungrammatical words.

"You ... I ... go Helmuth," suggested Luna suddenly, waving a delicate hand.

I agreed, wondering what a Helmuth was. So we walked down the avenue of bamboo, and came to a large area of lawn, dotted with gigantic palm trees, their trunks covered with parasitic plants and orchids. Then we walked through these towards a long, low red-brick building, while the hummingbirds flipped and whirred round us, gleaming and changing with the delicate sheen one sees on a soap bubble. Luna led me through gauze-covered doors into a large cool dining room, and there, devouring breakfast at a huge table, was a man of about thirty with barley-sugar-coloured hair, vivid blue eyes and a leathery, red, humorous face. He looked up as we entered and gave us a wide, impish grin.

"Helmuth," said Luna, pointing to this individual; an Austrian, I was to learn, who had left Europe after the war. Helmuth rose from the table and extended a large, freckled hand.

"Hullo," he said, crushing my hand in his, "I'm Helmuth. Sit down and have some breakfast, eh?"

I explained that I had already had some breakfast, and so Helmuth returned to his victuals, talking to me between mouthfuls, while Luna drooped languidly in a chair and hummed softly to himself.

"Charles tells me you want animals, eh?" said Helmuth. "Well, there *are* animals, of course, up in the hills, but I don't know what you'll get in the villages. However, we go see, eh?"

When Helmuth had assured himself that there was nothing edible left on the table, he hustled Luna and myself into his station wagon, and drove down to the village.

It was a fairly typical one, consisting of small whitewashed shacks, each standing in its own little patch of ground, surrounded by a bamboo fence. Helmuth stopped at one of these little shanties and peered hopefully into the riot of pomegranate trees, covered with red flowers, that filled the tiny garden.

"Here, the other day, I think I see a parrot," he explained.

We left the station wagon, clapped our hands and waited patiently at the gate. Presently, from inside the shack, erupted a brood of chocolate-coloured children, all dressed in clean but tattered clothing, who lined up like a defending army, each sucking its thumb vigorously. They were followed by their mother, a short, rather handsome Indian woman with a shy smile.

"Enter, *senõres*," she called, beckoning us into the garden.

We went in, and Helmuth, exuding goodwill and personality, beamed at the woman.

"This *señor*," he said, gripping my shoulder tightly, as if fearful that I might run away, "this *señor* wants *bichos*, live *bichos*, eh? Now, the other day when I passed your house, I saw that you possessed a parrot, a very common and rather ugly parrot which I have no doubt the *señor* will despise. Nevertheless, I am bound to show it to him, worthless though it is."

The woman bristled.

"It is a beautiful parrot," she said shrilly and indignantly, "a very beautiful parrot, and one, moreover, of a kind that is extremely rare."

"Nonsense," said Helmuth firmly, "I have seen many like it in the market in Jujuy, and they were so common they were practically having to give them away."

I felt it was about time I entered the fray.

"Er ... Helmuth," I said tentatively, "I don't want to interfere, but wouldn't it be a good idea if I saw the bird first, before we start bargaining?"

"Yes," said Helmuth, struck by the novelty of this idea, "yes, let us see the bird."

He turned and glared at the woman.

"Where is this wretched bird of yours?" he inquired.

The woman pointed silently over my left shoulder, and turning round I found that the parrot had been perching among the green leaves of a pomegranate tree some three feet away, an interested spectator of our bargaining. As soon as I saw him I knew that I must have him, for he was a red-fronted Tucuman Amazon. His plumage was a rich grass-green with tinges of yellow here and there; he had bare white rings round his dark eyes, and the whole of his forehead was a rich scarlet. Above each foot he appeared to be wearing orange garters. Trying to wipe the acquisitive look off my face I turned to Helmuth and shrugged, with elaborate unconcern.

"It's a rarity," I said, trying to infuse dislike and loathing for the parrot into my voice, "I must have it."

"You see?" said Helmuth, returning to the attack, "the *señor* says it is a very common bird, and he already has six of them down in Buenos Aires."

The woman regarded us both with deep suspicion, while I tried to look like a man who possessed six Tucuman Amazons. She wavered, and then played her trump card.

"But this one *talks*," she said triumphantly.

"The *señor* does not care if they talk or not," Helmuth countered quickly. "We will give you thirty pesos for it."

"Two hundred," said the woman, "for a parrot that talks, two hundred is cheap."

"Nonsense," said Helmuth. "Anyway, how do we know it talks? It hasn't said anything."

"Blanco, Blanco," cooed the woman, "speak to Mama ... speak, Blanco."

Blanco eyed us all in a considering way.

"Fifty pesos, take it or leave it," said Helmuth flatly. "That's a lot of money for a bird that won't talk."

"Blanco, Blanco, speak," wailed the woman, "say something for the *señores* ... please."

The parrot shuffled his green feathering with a silken sound, put his head on one side and spoke.

"*Hijo de puta*," he said, clearly and slowly.

The woman stood as though transfixed, her mouth open, unable to believe in the perfidy of her pet. Helmuth uttered a great sigh as of someone who knows the battle is won. Slowly, and with a look of utter malignancy, he turned to the unfortunate woman.

"So!" he hissed, like the villain in a melodrama. "So! This is your idea of a talking parrot, eh?"

"But, *señor* ..." began the woman faintly.

"Enough!" said Helmuth, cutting her short. "We have heard enough. A stranger enters your gates, in order to help you by paying you money for a worthless bird. And what do you do? You try and cheat him by telling him your bird talks."

"But it *does* talk," protested the woman faintly.

"Yes, *but what does it say*?" hissed Helmuth. He paused, drew himself up to his full height, took a deep breath and roared: "It insults not only this good-natured, kindly *señor*, but also his mother."

The woman looked down at the ground and twiddled her bare toes in the dust. She was beaten and she knew it. Helmuth turned to me.

"We have got her," he said in a pleading tone of voice, "all you have to do is to try and look insulted."

"But I am insulted," I said, trying to suppress the desire to giggle.

"Never, in fact, in a long career of being insulted, have I been so insulted."

"You're doing fine," said Helmuth, holding out both hands as if begging me to relent. "Now give in a bit."

I tried to look stern but forgiving. "All right," I said in a reluctant tone, "but only this once. Fifty, you said?"

"Yes," said Helmuth, and as I pulled out my wallet he turned again to the woman. "The *señor*, because he is the very soul of kindness, has forgiven you the insult. He will pay you the fifty pesos that you demanded, in your greed."

The woman beamed. I paid over the grubby notes, and then approached the parrot. I held out my finger, and he gravely climbed on to it, and then made his way up to my shoulder. Here he paused, gave me a knowing look, and then, as we closed the bamboo gate behind us and were getting into the car, he turned and fired his parting shot.

"*Estupido*," he called to his late owner, "*muy estupido*."

"That parrot," said Helmuth, hastily starting the car, "is a devil."

I was inclined to agree with him.

Our subsequent tour of the village was not entirely unproductive. By cross-questioning nearly everyone we met we managed to run to earth five yellow-fronted Amazon parrots, an armadillo and two grey-necked guans. These latter are game birds which look, at first glance, rather like slim hen pheasants. But under the chin they have two drooping red wattles, and the feathers on their heads, when they get excited, stand up in a kind of crest that looks like a lengthy crewcut. They were both young birds and were ridiculously tame. The Amazon parrots were also tame, but none of them had the knowingness or the vocabulary of Blanco. All they could do was to whistle and mutter "*Lorito*", which is the Argentine equivalent of "Polly". Nevertheless, I carried my purchases back in triumph to the house, where Joan Lett had kindly allowed me to use their empty garage as a storehouse for my creatures.

As I had no cages ready I had to let them all loose in the garage, and to my surprise this arrangement worked very well. The parrots all found themselves convenient perches, just out of pecking range of each other and, though it had obviously been agreed that Blanco was the boss, there was no unmannerly squabbling. The guans also found themselves perches, but these they used only to sleep on, preferring to spend their days stalking about the floor, occasionally throwing back their heads and letting forth their ear-splitting cry. The armadillo, immediately on being released, fled behind a large box and spent all day there meditating, only tiptoeing out at night to eat his food, casting many fearful glances at the sleeping birds.

In the following days the news spread through the village that there had arrived a mad gringo who was willing to pay good money for live animals, and the trickle of specimens started. Among the first arrivals was an Indian clasping a large straw hat tenderly to his bosom. After a polite exchange of greetings he held it out, beaming hopefully at me, and I saw reclining at the bottom the most delightful kitten. It was a baby Geoffroy's cat, a small species of wild cat which is getting increasingly rare in South America. Its basic colouring was a pale fawny-yellow, and it was dappled all over with neat, dark brown spots. It regarded me with large bluey green eyes, as if pleading to be picked up. I should have known better. Misled by its seraphic expression, I tried to grasp it by the scruff of the neck. The next moment I had a bad bite through the ball of my thumb and twelve deep red grooves across the back of my hand. As I withdrew my hand, cursing, the kitten resumed its innocent pose. While I sucked my hand like a half-starved vampire, I bargained with the Indian and eventually purchased my antagonist. Then I tipped it, hissing and snarling like a miniature jaguar, into a box full of straw. There I left it for an hour or so to settle down.

When I thought it would be willing to accept my overtures of friendship, I removed the lid of the box and peered in hopefully. I missed losing my left eye by approximately three millimetres. I wiped the blood from my cheek thoughtfully; obviously my latest specimen was not going to be easy. Wrapping my hand in a piece of sacking I placed a saucer of raw egg and minced meat in one corner of the box, and a bowl of milk in the other, and then left the kitten to its own devices. The next morning neither of the two offerings had been touched. A bottle seemed the only way of getting any nourishment down it. With a premonition that this was going to hurt me more than the kitten, I filled one of my feeding-bottles with warm milk, wrapped my hand in sacking and approached the box.

Now I have had a fair amount of experience in trying to get frightened, irritated or just plain stupid animals to feed from a bottle, and I thought

337

that I knew most of the tricks. But after half an hour of struggling with the Geoffroy's kitten I was covered in milk and blood and thoroughly exhausted, whereas the kitten regarded me with blazing eyes and seemed quite ready to continue the fight. In this stubborn mood, I knew that it was capable of quite literally starving itself to death. I put it back in its box, and was washing my wounds when Luna arrived, singing cheerfully.

"Good morning, Gerry," he said and then his eyes widened, for I was still bleeding profusely.

"What's this?" he asked.

"A cat ... *gato*," I said irritably.

"Puma ... jaguar?" he asked hopefully.

"No," I said reluctantly, "*chico gato montes*."

"*Chico gato montes*," he repeated incredulously, "do this?"

"Yes. The little fool won't eat. What it really needs is an example ..." My voice died away as an idea struck me. "Come on, Luna, we'll go and see Helmuth's wife. She can help."

"But, Gerry, Helmuth won't like it if Edna is bitten by a *gato montes*," Luna pointed out.

"She won't get bitten," I explained. "I just want her to give me a kitten."

Luna gazed at me with dark, puzzled eyes, but the conundrum was too much for him, and so he merely shrugged and followed me round to Helmuth's and Edna's comfortable sitting room, where Edna was ensconced over a huge pile of socks, darning placidly.

"Hullo," she said, giving us her wide, attractive smile, "the gin is over there, help yourself."

Edna had a beautiful and placid nature. I am sure that if you walked into her sitting room with fourteen Martians in tow she would merely smile and point out the location of the gin.

"Thank you, dear," I said, "but I didn't come for gin. I want a kitten."

"Today Gerry is *loco*," said Luna, with conviction.

"I have just bought a baby *gato montes*," I explained to Edna. "It's extremely wild. It won't eat by itself, and this is what it did when I tried to feed it on the bottle."

I displayed my wounds.

Edna looked stern. She folded up the sock she was darning.

"Have you put disinfectant on those cuts?" she inquired, obviously preparing herself for a medical orgy.

"Never mind the cuts .... What I want from you is an ordinary kitten.

Didn't you say the other day that you were infested with kittens over here?"

Edna considered. "If I give you a kitten will you let me disinfect your cuts?" she asked cunningly. I sighed.

"All right, blackmailer," I said.

So Edna disappeared into the kitchen quarters, whence came a lot of shrill exclamations and much giggling. Then she returned with a bowl of hot water and proceeded to minister unto my cuts, while a procession of semi-hysterical Indian maids filed into the room, carrying in their arms kittens of all ages and colours. Eventually I chose a fat, placid female tabby which was approximately the same size and age as my wild cat, and carried it back in triumph to the garage. Here I spent an hour constructing a rough cage. When it was ready I put the tabby kitten in first, and left it to settle down.

Most wild animals have a very strong sense of territory. In the wild state, they each have a particular bit of forest or grassland which they consider their own preserve, and will defend it to the death against any other member of their own species (or other animals, sometimes) that tries to enter it.

When you put a wild animal into a cage, the cage becomes its territory. So, if you want to confine two animals in the same cage, you generally have to employ low cunning. The best thing to do is to introduce the weaker of the two animals into the cage first. When it has settled down, you then put the stronger one in with it. The stronger one will, of course, still remain the dominant animal, but as far as he is concerned he has been introduced into someone else's territory, and this takes the edge off his potential viciousness.

In this case I was sure that the baby Geoffroy's was quite capable of killing the domestic kitten, if I introduced the kitten to it. So, once the tabby had settled down, I seized the Geoffroy's and pushed it, snarling and raving, into the cage, and stood back to see what would happen. The tabby was delighted. It came forward to the angry Geoffroy's and started to rub itself against its neck, purring loudly. The Geoffroy's, taken aback by its greeting as I had hoped, merely spat rather rudely and retreated into a corner, while the tabby, having made the first overtures, proceeded to wash itself with a self-satisfied air. I covered the front of the cage with a piece of sacking and left them to settle down, for I was sure now that the Geoffroy's would do the tabby no real harm.

That evening I found them lying side by side, and the Geoffroy's, instead of spitting at me as it had done up until now, contented itself with merely lifting its lip in a warning manner. I carefully inserted a large bowl of milk into the cage, and a plate containing finely chopped meat and raw egg. This was the crucial test, for I was hoping that the tabby would fall upon this delicious fare and, by example, encourage the Geoffroy's to eat. Sure enough, the tabby, purring like an ancient outboard engine, flung itself at the bowl of milk, took a long drink and then settled down to the meat and egg. I had retreated to a place where I could see without being seen, and I watched the Geoffroy's carefully. To begin with it took no interest at all, but eventually the noise the tabby was making—it was a rather messy feeder—attracted its attention. It rose cautiously and approached the plate, while I held my breath. Delicately it sniffed round the edge of the plate, while the tabby lifted a face that was dripping with raw egg and gave a mew of encouragement. The Geoffroy's stood pondering for a moment and then, to my delight, sank down by the plate and started to eat. I watched until they had cleaned both plates, which I replenished before going off to bed. The next morning both plates were spotless, and the kittens were locked in each other's arms, fast asleep, their stomachs bulging like two little hairy balloons. My battle with the Geoffroy's was won.

A City of "Bichos"

Ever since my arrival in Calilegua, Luna had been pestering me to accompany him to a town called Oran, which lay some fifty miles away, and where, he assured me, I would get plenty of *bichos*. I was a bit chary about this, for I knew how easy it is to rush frantically from one place to another on a collecting trip, and achieve very little. One evening I decided to discuss it with Charles.

"Why is Luna so keen on Oran?" I asked.

"Well," said Charles drily, "it's his home town, for one thing, but this might prove an advantage, for it means that he knows everyone. I think you could do worse than go and investigate, Gerry."

"Can Luna get the time off?" I asked.

Charles smiled his gentle smile.

"I don't think that we would notice his absence for three days," he said, "and that should give you time to denude Oran of whatever fauna is lurking there."

"Wonderful," I said, "and now I must go and see Edna."

"Why Edna?"

"Well, someone's got to feed my animals while I'm away, and I'm hoping Edna has a kind heart."

I found Helmuth, Edna and Luna arguing over the relative merits of two folksongs which they kept playing over and over again on the gramophone. Edna pointed silently to the drinks; I helped myself, and then went and sat on the floor at her feet.

"Edna," I said, during a lull in the argument, "I love you."

She raised one eyebrow sardonically and regarded me.

"If Helmuth wasn't bigger than me I would suggest that we elope," I went on. "Since I first saw you I have been mad about you."

"What do you want?" she inquired.

I sighed. "You have no soul," I complained. "Well, Charles says that Luna and I can go to Oran for three days. Will you look after my animals?"

"But, of course," she said.

"But, of course," echoed Helmuth. "Gerry, you are very stupid. I tell you we will help all we can." He splashed gin into my glass. "Except," he added reluctantly, "let you elope with my wife."

So, early one morning, Luna and I set out in a small station wagon driven by a gay, semi-inebriated individual, sporting a moustache so large it looked like a nature reserve. We took with us only the bare essentials of travel: Luna's guitar, three bottles of wine, my wallet well stuffed with pesos, the recording machine and cameras. We also had a clean shirt each, which our driver placed reverently in a pool of oil.

All the previous night it had rained with a loudness and thoroughness that only the tropics can achieve; and the earth road had turned into something resembling a badly made blancmange. We had been travelling some three quarters of an hour when our driver slithered round a corner on two wheels and I saw something ahead that made my heart sink. Before us lay a torrent of red, froth-flecked water some four hundred yards across. At the edge of this, like a line of depressed elephants, stood three lorries, while in mid-stream another lorry was being laboriously dragged across to the opposite bank by a gigantic tractor, fitted with a winch and steel cable and run by two laconic-looking Indians. Our driver joined the line of waiting lorries, switched off his engine and beamed at us.

"*Mucha agua*," he pointed out to me, in case I had missed noticing the miniature Bay of Biscay we had to cross. The previous day this broad torrent had probably been a mere trickle, glinting over its bed of pebbles, but one night's tropical rain had swollen it into a full-sized river.

At length, after an hour, the last of the lorries had been hauled over and it was our turn. The hawser was attached to our bumper and the tractor gingerly drew us into the flood. Slowly the water rose higher and higher, until it was spurting in through the cracks of the door. Gradually it rose until it covered our shoes.

We were now approximately halfway across, and the force of the water was kindly but firmly pushing us downstream of the tractor so that I felt as though we were some gigantic fish that the two Indians were playing. The icy water reached the level of the seats; here it paused for a moment and then overflowed generously under our behinds. At this crucial moment, we heard the winch stop.

"Arrr!" roared our driver, sticking his head out of the window, his moustache quivering impressively, "*Que pasa?*"

By now the tractor was well up on the opposite shore. One of the Indians leaped off it and loped slowly off down the road; the other pushed his big straw hat onto the back of his head and slowly approached the bank of the river.

"*Nafta no hay*," he explained, scratching his stomach with every evidence of satisfaction.

"Fine time for them to run out of petrol," I said irritably.

Half an hour passed. Then an hour. Our nether regions were so frozen that we were all shifting uneasily in our seats, making noises like a troupe of hippopotami enjoying a wallow in a succulent swamp. At last the first Indian appeared carrying a can of petrol. The tractor sprang into life, the hawser tightened and we were drawn slowly towards the bank.

When we reached dry land we all got out, removed our trousers and wrung them out, while our driver roared insults at the Indians, who both grinned at us amiably. Then we turned our attention to drying out the engine, and at last piled in again and jolted off down the road, the Indians waving their straw hats in gay farewell.

Eventually we reached Oran. Luna's charming family greeted us with delight, whipped our clothes away to be dried, and sat us down to eat an enormous meal in an inner courtyard overflowing with flowers. While we ate and drank, Luna sent an apparently endless stream of his smaller relatives on mysterious missions, and they kept reappearing to whisper reports to him, whereupon he would nod his head portentously and smile, or else scowl ferociously.

Everyone had an air of suppressed excitement and I began to feel as though I was having lunch with the Duke of Wellington on the eve of Waterloo. At last he leaned forward and grinned at me, his big black eyes sparkling with suppressed excitement.

"Gerry," he said in Spanish, "I have found you some *bichos*."

"Already?" I asked in English. "But how?"

He waved a hand. "I have sent my family to make inquiries. Now it only remains for us to go and buy the *bichos*."

"Wonderful," I said enthusiastically, finishing my wine at a gulp, "let's go, shall we?"

So Luna and I set off to quarter Oran like huntsmen, preceded by Luna's pack of young and excited relatives. Everywhere we went, Luna was greeted with cries of joy, and we refused many invitations of a bibulous variety. Luna, with a reluctant gleam in his eye, sternly turned his back on such frivolity. Eventually, one of our retinue ran on ahead and beat a loud tattoo on the door of a large house. It was opened by an ancient woman dressed in black, which made her look like a somewhat dilapidated cockroach. Luna gave her a grave good evening, to which she bowed slightly. "I know that you have in your house a parrot," said Luna with the air of a policeman daring a criminal to deny the existence of a corpse which he knows to be concealed beneath the sofa.

"That is so," said the woman, mildly surprised.

"This English *señor* is collecting for his *jardin zoologico*," Luna went on, "and it is possible that he may wish to purchase this bird of yours."

The woman surveyed me, without curiosity. "You are welcome to him," she said, "for he is a dirty bird and he does not talk. Come in, *señores*, and see him."

She shuffled ahead of us and led us into the inevitable courtyard in the well of the house. When I saw the bird it was all I could do to stifle a yelp of delight, for it was a yellow-naped macaw, a rare member of the parrot family. Luna gave me a quick glance, and I nodded my head vigorously. He took a deep breath, surveyed the macaw with loathing, and then turned to the woman. "One of the commoner ones, I see," he said carelessly. "You realize, of course, that for such a common bird, and one, moreover, that does not talk, the *señor* would not dream of paying anything more than, say, twenty-five pesos."

Then he folded his arms and looked at the woman, waiting for her outburst of indignation at the mere mention of such a low price.

"All right," said the woman, "you can have him."

While Luna regarded her open-mouthed she picked the macaw off its perch, plonked him unceremoniously on my shoulder, and held out her wrinkled palm for the notes which I was hastily counting out from my wallet. We were back in the street again before Luna recovered the power of speech. Then he shook his head despondently.

"For your sake," he said gloomily, "I am glad to get the bird so cheap.

But it makes me fear for the future of Argentina when I meet someone who will not bargain, but accepts the first price offered." And he continued to grumble over the woman's behaviour for the rest of our tour.

We continued on our way until it grew dark, by which time all of us were carrying what amounted to a small zoo. There were five parrots (including, to my delight, another yellow-naped macaw), two pygmy Brazilian rabbits, with ginger paws and white spectacles of fur round their eyes, and an agouti, a large rodent with the disposition of a racehorse suffering from an acute nervous breakdown.

We carried this assortment of wildlife back to Luna's house, let them all loose in the patio, and spent the next two hours building suitable habitations for the creatures out of empty wooden boxes and wire netting. At length, when the last of them had been placed in its cage, Luna and I ate and drank heartily at the table nearby. Then, a tumbler of good wine by my side, I sat down in front of the cages to examine my charges by lamplight, while Luna called for his guitar and sang the soft, mournful folksongs of Argentina.

Apart from the macaws, the parrots were all blue-fronted Amazons. We had caged these together, and now in the lamplight they sat in a row, like a highly coloured jury, regarding me with the ancient, reptilian and falsely wise expressions that parrots are such masters at adopting. Gently I lowered a piece of sacking over the front of their cage and heard them all fluff and rearrange their feathers (a sound like someone riffling through a pack of cards) preparatory to sleep.

Next I turned my attention to the macaws, and gloated over them for some time. We had, experimentally, caged them together, and the way they had immediately started to bill and coo inclined me to think that they were a true pair. Their colouring was a deep rush-green, only relieved on the neck where they had a broad half-moon-shaped patch of bright canary-yellow. They gurked gently to me and to each other, their pale eyelids drooping sleepily over their bright eyes.

Next to the macaws the Brazilian rabbits were the creatures I was most delighted to have obtained. The two we had got were only babies, and I lifted them out of their cage and they sat, one in each hand, comfortably filling my palms with the soft, fat warmth of their flecked, brown bodies, their noses wiffling with all the strange scents of the patio. When they were fully adult they would still be among the dwarfs of their breed, being only half the size of the European wild rabbit. As far as I knew, no zoo in the world possessed these interesting little creatures, and I hoped they would settle down satisfactorily.

When I lifted the sacking off the front of the agouti's cage she leaped straight up into the air and landed with a crash in her straw bed, quivering in every limb, with the expression of an elderly virgin who, after years of looking under the bed, has at last found a man there. However, with the aid of a piece of apple I managed to soothe her into a fairly reasonable state, and she actually allowed me to stroke her. Agoutis are not the most prepossessing of the rodent family. They look like a cross between one of the smaller forerunners of the horse and a rather lugubrious rabbit. Their basic colouring is a rich, shining mahogany, fading to reddish-ginger on their rumps. Their long, slender legs are chocolate brown, and end in a bunch of frail, artistic toes. Their backside is out of all proportion, so that the creatures look as though they have a hump-behind. They have large, fine eyes, neat rounded ears and a mass of black whiskers which are in a constant state of agitation about everything. Musing on the beast's neurotic temperament, I lowered the sacking over the front of my agouti's cage, and she immediately leaped once more into the air and came down shaking in every limb. I left an apple in the cage for her, and then joined Luna where he sat at the table, humming softly like a drowsy bee. We had a final glass of wine and, yawning prodigiously, stumbled off to bed.

I was awoken next morning at a most uncivilized hour by a burst of song from Luna's bed, in the opposite corner of the room. Song and music ran through Luna's being as naturally as the blood flowed through his

veins. He is the only man I have ever met who can burst into song at five in the morning. But he sang so pleasantly that you forgave him and, after knowing him some time, you took no more notice of it than you would have done of a dawn chorus of birds.

"The moon is like a little white drum in the sky," he sang, from under a pile of bedclothes, "leading me to my love with the dark hair and the magic eyes, behind the mountains of Tucuman."

"If you sing to your female acquaintances at this hour of the morning," I said drowsily, "I should think you lead a pretty lonely life in bed. These things get around, you know."

He chuckled and stretched luxuriously.

"Today is going to be a fine day, Gerry," he said. I wondered how he knew. The window shutters were tightly closed, for the night air, in which the Argentine will sit as late as he pleases becomes, as soon as he retires to bed, a deadly gas waiting to strangle him. However, when we had dressed and gone out into the patio for breakfast, I found he was right, for it was flooded with sunshine.

We were finishing our last cup of coffee when our troupe of spies, apparently having been out at the crack of dawn, appeared to report. So when the animals had been fed we started once more on our search of the town, and during the morning we ran to earth three more pygmy rabbits, two seriemas, a strange, leggy bird, and two coatimundis, the odd little raccoon-like predator of South America. Then, after a hearty lunch, we set out to explore the outer limits of Oran in an ancient borrowed car.

Luna had learned, by some MI5 methods of his own, that in one of the more far-flung portions of the town there was a wild cat of some sort. Its possessor turned out to be a large, dark, unclean-looking man of about forty, with an unhealthy paunch and beady black eyes that were alternately cringing or cunning.

Yes, he admitted, he had got a wild cat, an ocelot; and then, while he eulogized the animal's beauty, tameness, value, size, he led us round into a filthy backyard and lumbered over to a rough wooden cage which would have been small for the average rabbit. He opened the door, caught hold of a chain inside and hauled out onto the ground one of the most pathetic sights I have seen. It was a half-grown ocelot, and how it managed to fit in such a small cage was a mystery. But it was its condition that was so appalling. Its coat was filthy, it had a large, running sore on one flank, and it was so thin that you could see its ribs and backbone clearly. Indeed, it was so weak that it wavered from side to side like a drunk, and eventually gave up the attempt to stay upright, and sank dejectedly onto its dirty belly.

"You see how tame it is?" inquired the man. "Never has she been known to bite." He was patting the cat as he spoke, and I could see that it was not tameness that stopped the animal from turning on him, but sheer inertia due to lack of food.

"Luna," I said, making a valiant attempt to keep my temper, "I will pay fifty pesos for this cat. No more. Even that is too much, for she will probably die. I won't bargain, so tell this bloated imbecile that he can take it or leave it. Here is the money."

Luna translated my message, tactfully leaving out my character rendering. The man clasped his hands in horror. Surely we were joking? For such a magnificent animal three hundred pesos would be a beggarly sum to pay. Surely the *señor* could see what a wonderful creature... But the *señor* had seen enough. I spat loudly, turned on my heel and walked back to the road. I could hear Luna and the man arguing, and  presently, when I detected a weakening note in the repulsive man's voice, I roared at Luna not to waste time. Within thirty seconds he appeared with the box and put it in the back seat of the car. We drove off in silence.

Presently, when I had finished mentally working out what I would like to have done to the cat's late owner, I sighed and lit a cigarette. "We must get home quickly, Luna. That animal's got to have a decent cage and some food or she's going to die," I said. "Also I shall want some sawdust."

"*Si, si*," said Luna, his dark eyes worried. "I have never seen anyone keep an animal like that. She is half dead." We drove in silence along the rutted road for some way before Luna spoke. "Gerry, you do not mind stopping once more, only for a minute?" he inquired anxiously. "It is on our way. I hear of someone else that has a cat they might sell."

"Yes, all right, if it's on the way."

Presently Luna ran the car off the road onto a sizeable stretch of greensward where stood a dilapidated-looking marquee, a battered roundabout and a couple of small booths made of faded, striped canvas. Three fat, glossy horses grazed nearby, and round the marquee and the booths trotted a number of professional-looking dogs.

"What is this? It looks like a circus," I said to Luna.

"It is," said Luna, grinning, "only a very small one."

I was amazed that any circus could make a living in a place as small as Oran, but this one appeared to be doing all right, for although the props were somewhat decrepit, the animals looked in good condition. As we left the car a muscular, ginger-haired man appeared from the marquee. We shook hands, and Luna explained our business.

"Ah, you want my puma," he grinned. "But I warn you I want a lot of money for her ... she's a beauty. But she eats too much, and I can't afford to keep her. Come and see her, she's over here."

He led us to a large cage in one corner of which crouched a beautiful young puma, about the size of a large dog. She was fat and glossy, and still had her baby paws which, as in all young cats, look about three times too big for the body. Her coat was a rich amber colour, and her piercing, moody eyes a lovely leaf-green. As we approached the cage she lifted one lip and showed her teeth in a scornful snarl.

The bargaining lasted for half a hour, and at length I agreed to a fair price. Then I asked the man if he would keep her until the following day for me, for I knew that she would be in good hands, and I had no cage ready for her. This our amiable ginger friend agreed to and Luna and I drove back home to try to resurrect the unfortunate ocelot.

When I had built a cage for her, and one of Luna's lesser relatives had appeared with a large sackful of sweet-smelling sawdust, I got the poor creature out of her box and dressed the wound on her thigh. She just lay on the ground apathetically, though the washing of the wound must have hurt considerably. Then I gave her a large shot of penicillin. The third operation was to try and dry her coat out a bit, for she was soaked in her own urine. All I could do was to cover her in sawdust, rubbing it well into the fur to absorb the moisture and then gently dusting it out again. Then I unpicked the more vicious tangles in her fur, and by the time I had finished she had begun to look faintly like an ocelot. But she still lay on the floor, uncaring. I cut the filthy collar away from her neck, and put her in her new cage on a bed of sawdust and straw. Then I placed in front of her a bowl containing one raw egg and a small quantity of finely minced fresh steak. At first she displayed no interest in this, and my heart sank, for I thought she might well have reached the stage of starvation where nothing would induce her to eat. In sheer desperation I ducked her face into the raw egg. Even this indignity she suffered without complaint, but she sat back and licked the dripping egg off her lips, slowly, carefully, like someone sampling a new, foreign and probably dangerous offering. Then she eyed the dish with a disbelieving look in her eye and, while I held my breath, leaned forward and lapped experimentally at the

raw egg. Within thirty seconds the plate was clean, and Luna and I were dancing a tango of delight round the patio, to the joy of his younger relatives.

"Give her some more, Gerry," panted Luna, grinning.

"No, I daren't," I said. "When a creature's that bad you can kill it from overfeeding. She can have a bowl of milk later on, and then tomorrow she can have four small meals during the day. But I think she'll be all right now."

"That man was a devil," said Luna shaking his head.

I drew a deep breath and, in Spanish, gave him my view on the cat's late owner.

"I never knew you knew so many bad things in Spanish, Gerry," said Luna admiringly. "There was one word you used I have never heard before, but I hope you say nothing like that tonight."

"Why? What's happening tonight?"

"Because we are leaving tomorrow, my friends have made an *asado* in your honour, Gerry. They will play and sing very old Argentine folksongs. You like this idea?" he asked anxiously.

"There is nothing I like better than an *asado*," I said, "and an *asado* with folksongs is my idea of heaven."

So, at about ten o'clock that evening, a friend of Luna's drove us out to the *estancia* where the *asado* had been organized in a eucalyptus grove, an area of bare earth that told of many dances. The long wooden benches and trestle tables were lit with the soft buttercup glow of oil lamps, and outside this circle of light the moonlight was silver brilliant. There were about fifty people there, few of them over the age of twenty. They greeted us uproariously, almost dragged us to the tables, which were groaning under the weight of food, and placed great hunks of sizzling steak in front of us.

The wine bottles passed with monotonous regularity, and within half an hour Luna and I were thoroughly in the party spirit. Guitars, drums and flutes appeared as if by magic, and the entire crowd burst into song. They sang and sang, and each time they came to the end of a song, someone would think of a new one, and they would start again. Sometimes a shy, grinning youth would be pushed to the front of the circle as the only person there capable of rendering a certain number. Then it would be a girl's turn to sing the solo refrain in a sweet-sour voice, while the lamps glinted on her dark hair, and the guitars shuddered and trembled under the swiftly-moving fingers. They danced in a row on a flagstone path, their spurs striking sparks. They danced the delightful handkerchief dance

350

with its lilting tune, and they danced tangos that made you wonder if the stiff, sexless dance called by that name in Europe was a member of the same family. These teenagers revelled in the old and beautiful songs of their country, and the old and beautiful dances, their faces flushed with delight at my delight, honouring a stranger they had never seen before and would probably never see again.

Now they had reached the peak. Slowly they started to relax, the songs getting softer and softer, more and more plaintive, until we all reached the moment when we knew that to continue longer would be a mistake. They had sung themselves from the heavens back to earth, like a flock of descending larks. Flushed, bright-eyed, happy, our young hosts insisted we travel back to Oran with them in the big open back of the lorry in which they had come. As it roared off down the road the guitarists started strumming and everybody, revived by the cool night air, took up the refrain once more, and we roared along through the velvet night like a heavenly choir.

A Wagonload of "Bichos"

On my return from Oran the Letts's garage almost overflowed with animals. One could scarcely make oneself heard above the shrill conversations of the parrots, the trumpeting song of the seriemas, the chittering of the coatimundis, and an occasional dull rumble, as of distant thunder, from the puma, whom I had christened Luna in the human Luna's honour.

Soon after getting back, I had set about building a new cage worthy of the puma's beauty and grace. I had just finished it when Luna's godfather arrived and offered to help me in the tricky job of getting her to pass into it from her present quarters. We carefully closed the garage doors so that, if anything untoward happened, the cat would not go rampaging off across the countryside. It also had the advantage, as the human Luna pointed out, that we would be locked in with her, a prospect he viewed with alarm and despondency. I soothed his fears by telling him that the puma would be far more frightened than we were, and at that moment she uttered a rumbling growl of such malignancy and fearlessness that Luna paled visibly.

The plan of campaign was that the large crate in which the puma now reposed would be dragged opposite the door of the new cage, a few slats removed from the side, and the cat would then walk from the crate into the cage without fuss. Unfortunately, owing to the construction of the new cage, we could not wedge the crate close up to its door: there was a gap of some eight inches. Undeterred, I placed planks so that they formed a short tunnel between the two boxes, then removed the end of the crate so that the puma could get out. During this process a golden paw the size of a ham suddenly appeared in the gap and a nice, deep slash appeared across the back of my hand.

"Ah!" said Luna gloomily, "you see, Gerry?"

"It's only because she's scared of the hammering," I said. "Now, I think I've removed enough boards. All we have to do is wait."

We waited. After ten minutes I peered through a knot-hole and saw the wretched puma drowsing peacefully in her crate, and showing not the slightest interest in passing down our rickety tunnel into her spacious new quarters. There was obviously only one thing to do. I lifted the hammer and brought it down on the back of the crate with a crash. Two things happened at once. The puma, startled out of her half-sleep, leaped up and rushed to the gap in the crate, and the force of my blow knocked down the piece of board which was forming Luna's side of the tunnel. In consequence he looked down just in time to see an extremely irritable-looking puma sniffing meditatively at his legs. He uttered a tenor screech which I have rarely heard equalled, and leaped vertically into the air. It was the screech that saved the situation. It so unnerved the puma that she fled into the new cage as fast as she could, and I dropped the sliding door, locking her safely inside. Luna leaned against the garage door, wiping his face with a handkerchief.

"There you are," I said cheerfully, "I told you it would be easy."

Luna gave me a withering look. "You have collected animals in South America and Africa for fourteen years?" he inquired. "That is correct, is it not?"

"Yes."

"You are now thirty-three?"

"Yes."

Luna shook his head, like a person faced with one of the great enigmas of life.

"How you have lived so long only the good God knows," he said.

"I lead a charmed life," I said. "Anyway, why did you come to see me, apart from wanting to wrestle with your namesake?"

"Outside," said Luna, still mopping his face, "is an Indian with a *bicho*. I think it is a pig."

We found the Indian squatting on the lawn, and in front of him was a box from which issued a series of falsetto squeaks and muffled grunts. The Indian grinned, removed his big straw hat, ducked his head and then drew forth from the box the most adorable little creature. It was a very young collared peccary, the wild pig that inhabits the tropical portions of South America.

"This is Juanita," said the Indian, smiling as he placed the diminutive creature on the lawn, where it uttered a shrill squeak of delight and started to snuffle about hopefully.

Now, I have always had a soft spot for the pig family, and baby pigs I cannot resist, so within five minutes Juanita was mine at a price that was double what she was worth, speaking financially, but only a hundredth part of what she was worth in charm and personality. She was about eighteen inches long and twelve inches high, clad in long, rather coarse greyish fur and a neat white band that ran from the angle of her jaw up round her neck, so that she looked as though she was wearing an Eton collar. She had a slim body, with a delicately tapered snout ending in a delicious retroussé nose, and slender, fragile legs tipped with neatly polished hoofs the circumference of a sixpence. She had a dainty, ladylike walk, moving her legs very rapidly.

She was ridiculously tame, and had the most endearing habit of greeting you—even after only five minutes' absence—as if you had been away for years, and as if, for her, those years had been grey and empty. She would utter strangled squeaks of delight, and rush towards you to rub her nose and behind against your legs in an orgy of delighted union, giving seductive grunts and sighs. Her idea of heaven was to be picked up and held on her back in your arms, as you would nurse a baby, and then to have her tummy scratched. She would lie there, her eyes closed, gnashing her baby teeth together in an ecstasy of delight.

I still had all the less destructive creatures running loose in the garage, and as Juanita behaved in such a ladylike fashion I allowed her the run of the place as well, only shutting her in a cage at night. At feeding time it was a weird sight to see Juanita, her nose buried in a large dish of food, surrounded by an assortment of creatures—seriemas, parrots, pygmy rabbits, guans—all trying to feed out of the same dish. She always behaved impeccably, allowing the others plenty of room to feed, and never showed any animosity, even when a wily seriema pinched titbits from under her pink nose. The only time I ever saw her lose her temper was when one of the more weak-minded of the parrots, who had worked himself into a highly excitable state at the sight of the food plate, flew down squawking joyously and landed on Juanita's snout. She shook him off with a grunt of indignation and chased him, squawking and fluttering, into a corner, where she stood over him for a moment champing her teeth in warning, before returning to her interrupted meal.

By now my collection of creatures had grown to such an extent that it was time to plan my return to Buenos Aires. I found I would have to go by train, a two-day and three-night journey that I did not relish. But Charles arranged the whole thing for me with a speed and efficiency that was typical of him, and I hammered and sawed in the garden, getting cages ready for the journey.

The biggest of the still-uncaged animals were the coatimundis, Martha and Mathias who, on collars and chains, were tethered under the trees. Coatimundis are not everyone's idea of the most charming of animals, but I find something very appealing about their long, rubbery, tip-tilted noses, their pigeon-toed, bear-like walk, and the way they hold their long, ringed tails straight up in the air when they move, like furry exclamation marks. In the wild state they are gregarious, travelling through the forest in quite large parties, and like most small gregarious mammals they have an extensive vocabulary. Mathias would converse with me by the hour in a series of bird-like squeaks and trills; if, when investigating a rotten log or a stone, he thought he was nearing a succulent beetle or slug, the sounds would turn to snuffling grunts, pitched in different keys and interspersed with a strange champing noise made by chattering his teeth together at great speed.

Both the coatimundis had fairly long leashes which were attached to a convenient tree. When they had uprooted and investigated every log and stone within the circle of the leash, they were moved to a fresh tree. Every time this happened, Mathias would spend ten minutes or so marking out his territory with the scent gland at the base of his tail. He would solemnly shuffle his way round in a circle, a look of immense concentration on his face, squatting down at intervals to rub his hindquarters on a convenient rock or stick.

Having thus, as it were, hoisted the coatimundi equivalent of the flag, he would relax and settle down to the task of beetle-hunting with a clear conscience. If any of the local dogs were so misguided as to approach his territory, they never did it a second time. He would walk slowly towards them, champing his teeth alarmingly, his tail erect, stiff as a poker, and puffed up to twice its normal size. Having got within range he would suddenly dart forward in a curious, rolling run, uttering ear-splitting whistling screams. This ghastly noise had the effect of undermining the morale of any but the bravest dog, and when they had hurriedly retreated

Mathias, quietly chattering and trilling to himself, would wend his way round in a circle, re-marking his entire territory.

All the other creatures I had acquired were doing splendidly. Juanita, the peccary, grew fatter and more charming each day, and lorded it over the parrots.

To my delight I had found the perfect mate for her, a fully adult male peccary, called Juan. They seemed to be delighted with each other, and I had hopes of eventually arranging a successful marriage. The little Geoffroy's was now quite reconciled to captivity, and played such strenuous games with his tabby kitten companion that I began to wonder if I would get them to Buenos Aires alive, let alone Jersey. Luna the puma had tamed down a lot, and even condescended to allow me to scratch her behind the ears, while she rumbled contentedly deep in her throat. The poor half-starved ocelot was now fat and glossy. Having lost the apathy of starvation, she was very full of herself, and the process of cleaning her out or feeding her was fraught with danger. Thus are one's kindnesses sometimes repaid.

Among the new creatures which I had added to my collection were two of the most enchanting members of the monkey tribe, a pair of douroucoulis brought to me by an Indian hunter. Douroucoulis are remarkable as being the only nocturnal monkeys in the world. When you add to that the fact that they look like a cross between an owl and a clown, that they are the gentlest of monkeys, and that they spend a lot of time clasped in each other's arms exchanging the most human kisses, then douroucoulis become, so far as I am concerned, irresistible. They have huge, nocturnal eyes, surrounded by a white facial mask edged with black, and their mouth seems just about to break into a rather sad, slightly pitying smile. The only time they make any sound is when feeding.

I used to dig large red beetles out of the rotting palm trees for them, insects of which they were inordinately fond. They would watch my approach with the titbits, their eyes wide, their hands held out beseechingly, trembling slightly, uttering faint squeaks of excitement. They would clasp the wriggling beetles in their hands with the awkward grace of a young child accepting a stick of rock, and scrunch their way through them, pausing now and again to utter squeaks of joy. When the last piece had been swallowed they would carefully examine their hands, both back and front, to make sure there was none left, and then examine each other for the same reason. Having convinced themselves that no fragment remained, they would clasp each other and kiss passionately for five minutes or so, in what appeared to be an orgy of mutual congratulation.

It was just after I had acquired these delightful monkeys that I met a man who deserves to head the list of all the curious and interesting human beings I have encountered during the course of my perambulations about the world.

My introduction to him was due to Luna. He appeared one morning and said that business was to take him to a village a few miles away from Calilegua, where he had heard rumours of a man who was interested in animals.

"All I can find out is that his name is Coco, and everyone there says he is *loco*, Gerry," said Luna, "but you might like to come and see."

"All right," I said, nothing loath to leaving carpentry.

The village, when we reached it, proved to be a straggling, ill-kempt one, with a curious dead air about it. But everyone appeared to know Coco, for when we inquired in the local bar where he lived a forest of hands directed us.

His house was very noticeable anyway, for in comparison to the rest of the village, it gleamed like a gem and its front garden was neatly tended. In response to our clapping a slight, dark woman appeared, who admitted to being Coco's wife, but said that he was not at home: he worked during the day at the local sawmill. Luna explained my mission, and the wife's face lighted up.

"Oh," she said, "I will send one of the children to fetch him. He would never forgive me if he missed meeting you. Please come round to the back and wait ... he will come in a few moments."

The garden at the back of the house was as well tended as the front and, to my surprise, contained two well-constructed and spacious aviaries. I peered into them hopefully, but they were both empty.

We did not have to wait long for Coco. He appeared from the path leading to the sawmill at a brisk trot. He was a short, well-built man with coal-black curly hair and a thick black beard and moustache, carefully trimmed. His eyes were dark, and shone with eagerness as he held out a well-shaped brown hand to Luna and myself.

"Welcome, welcome," he said. "You must excuse, please, my English. I have no chance to practise."

The fact that he could speak English at all amazed me.

"You have no idea what this means to me," he said eagerly, wringing my hand, "to speak with someone who has an interest in Nature ... I could not believe it when my son told me ... an Englishman to see me, and about animals, too." He smiled at me, his face awe-stricken at this miracle that had happened.

"Well," said Luna, having obviously decided that he had done his job by bringing one lunatic in contact with another, "I will go and do my work and see you later."

He drifted off, humming to himself, while Coco seized my arm gently, as though it were a butterfly's wing that he might damage, and urged me up the steps and into the living room. Here his wife had produced wonderful lemonade made from fresh lemons, and we sat at the table and drank this while Coco talked. He spoke quietly, stumbling occasionally in his English and saying a sentence in Spanish. It was an extraordinary experience, like listening to a man who has been dumb for years suddenly recover the power of speech. He had been living for so long in a world of his own, for neither his wife, children nor anyone in the fly-blown village could understand his interests. To him I was the incredible answer to a prayer, a man who could understand what he meant when he said that a bird was beautiful, or an animal was interesting. All the time he spoke he watched me with an embarrassing expression, a mixture of awe and fear—awe that I should be there at all, and fear that I might suddenly disappear like a mirage.

"It is the birds that I am particularly studying," he said. "I know the birds of Argentina are catalogued, but who knows anything about them? Who knows their courtship displays, their type of nests, how many eggs they lay, how many broods they have, if they migrate? In this field I am trying to help, as well as I can."

"This is the problem all over the world," I said. "We know what creatures exist—or most of them—but we know nothing of their private lives."

"Would you like to see the place where I work? I call it my study," he explained deprecatingly. "It is very small ...."

"I would love to see it," I said.

Eagerly he led me outside to where a miniature wing had been built on to the side of the house.

As he pulled a key from his pocket he smiled at me. "I let no one in here," he explained simply, "they do not understand."

Up until then I had been greatly impressed with Coco. But now, being led into his study, I was speechless. It was about eight feet long and six feet wide. In one corner was a cabinet which housed his collection of bird and small mammal skins, and various birds' eggs. Then there was a long, low bench on which he did his skinning, and nearby a rough bookcase containing some fourteen volumes on natural history, some in Spanish, some in English. Under the one small window stood an easel, and on it the half-finished watercolour of a bird.

"Did you do *that?*" I asked incredulously.

"Yes," he said shyly, "you see, I could not afford a camera, and this was the only way to record their plumage."

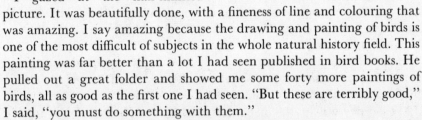

I gazed at the half-finished picture. It was beautifully done, with a fineness of line and colouring that was amazing. I say amazing because the drawing and painting of birds is one of the most difficult of subjects in the whole natural history field. This painting was far better than a lot I had seen published in bird books. He pulled out a great folder and showed me some forty more paintings of birds, all as good as the first one I had seen. "But these are terribly good," I said, "you must do something with them."

"Do you think so?" he inquired doubtfully, peering at the paintings. "I have sent some to the man in charge of the museum at Cordoba, and he liked them. He said we should have a small book printed when I have enough of them, but this I think is doubtful, for you know how costly such a production would be."

He talked on enthusiastically for an hour or so, telling me what he had accomplished and what he hoped to do, that he was saving to buy a small cinecamera, for there were certain things that could be captured only on film. I had to keep reminding myself that this was a man who worked in a sawmill and lived in a house which, though spotless, no so-called "worker" in England would have been seen dead in. To find him here in this remote, unlikely spot was like suddenly coming across a unicorn in the middle of Piccadilly. And, although he explained to me the difficulties of saving enough money to buy paints and his dream cinecamera, there was never once the slightest suggestion that financial aid might be forthcoming from me. To him I must have represented a millionaire, yet I knew that if I offered him money I, too, would become a person who did not understand. The most I could do was to promise to speak to the museum in Buenos Aires (for good bird painters are not two a penny) and tell him that if there was anything that he wanted from England to let me know and I would send it to him. When, eventually, Luna reappeared and we simply had to leave, Coco said goodbye wistfully, rather like a child who had been allowed to play with a new toy and then had it taken away.

When I got back to England, and Christmas came, I sent Coco a card, and in it I reiterated the offer I had made him. Then he wrote to me, a charming letter, in which he gave me news of his birds and his painting. But there was not a single request. So, at the risk of offending him, I packed up a parcel of books and shipped them off. And now, when I get irritated because I can't afford some new animal, or a new gadget for my camera, I remember Coco in his tiny study, working hard and enthusiastically with inadequate tools and money. I hope that some day I may have the privilege of meeting him again.

At last the day came when I had to leave Calilegua. I did not want to leave a bit, for everyone had been so kind to me. Joan and Charles, Helmuth and Edna, and the human nightingale Luna, had accepted me, a complete stranger, into their lives, allowed me to disrupt their routine, and done everything possible to help me. To say that I was sorry to leave these friends was putting it mildly.

My journey was, in the first stages, slightly complicated. I had to take the collection on the small railway that ran from Calilegua to the nearest big town. Here everything had to be transhipped onto the Buenos Aires train.

Charles, realizing that I was worried about the transhipment, insisted, despite my protests, that Luna should travel with me as far as the main town, and said that he, Helmuth and Edna (Joan was ill) would drive into the town and meet us there, to sort out any difficulties. So, on the morning of departure, a tractor dragging a giant flat cart arrived outside Charles's house, and the crates of animals were piled up on it and then driven slowly to the station. Here we stacked them on the platform, and awaited the arrival of the train.

When it eventually came into view it was startling. The carriages were wooden, and looked like the ones you see in old Western films. But it was the engine that was so remarkable. It was obviously an old one with a gigantic cowcatcher in front, but it had been streamlined with sheets of metal, painted in broad orange, yellow and scarlet stripes. It was, to say the least, the gayest engine I had ever seen; it looked as though it had just come straight from a carnival, as it swept down towards us at a majestic twenty miles an hour, the riotous undergrowth covering the worn-down rails so successfully that it appeared to be coming straight across country.

360

It roared into the station with a scream of brakes, and then proudly let out a huge cloud of pungent black smoke that enveloped us all. Hastily we pushed the animal crates into the guard's van, Luna and I got ourselves a seat in the compartment next door, and then, with a great jerk and a shudder, the train was off.

For most of the way the road ran along the railway, only separated by a tangle of grass and shrubs and a low barbed-wire fence. So Charles, Helmuth and Edna drove parallel with our carriage, shouting insults at us, shaking their fists and accusing Luna and myself of a rich variety of crimes.

The other passengers were at first puzzled, and then, when they realized the joke, they joined in heartily, even suggesting a few choice insults we could shout back. It was childish, but it was fun. At each of the numerous little stations we had to stop at, the idiots in the car would drive on ahead and be there on the platform to present me with a huge bouquet of wilting flowers, after which I would make an impassioned speech in modern Greek, to the complete mystification of the passengers who had only just joined the train, and who obviously thought that I was some sort of visiting politician.

When we reached the town where I was to change trains we piled the collection of animals on the platform. The Buenos Aires train, with just an ordinary engine, rumbled its way into the station and, while Charles put my things inside my sleeping berth, Helmuth, Luna and I carefully stacked the animals into the van that I had hired. Then, with nothing to do but wait for departure, I squatted on the steps leading down from my carriage, while the others gathered in a group round me. Edna fumbled in her bag, and held up something that glinted in the dim lights of the station. A bottle of gin.

"Helmuth," I said, as Luna went off in search of tonic water and glasses, "you have a wife in a million."

And there on the station we toasted each other. I had just finished my drink when the guard's whistle squealed, and the train started to move. Still clutching their drinks the others ran alongside to shake my hand, and I nearly fell out of the train kissing Edna goodbye. The train gathered speed, and I saw them in a group under the dim lights, holding up their glasses in a last toast, before they were lost to view.

The train journey was not quite as bad as I had anticipated. My problem was that I could get to my animals only when the train was in a station, for their van was not connected by the corridor to the rest of the train. Here the sleeping-car attendant came into his own. He would warn me ten minutes before we got to a station, which gave me time to wend my way down the train until I reached the animal van and, when the train pulled up, to jump out and minister to their wants. The three carriages I had to go through were third class, and on the wooden benches therein was a solid mass of humanity surrounded by babies, bottles of wine, mothers-in-law, goats, chickens, pigs, baskets of fruit, and other necessities of travel. When this exuberant, garlic-breathing crowd learned the reason for my curious and constant peregrinations, they united in their efforts to help.

As soon as the train stopped they would find the nearest water tap for me, send their children scuttling in all directions to buy me bananas or bread or whatever was needed for the animals, and then, when I had finished my chores, they would hoist me lovingly on board the slowly moving train, and make earnest inquiries as to the puma's health, or how the birds were standing up to the heat, and was it true that I had a parrot that said *"hijo de puta"?* Then they would offer me sweetmeats, sandwiches, glasses of wine or pots of meat, show me their babies, their goats or chickens or pigs, sing songs for me, and generally treat me as one of the family. They were so charming and kind, that when we eventually pulled slowly into the huge echoing station at Buenos Aires, I was almost sorry the trip was over. The animals were piled into a lorry, my hand was wrung by a hundred people, and we roared off to take the creatures, all of whom had survived the journey remarkably well, to join the rest of the collection.

The Customs of the Country

When you have a large number of animals to transport from one end of the world to the other you cannot, as a lot of people seem to think, just hoist them aboard the nearest ship and set off with a gay wave of your hand. There is slightly more to it than this. Your first problem is to find a shipping company who will agree to carry animals. Most shipping people, when you mention the words "animal cargo", grow pale, and get vivid mental pictures of the captain being eviscerated by a jaguar, the first officer being slowly crushed in the coils of some enormous snake, while the passengers are pursued from one end of the ship to the other by a host of repulsive and deadly beasts.

Once you have surmounted this psychological hurdle, there are still many problems. There are consultations with the chief steward as to how much refrigerator space you can have for your meat, fish and eggs; and with the chief officer as to where your cages are to be stacked, and how they are to be secured for rough weather. Then you pay a formal call on the captain, and you tell him (almost with tears in your eyes) you will be so little trouble aboard that he won't even notice you are there—a statement which neither he nor you believe. But, most important of all, you have to have your collection ready for embarkation a good ten days or so before the ship is scheduled to leave, for a number of things may happen that will change the sailing date.

However, we had now, it seemed, surmounted all these obstacles, and everything appeared to be running smoothly. It was at this precise juncture that Juanita, the peccary, decided to catch pneumonia.

I had given up the villa, and the animals were now in a huge shed in the museum grounds, which had no heating. While this did not appear to worry any of the others unduly, Juanita decided to be different. Without so much as a preliminary cough, she succumbed. In the morning she was full of beans, and devoured her food avidly; in the evening, when we went to cover the animals for the night, she looked decidedly queer. She was, for one thing, *leaning* against the side of her box as if for support, her eyes half closed, her breathing rapid and rattling in her throat. Hastily I opened the door of the cage and called her. She made a tremendous effort, stood upright shakily, tottered out of the cage and collapsed into my arms. It was in the best cinematic tradition, but rather frightening. As I held her I could hear her breath wheezing and bubbling in her tiny chest, and her body lay in my arms limp and cold.

In order to husband our rapidly decreasing money supplies two friends in Buenos Aires had rallied round and allowed my secretary, Sophie, and me to stay in their respective flats. I was occupying a camp bed in the flat of one David Jones, who was with me at the moment when I discovered Juanita's condition.

"Anything we can do?" he said hopefully for, like me, he had grown tremendously fond of the little pig.

"Yes, she's got to have a whacking great shot of penicillin and as much warmth and fresh air as she can get."

I looked at him hopefully. "Let's take her back to the flat," said David, as I had hoped he would. We wasted no more time.

At the flat I laid the by now completely unconscious Juanita on David's sofa, turned on the electric fire and then opened all the windows that would not create draughts. Rapidly we boiled my hypodermic and I gave Juanita the biggest dose of penicillin I dared. Then we sat and watched her. At the end of an hour I persuaded myself that her breathing was a little easier, but she was still unconscious and I knew she was a very long way from recovery.

"Look," said David, when I had listened to Juanita's chest for the fourteen-hundredth time, "are we doing any good, just sitting here looking at her?"

"No," I said reluctantly, "I don't think we'll really see any change for about three or four hours, if then."

"Well," said David practically, "let's get something to eat at Olly's. We needn't be more than three quarters of an hour."

"OK," I said reluctantly, "I suppose you're right."

So, having made sure that Juanita was comfortable, we drove down to Olly's Music Bar in 25 de Mayo, a street lined with tiny clubs, some of which have the most delightful names like "My Desire", "The Blue Moon Hall of Beauties", and, perhaps slightly more mysteriously, "Joe's Terrific Display".

The bar my friends and I liked best was Olly's. There were many reasons for liking it. First, was the walnut-crinkled Olly himself and his lovely wife. Second, Olly not only gave you fair measure in your glass, but frequently stood you a drink himself. Third, his bar was well lit, so that you could actually see your companions. Fourth, his hostesses were not allowed to irritate you by constantly suggesting you bought them drinks, and fifth, there was a brother and sister with a guitar who sang and played delightfully. Lastly, and perhaps most important, I have seen the hostesses at Olly's, when their night's work was done, kiss Olly and his wife goodnight as tenderly as if they had been the girls' parents.

So David and I made our way down the stairs into Olly's and were greeted with delight. The reason for our depression being explained, the whole bar was full of commiseration; Olly stood us each a large vodka, and the hostesses gathered round to tell us how they were sure Juanita would get well. But, as we stood there eating hot sausages and sandwiches, not even the gay *carnavalitos* the brother and sister played and sang specially for us could cure my depression. I felt sure that Juanita was going to die, and I had grown absurdly fond of the little creature. Eventually we said goodbye and climbed the steps that led to the road.

"Come tomorrow and tell us how the animal is," called Olly.

"*Si, si*," said the hostesses, like a Greek chorus, "come tomorrow and tell us how the *pbroecíta* is."

By the time we had got back to David's flat I was convinced that we should find Juanita dead. I gazed at the pile of blankets on the sofa, and had to force myself to go and look. I lifted one corner of a blanket gently and a twinkling dark eye gazed up at me lovingly, while a pink plunger-shaped nose wiffled, and a faint, very faint, grunt of pleasure came from the invalid.

"Good heavens, she's better," said David incredulously.

As if to second this Juanita gave another grunt.

In order to make sure that Juanita did not kick off her blankets during the night I took her to bed with me on the sofa. She lay very quietly across my chest and slept deeply. I was awoken the following morning by a cold, rubbery nose being pushed into my eye, and hearing Juanita's wheezy grunts of greeting, I unwrapped her and saw she was a different animal. Her eyes were bright, her temperature was normal, her breathing was still wheezy, but much more even and, best of all, she stood up for a brief, wobbly moment.

From then on she never looked back. But the better she felt the worse patient she made. As soon as she could walk without falling over every two steps, she insisted on spending the day trotting about the room, and was most indignant because I made her wear a small blanket, safety-pinned under her chin, like a cloak. But it was during the nights that I found her particularly trying. We seemed to have different ideas about the purposes for which one went to bed. I went in order to sleep, while Juanita thought it was the best time for a glorious romp. Sometimes she would do a  porcine tango with her sharp hoofs along my stomach and chest, and at other times she would simply chase her tail round and round. She would occasionally break off her little dance in order to come and stick her hard, wet nose into my eye, to see how I was enjoying it. At other times she would become obsessed with the idea that I had, concealed about my person somewhere, a rare delicacy, and she would make a thorough search with nose, tusks and hoofs, grunting shrilly and peevishly when she couldn't find anything. Round about three am she would sink into a deep, untroubled sleep. Then, at five thirty, she would take a quick gallop up and down my body to make sure I woke up in good shape. This lasted for four soul-searing nights, until I felt she was sufficiently recovered, and then I banished her to a box, to her intense and vocal indignation.

I had only just pulled Juanita round in time, for no sooner was she better than we got a message to say that the ship was ready to leave.

So, on the appointed day, our two lorry-loads of equipment and animal cages rolled down to the dock, and then began the prolonged business of hoisting the animals on board, and arranging the cages on the hatch. This is always a nerve-racking time, for as the great nets, piled high with cages, soar into the air, you are always convinced that a rope is going to break and deposit your precious animals either into the sea or else in a mangled heap on the dockside. But by evening the last cage was safely aboard, and the last piece of equipment stowed away in the hold, and we could relax.

All our friends were there to see us off, and if in one or two people's eyes was a semi-repressed expression of relief, who was to blame them? I had made martyrs of them all in one way or another. However, we were all exhausted but relaxed, everything was on board, and now all we had to do was to have a farewell drink in my cabin, for in an hour the ship was sailing.

Just as I was replenishing everyone's glass for the fifth toast, a little man in customs uniform appeared in the doorway, rustling a sheaf of papers. I gazed at him fondly, without any premonition of danger.

"Señor Durrell?" he asked politely.

"Señor Garcia?" I inquired.

"*Si*," he said, flushing with pleasure that I should know his name.

It was Marie who scented danger. "Is anything wrong?" she asked.

"*Si, si, señorita*, the *señor's* papers are all in order, but they have not been signed by a *despachante*. Without the *despachante's* signature we cannot let the animals be taken."

I felt as though someone had removed my entire stomach in one piece, for we had about three quarters of an hour.

"But is there no *despachante* here at the dock who will sign them?" asked Marie.

"*Señorita*, it is late, they have all gone home," said Señor Garcia.

This is, of course, the sort of situation which takes about twenty years off your life. I could imagine the shipping company's reaction if we now went to them and told them that, instead of gaily casting off for England, they would be delayed for five hours while they unloaded all my animals. But by now my friends were used to crises like this, and they all fled in different directions. Mercedes, Josefina and David went to argue with the chief of customs, while Willie Anderson, another friend of ours, went off with Marie to the private home of a *despachante* he knew on the outskirts of Buenos Aires. They would have to drive like the devil to get back in time. Sophie and I could only wait and hope, while I mentally rehearsed how I could phrase the news to the captain without being seriously maimed, if we had to unload everything.

Presently the party who had been arguing with the chief of customs returned despondently.

"No use," said David, "he's adamant. No signature, no departure."

We had about twenty minutes to go. At that moment we heard a car screech to a halt on the docks outside. We piled out onto the deck, and there, smiling triumphantly, were Marie and Willie, waving the necessary documents, all beautifully signed by what must be the finest, noblest *despachante* in the business. So we all had a last drink. I even gave Señor Garcia one.

Then sadly we said our goodbyes. Ropes were cast off, and slowly the gap between the ship and the dock widened, so we could see the shuddering reflection of the quay lights in the dark waters. Presently the ship gained speed, and soon our friends were lost to sight, and all we could see was the great heap of multicoloured lights that was Buenos Aires.

As we turned away from the rail and made our way to our cabins, I remembered Darwin's words, written a century before. When speaking of the travelling naturalist he said: "He will discover how many truly kind-hearted people there are with whom he had never before had, or ever again will have, any communication, who yet are ready to offer him the most disinterested assistance."

Gerald Durrell

Gerald Durrell was born in India in 1925 and spent his childhood in Corfu. By his teens he knew that the only things he really wanted were to study animals and to own a zoo. After joining the staff of Whipsnade Zoo in 1945 he organized animal-collecting expeditions all over the world, and started writing in order to finance them. His first book, *The Overloaded Ark*, was an instant success, and he has been writing equally popular books ever since. In 1958 he achieved his ambition by founding the Jersey Wildlife Preservation Trust, a zoo which specializes in breeding animals which in the wild are threatened with extinction.